Teaching Social Studies to Multilingual Learners of English

Fatima Aldajani, Mary Brennan, Peggie Cypher, Kaedmon Fulton, Andy Jiahao Liu

This book has a companion website. Go to www.tesol.org/socialstudies-book for additional resources.

TESOL International Association	**National Council for the Social Studies**
1925 Ballenger Avenue, Ste. 550	8403 Colesville Road, Ste. 1100,
Alexandria, VA 22314 USA	Silver Spring, MD 20910 USA
www.tesol.org	www.socialstudies.org
Associate Director of Publications: Tomiko Breland	Executive Director: Kelly McFarland Stratman
Head of Education and Events: Sarah Sahr	Interim Director of Publications: Laura Godfrey
	Production: Rich Palmer
	Editorial Staff on this Publication: Laura Godfrey, Nancy Driver, Jennifer Bauduy

Reviewers: Katherine Miller, Jerry Parker, Cinthia Salinas

Recommended citation:
Aldajani, F., Brennan, M., Cypher, P., Fulton, K., & Liu, A. J. (2026). *Teaching social studies to multilingual learners of English*. TESOL Press & National Council for the Social Studies.

Library of Congress Cataloging-in-Publication Data

Names: Aldajani, Fatima author | Brennan, Mary (Teacher) author | Cypher, Peggie author | Fulton, Kaedmon author | Liu, Andy Jiahao author
Title: Teaching social studies to multilingual learners of English / Fatima Aldajani, Mary Brennan, Peggie Cypher, Kaedmon Fulton, and Andy Jiahao Liu.
Description: Silver Spring, MD : National Council for the Social Studies, [2025] | Includes bibliographical references and index. | Summary:
"Teaching Social Studies to Multilingual Learners of English calls for educators to view multilingual learners of English as essential participants in civic learning. This book provides real-life examples, research-based strategies, and lesson plans to help teachers integrate language and content instruction while maintaining academic rigor and fostering students' strengths"—Provided by publisher.
Identifiers: LCCN 2025024900 (print) | LCCN 2025024901 (ebook) | ISBN 9781953745521 paperback | ISBN 9781953745538 ebook
Subjects: LCSH: Social sciences—Study and teaching (Secondary)—United States | English language—Study and teaching--Foreign speakers | Multilingual education—United States
Classification: LCC H62.5.U5 A43 2025 (print) | LCC H62.5.U5 (ebook)
LC record available at https://lccn.loc.gov/2025024900
LC ebook record available at https://lccn.loc.gov/2025024901

Purchase Orders and Bulk Purchases

Discounts are available for tax-exempt purchase orders and bulk purchases.

Please contact publications@tesol.org for more information.

Contents

Preface vi

Introduction 1

    Importance of Social Studies for Multilingual Learners of English 3

    Who We Are 3

    About This Book 4

    Classroom Connections 4

    Conclusion 5

Chapter 1. Understanding Multilingual Learners of English 7

    Assets That Multilingual Learners of English Bring to Social Studies 7

    Barriers That May Affect Multilingual Learners of English in Social Studies 12

    Conclusion: Every Student Is an Individual 22

    Classroom Connections 23

Chapter 2. Supporting Multilingual Learners of English at the Lesson-Planning Level 29

    Integrating Language Learning Objectives With Social Studies Standards 31

    Disciplinary Literacy: Reading and Writing in Social Studies 33

    Collaborative Learning 40

    Supporting Multilingual Learners of English in Assessments 44

    Conclusion: Planning for Success 55

    Classroom Connections 56

Chapter 3. Supporting Multilingual Learners of English at the Lesson-Delivery Level: Teaching Strategies and Activities 59

    Build and Activate Background Knowledge 62

    Incorporate Visuals and Multimedia 64

    Simplify Language 68

    Explicitly Teach Vocabulary 72

    Support Note-Taking and Other Academic Skills 79

    Support Writing 81

    Conclusion: Strategies to Enhance Your Lessons 84

    Classroom Connections 84

Chapter 4. Supporting Multilingual Learners of English in Our Classrooms: Equity and Inclusion in Social Studies 87

    Language Justice in Education 89

    Culturally Responsive Teaching 95

    Addressing Bias and Stereotypes in Curriculum and Instruction 103

    Creating an Inclusive and Equitable Curriculum 108

    Conclusion: Every Teacher Is a Changemaker 109

    Classroom Connections 109

Chapter 5. Supporting Multilingual Learners of English at the School Level: Guidance and Resources for Administrators 111

    Teachers' Perspectives 113

    An Administrator's Guide 115

    Professional Development Resources for Administrators 120

    Classroom Observations 124

    Conclusion: Leaders of Changemakers 127

    Classroom Connections 128

Chapter 6. Supporting Multilingual Learners of English Through Technology ... 131

    Overview of Technology and AI for Teachers 132

    The Ethics of Using AI in the Social Studies Classroom 133

    Digital Literacy 139

    Strategies for Integrating Technology and AI Into
        Social Studies Instruction 142

    Digital Resources for Supporting Language and Social Studies Content ... 143

    Conclusion: Purposeful Integration of Technology 145

    Classroom Connections 146

Chapter 7. Lesson Plans for Supporting Multilingual Learners of English 149

    Key Features of the Lessons 149

    Teaching History, Building Language: Instruction for Multilingual Learners
        of English in the Middle School Classroom 151

        Lesson 1: The American Civil War 151

        Lesson 2: Ancient Egypt 158

        Lesson 3: Understanding Supply and Demand 163

        Lesson 4: Exploring Landforms and Physical Features 167

        Lesson 5: Thanksgiving 173

Access and Engagement: Designing Instruction for Multilingual Learners
of English in the High School Classroom 180
    Lesson 6: Articles of Confederation.. 180
    Lesson 7: The Bill of Rights 184
    Lesson 8: Jim Crow Laws 189
    Lesson 9: The Industrial Revolution 193
    Lesson 10: Women's Suffrage 210
    Lesson 11: Causes of World War I 213

Conclusion 223
Appendix A. Common Terminology 225
Appendix B. Digital Resources for Language Support 226
Appendix C. Recommended Reading Resources 228
Appendix D. Types of Programs 230
References 232
About the Authors 242

Preface

At the 2022 FIFA World Cup Opening Ceremony in Qatar, a dialogue between Morgan Freeman and Ghanim Al Muftah inspired the world with their powerful message of unity—of bridging and coming together as one global community:

Morgan Freeman: I heard something beautiful, not just music, but also this call to celebration. This is all so new. All that I have known before was a land that seemed to be in turmoil, with families forgotten and I stopped hearing your voice.

Ghanim Al Muftah: Come on over.

Morgan Freeman: I'm not sure. Am I welcome?

Ghanim Al Muftah: We sent out the call because everyone is welcome. This is an invitation to the whole world.

Morgan Freeman: I remember, even after hearing the call, instead of seeing another way, we dismissed it and demanded our own way. And now, the world feels even more distant and divided. How can so many countries, languages, and cultures come together, if only one way is accepted?

Ghanim Al Muftah: We were raised to believe that we were scattered on this earth as nations and tribes, so we could learn from each other and find beauty in our differences.

Morgan Freeman: I can see it. What unites us here in this moment is so much greater than what divides us. How can we make it last longer than just today?

Ghanim Al Muftah: With tolerance and respect, we can live together under one big home. In Arabic, *Bayt al sha'ar* is the Bedouin tent. Wherever it is built, that is home. And when we call you here, we welcome you into our home.

Morgan Freeman: So we gather here as one big tribe and earth is the tent we all live in.

Ghanim Al Muftah: Yes. And together, we can send out the call for all the world to join us.

Morgan Freeman: In celebration, in hearing from our heroes through all the differences in language, there is a common thread of hope, jubilation, and respect. We may or may not understand the words, but in the deepest part of us, we must understand and appreciate the emotions that connect us all. (FOX Soccer, 2022)

Introduction

Many professional resources are available to social studies teachers; hundreds of books have been written on the topic of teaching students history in an engaging and authentic way. Likewise, there is a wealth of books for teachers who want to increase their ability to teach English to multilingual learners of English (MLEs), many of which apply language acquisition principles to the English language arts classroom. However, there are not many resources that focus on integrating social studies instruction with English language development. We wrote this book to fill this gap.

We also had another gap in mind in writing this book: The disconnect we have observed between typical instructional practices and the needs of our MLE students, with the unique assets and barriers they bring to the classroom. In many classrooms, MLEs are on the sidelines, sitting silently while others speak, copying off the board words they do not understand and will not remember. Their teachers *know* they are not learning what they need to learn but do not know how to help them.

But things could be different.

We have seen classrooms where MLEs, empowered by clear and consistent language supports, write incredible document-based essays. We have observed MLEs shifting fluidly between their home languages and English as they work with other students to determine the meaning of a primary source. We have seen how powerful it can be for non-MLE peers to hear the first-hand experience of a refugee whose family was caught up in ethnic conflicts left behind by the retreat of colonial powers from Africa. History comes alive in these classrooms—for MLEs and non-MLEs alike.

There is a great opportunity here to transform the way we teach social studies.

The changes we propose in this book are needed today more than ever. MLEs are an increasingly prominent population in U.S. public schools. According to the National Center for Education Statistics (NCES, 2024), as of fall 2021, MLEs accounted for 10.6% of the student body (5.3 million students). States like Texas (20.2%), California (18.9%), and New Mexico (18.8%) have the highest proportions of MLEs, while states such as West Virginia (0.8%) report lower percentages.

Teachers now encounter linguistically diverse classrooms, where students may speak home languages such as Spanish (76.4%), Arabic (2.5%), Chinese (2.2%), Vietnamese (1.8%), and Portuguese (1.0%; NCES, 2024). This linguistic diversity underscores the need for social studies instructors to address the unique characteristics of MLEs, as language classes alone are insufficient to meet their comprehensive learning needs.

Legal cases worldwide have also shaped the conversation around equitable education for linguistically and culturally diverse students:

- *Casteñeda v. Pickard* **(1981):** This landmark U.S. case highlighted the inadequacies of a school district's bilingual education program, which failed to address linguistic barriers preventing equal participation. It was a foundational moment for addressing bilingual education inequalities in the United States.

- *Lovelace v. Ontario* **(2000):** In Canada, Sandra Lovelace successfully argued that denying funding for Indigenous education programs violated constitutional equality provisions. The Supreme Court of Canada's ruling emphasized the need for equitable funding to address systemic disadvantages faced by Indigenous communities.
- *Governing Body of Mikro Primary School v. Western Cape Minister of Education* **(2005):** This South African case underscored how language can be used as a proxy for racial discrimination, challenging the lingering inequalities of apartheid. The court reinforced the right to equitable access to education, regardless of language or race.

These cases reveal a common theme: linguistic and cultural barriers often perpetuate systemic inequities in education, necessitating comprehensive policies and advocacy efforts. Modern policies have sought to address these systemic challenges:

- **Every Student Succeeds Act (ESSA, 2015):** By shifting responsibility for MLE education to the states, ESSA allows local solutions tailored to specific needs. However, states with what the ESSA terms "local control" often struggle to implement consistent policies, structures, and evaluations.
- **Bilingual Education Act (Title VII):** This U.S. legislation provides federal funding for bilingual and dual-language programs, aiming to improve outcomes for MLEs.
- **State and Local Initiatives:** Policies like California's Proposition 58 promote multilingual education programs. These initiatives highlight the importance of state-level advocacy for equitable education.

Together, these frameworks offer opportunities to address the needs of MLEs but require robust implementation and advocacy to achieve their goals at district and building levels. Despite progress, significant challenges remain:

- **Immigration Policies:** Immigration laws and policies, such as the Deferred Action for Childhood Arrivals (DACA) program in the United States, can affect MLEs and their families. Students from mixed-status families or those without legal status may experience fear and uncertainty about their future.
- **Resource Disparities:** Schools with high populations of MLEs often face disparities in resource allocation. Funding cuts can lead to a lack of support services such as English language programs and counseling, impacting MLEs' ability to succeed academically.
- **Discrimination and Racism:** Systemic racism and discrimination can affect MLEs by limiting their opportunities and affecting their self-esteem. Biases in the education system, such as lower expectations or unequal treatment, can hinder MLEs' academic and social development.
- **Political Climate:** The political climate and rhetoric around immigration can create a hostile environment for MLEs. Negative or inflammatory language about immigration can affect students' sense of safety and belonging in school.

While legal victories and policy advancements have laid a foundation, ongoing advocacy is crucial to overcoming these persistent barriers. By fostering inclusive classrooms, advocating for equitable resources, and addressing systemic inequities, educators and policymakers can ensure MLEs thrive in social studies education and beyond.

Importance of Social Studies for Multilingual Learners of English

Social studies education plays a pivotal role in the academic and social development of students, especially MLEs in Grades 6–12. Social studies, encompassing the disciplines of history, geography, civics, economics, cultural studies, and others, offers MLEs more than just knowledge acquisition. It nurtures language development, cultural competence, critical thinking, civic engagement, and college and career readiness.

- **Language Development**: Social studies introduces MLEs to academic language and subject-specific vocabulary, enhancing their ability to understand historical events, geographic concepts, and civic responsibilities. Discussions, readings, and writing exercises support proficiency in both English and MLEs' home languages.
- **Cultural Understanding**: By exploring diverse cultures, histories, and perspectives, social studies fosters cultural awareness and empathy. This broadens MLEs' understanding of global societies and their own cultural identities.
- **Critical Thinking and Analysis**: Analyzing primary and secondary sources, interpreting geographic data, and evaluating historical events build MLEs' critical thinking and problem-solving skills.
- **Civic Engagement**: Social studies empowers MLEs with knowledge of democratic principles, rights, and responsibilities, encouraging active participation in civic life and advocacy for social justice, making them changemakers in their communities.
- **College and Career Readiness**: The skills developed in social studies, such as research, writing, and synthesizing complex information, prepare MLEs for success in higher education and future careers.

Who We Are

We are professional educators with more than 80 combined years of experience in the classroom. We have taught in urban, suburban, and rural public schools from kindergarten to graduate school. Our teaching experience includes the United States, China, Japan, Ukraine, Jordan, Iraq, Indonesia, Egypt, and Palestine. Among us, we speak eight different languages, and two of us (Fatima and Andy) are MLEs ourselves.

Authors are listed alphabetically, as all contributed equally to the conceptualization, development, and writing of this book. Authorship order does not indicate rank or level of contribution.

About This Book

This book is intended for social studies teachers, English language teachers, and anyone who teaches social studies content to MLEs. Chapter 5 also includes information for school and district leaders who want to increase their support for MLE education.

In Chapter 1, we begin with a focus on MLEs and their contributions to the classroom: the assets and the barriers rooted in students' languages, cultures, and prior experiences. Then, we move from the students themselves to the teachers and the ways we can make our lessons, classrooms, and schools more welcoming. Chapter 2 explores small changes in planning, including objectives and awareness of disciplinary literacy practices that can have a big effect on MLEs' success. Chapter 3 looks at teaching for MLEs on the learning activity level and is the core of the book, exploring best practices and specific strategies for instructional delivery and differentiation of learning activities. In Chapter 4, we turn our attention to accessibility and inclusion at the classroom level, exploring ways our curriculum and teaching practices can unintentionally exclude MLEs and ways we can make our classroom more responsive to students from all cultural backgrounds. Next, Chapter 5 zooms out to look at MLE education at the school level; this chapter specifically addresses administrators and highlights collaborative structures in buildings to support teachers and MLEs in the classroom. In Chapter 6, we continue our discussion of practical strategies by looking at how technology, particularly artificial intelligence (AI), can enhance our application of these strategies. Finally, Chapter 7 provides lesson plans, covering a wide range of topics and grade levels, that show how the ideas in this book can be put into practice. The appendices of the book include common terminology, digital resources, recommended reading, and types of programs found around the world.

Companion Site

Many of the lessons, worksheets, and other resources featured in this book are also available for download on the companion site (www.tesol.org/socialstudies-book). These digital materials make it easy for you to access, adapt, and share content with your learners—whether you are teaching in person, online, or in a blended environment. The companion site includes ready-to-use handouts, templates, and graphic organizers that complement the book and save you valuable preparation time.

Classroom Connections

They say a picture is worth a thousand words. Perhaps the teaching version of this proverb would be, "An example is worth a thousand pages of explanation." We apply this proverb to this book by not only explaining best-practice strategies for teaching MLEs and the theory behind them but also including examples of what this looks like in the classroom through the stories of five focus students. You will meet the students in more depth in at the end of Chapter 1, but for now, here is a brief introduction:

- Viktor is a 10th grader from Ukraine with beginning English proficiency.
- Reem is a 6th grader from Syria with beginning English proficiency.
- Nyandeng is a 9th grader from South Sudan with intermediate English proficiency.
- Minh is an 11th grader from Vietnam with advanced English proficiency.
- Yadiel is an 8th grader from Cuba with advanced English proficiency.

Conclusion

Social studies provides MLEs with valuable opportunities for language development, cultural understanding, critical thinking, civic engagement, and preparation for future success. By implementing inclusive and engaging instructional practices, educators can empower MLEs to thrive academically and contribute meaningfully to a global society.

Chapter 1. Understanding Multilingual Learners of English

The backgrounds of multilingual learners of English (MLEs)—their languages, cultures, prior learning, and experiences—can have a profound effect on their learning in a variety of ways. In order to know how to help MLE succeed, teachers need to first understand the assets and barriers that MLEs bring to the classroom. Most obviously, MLEs bring knowledge of one or more languages other than English; this linguistic background can be an asset supporting their acquisition of English, even as their emerging English proficiency can at first limit their understanding of content. Beyond language, cultural factors can also affect MLEs' learning. Cultural norms, values, and traditions deeply influence how learners engage with education; these cultural differences can enrich social studies discussions but can also lead to misunderstandings unless teachers are aware of them. Equally significant are factors related to MLEs' experiences, including prior education, real-life experiences, displacement, and trauma. While these factors present challenges, they also help MLEs develop resilience, maturity, and unique perspectives that serve as assets to their learning. This chapter explores both sides.

In this chapter:
- Assets related to language, culture, and experience
- Linguistic barriers that affect MLEs
- Cultural differences and misunderstandings that can limit learning
- Gaps in background knowledge

Assets That Multilingual Learners of English Bring to Social Studies

While students who are learning English naturally face many challenges, these students also bring many assets into the classroom, assets that can facilitate their own learning as well as enhance learning for their peers. We begin our discussion of student background with an exploration of these assets.

Linguistic Assets

Learning a new language is a huge challenge. However, MLEs bring a huge advantage to this challenge in their knowledge of their home language (or languages, in many cases). There are many ways in which proficiency in one language can help students learn a new one, even if the languages appear to have nothing in common.

First-Language Literacy

An important language learning asset for many MLEs is literacy in their first language. Using reading and writing to learn is an important component of most school instruction (even more so in the United States over the past decade, as updates in standards emphasize the importance of literacy in all content areas). Research has shown that learners who can already read and write in their first language have a much easier time learning to read and write in English than those who have not acquired literacy in any language. This is especially true for learners whose first language uses the same alphabet as English, but it is not limited to these students. In fact, even if the student's first language uses a totally different writing system (such as Chinese characters that represent entire words rather than specific sounds or Arabic's system of using symbols for all consonants but only some vowels), the very fact that they already know one system of reading and writing is still a big advantage when learning to read and write in English.

Language Features That Transfer to English

While the many differences between English and other languages can make learning English difficult, there are also cases where transfer between languages is a benefit. There are thousands of cognates—words in two languages that mean the same thing and sound similar—between English and Spanish, as well as other romance languages such as French and Italian. These words are like free vocabulary for MLEs who speak those languages. Even MLEs who speak more distantly related languages will find words they already know in English. Many languages have very similar words for abstract concepts, political ideas, or recent technological or scientific developments. For example, a Ukrainian student will not need to spend much time studying the English words *constitution*, *ideology*, *empathy*, or *civilian*, as these words sound nearly the same in Ukrainian.

Beneficial language transfer extends beyond just vocabulary; grammatical concepts from a learner's first language can give them a "boost" in learning English. Students whose languages have singular and plural forms will quickly grasp the way adding an s changes the meaning of a word. If the learner's first language includes words that change in a more significant way when moving from singular to plural (such as Arabic, which has lots of plurals that involve an internal change in the word) even the more unusual plurals in English like *goose/geese* or *woman/women* will not be too surprising. Similarly, a learner's understanding (conscious or unconscious) of verb conjugations in their first language can help them grasp why in English, *I am* but *you are* and *she is*, or why one person *votes* but several *vote*. These examples of positive transfer between languages are just a few of the ways MLEs' first languages serve as an asset when they are learning English.

First Language as a Learning Tool

In addition to helping them learn English, MLEs' first languages are also a powerful tool that they can use to learn the content even while they are still building English proficiency. Taking advantage of MLEs' home language proficiency by using multiple languages in the classroom is known as translanguaging. This practice supports students both psychologically and academically by acknowledging the importance of learners' first language and making use of "students' full linguistic repertoire for teaching and learning"

(Qin & Llosa, 2023, p. 715). For instance, while teaching abstract and complex concepts and vocabulary from social studies, teachers can encourage MLEs to use their first languages to negotiate meaning and express their understanding. Students might read texts or watch videos in their first language or work together with a peer who speaks the same language to discuss what they are learning. More valuably, translanguaging can create safe zones for MLEs from the same language background to communicate concerns and find support.

Bilingualism as a Cognitive and Social Asset

Recent research has highlighted the cognitive benefits of bilingualism, such as improved higher level cognitive skills, problem-solving skills, and growth mindset. Bilingual students frequently have higher ability in activities requiring working memory and cognitive control due to their experience navigating multiple languages (Bialystok, 2001). Encouraging MLEs to use their language in the classroom enhances both cognitive growth and cultural interaction. This leads to deeper understanding and empathy to build a more inclusive learning environment where linguistic diversity is seen as an asset rather than a barrier, improving the learning environment for all students (Xia, 2024). In addition, Flores and García (2020) found that bilingual learners feel proud of their cultural identity and self-esteem.

For example, when studying the French Revolution, a student from the Democratic Republic of the Congo who speaks French was able to translate the text on a political cartoon. This experience positioned the student as an expert who could help her classmates with a challenging document and framed her multilingualism as an asset and a point of pride, rather than a factor that hampered her learning and separated her from her peers.

Cultural Assets

Diversity is a strength in any classroom, even more so in a subject where different cultures and perspectives are a major part of the content. In addition to making learning social studies easier for themselves, MLEs' cultural perspectives can enrich the learning of the entire learning community. MLEs also benefit from other cultural assets, such as resilience and community support.

Diverse Perspectives and Global Awareness in the Classroom

One of the most valuable assets MLEs bring to social studies classes is their unique perspectives on the world. Social studies stresses the idea that people see the world through many lenses, shaped by their experiences and cultural backgrounds, which impact how they interpret and understand events. MLEs provide a significant opportunity for students in homogeneous environments to explore and understand diverse perspectives authentically (Gay, 2018). Even in various settings where students are used to inclusiveness, including new perspectives improves discussions. By encouraging MLEs to share their perspectives on historical or contemporary issues, educators enhance critical thinking and foster a stronger link between past events and current global dynamics, resulting in a more inclusive and globally aware classroom environment (Banks, 2019).

Kaedmon, a high school world history teacher, observed the value of the diverse perspectives that MLEs bring to the classroom in a 10th-grade world history lesson on capitalism and communism. They and their coteacher had decided to introduce the economic systems through a simulation, in which students played two rounds of a paper airplane–making game. In the first round, simulating a capitalist system, students competed to make the best plane, which they could sell for a varying amount of candy. In the second round, representing communism, they worked in an assembly-line style to benefit the "mother country," which distributed a single candy to each student after completing the plane. At the end of both rounds of the game, the teachers asked students to reflect on which system they preferred and why. To their surprise, instead of an overwhelming support for the capitalist system, with its opportunities for creativity and huge candy profit, the MLEs in the class almost all chose the communist system. These students (most of whom came from cultures that value collective benefit rather than individualism) explained that they liked being able to help their "mother country"; it felt good to be working for everyone's benefit. This perspective benefitted the non-MLEs in the class because it helped them understand why so many people and countries throughout history have been attracted to communism. *All* the students who participated in this lesson were better prepared to understand the events of the Cold War because they had seen in their own classroom how people might have very different perspectives about the best way to organize an economy.

Cultural Resilience

One asset that MLEs bring to the classroom is their unique flexibility and ability to navigate multiple cultural contexts. These assets can enhance students' social studies learning and help them develop the skills needed for it.

MLEs are adept at shifting between cultural norms, whether at home, in the community, or in school. They code-switch between cultural expectations, much as they do between languages, modifying their behavior, communication, and attitudes according to the situation. This ability helps them comprehend and interpret historical and social contexts from many perspectives in the social studies classroom.

Some MLEs, particularly those who live apart from one or both parents, may accept responsibilities such as caring for siblings or managing household chores. These duties can help students build leadership, time management, and problem-solving skills that they can apply in the classroom where they can demonstrate resilience when handling assignments and engaging in debates.

Some MLEs serve as cultural brokers, interpreting for their parents or communities in public and private settings, such as doctor's visits or government offices. This experience improves critical thinking, communication, and negotiating skills, which are helpful when working with historical documents, primary sources, and debates in social studies.

In addition, some MLEs have been through extreme hardships, such as displacement, migration, violence, or exposure to colonization, which foster resilience, adaptability, and perseverance. These assets can help MLEs approach complex social studies issues like social justice, human rights, or historical events with a unique perspective and a deep understanding of adversity and survival. Social studies teachers may engage MLEs by allowing them, if the students are comfortable doing so, to share their experiences and use them as learning assets. Creating a learning environment that respects and honors these lived experiences can empower MLEs to connect with the content and contribute to discussions on complex global issues.

Background as Assets

Although differences in background knowledge and experiences can create many challenges for MLEs in understanding and participating in social studies learning, these differences can also be assets in certain circumstances, especially when teachers are able to shift their own perspectives.

Strong Prior Education

While some countries have struggling education systems that leave students behind their U.S. grade level, others are thriving and provide students with a much more robust background than the U.S. system. In particular, students from other countries may have more global consciousness than students who grew up in the United States, including better map skills.

In addition, while differences in curriculum can sometimes hamper MLEs' ability to understand social studies classes in the United States, these same students often have much deeper knowledge of the history of their home country or region than their non-MLE peers. This background knowledge can make world history classes much easier because they are studying information they already know and can focus their energy on acquiring the language to express their understanding. For example, Kaedmon's Ukrainian students typically have a very easy time during the Cold War unit of their world history class, as the Soviet period was an important chapter in their own history. Reading texts on this time period is less like learning new information and more like recognizing things they already know, just expressed in a different way.

Relevant Background Experiences

Many MLEs come into the classroom with firsthand experience of history topics that are hard for their U.S. peers to understand. They may have experienced ethnic cleansing, war, famine, civil unrest, economic crises, or oppressive governments. Additionally, they may practice or be familiar with the world religions covered in the curriculum. MLEs will find it much easier to understand these topics, especially if their teacher is aware of their background and highlights these connections. In this context, MLEs' background knowledge and experiences should be considered assets and can benefit the entire learning community if addressed appropriately. Talking to someone who is directly impacted by specific historical incidents makes the content seem more real to students, and the rest of the world feels closer and more relevant when students from China, Kenya, and Venezuela sit at desks in your classroom.

For example, when teacher Fatima's world history class discussed the end of World War II and the beginning of the Cold War, her Palestinian students from Gaza shared how these events affected them. The students shared family stories about the Nakba of 1948 when the Israeli occupation led to the displacement and massacres of millions of Palestinians by armed Zionist militias with the help of the British government. The students shared how their ancestors were forced to leave their lands, property, and homes behind and were displaced to other Palestinian cities, such as Gaza, or neighboring countries and how their family members continue to live under colonization, apartheid, and genocide in Palestine to this day. This personal connection to the discussion of the end of World War II and the beginning of the Cold War underscores how these political events affected and continue to affect Palestinians and provides a deeper understanding of how global events changed the political order in the region.

It is essential, however, when bringing MLEs' experiences into the classroom, to prioritize students' psychological safety and comfort. Many *non*-MLE students do not feel comfortable speaking in front of the entire class; this can be an even more intimidating prospect for students who are still learning to speak English! To make the experience more accessible for MLEs, keep the following guidelines in mind:

- When inviting students to share about their cultures and experiences, always make it clear that this is an option, not a requirement.
- Give students time to gather their thoughts. Avoid putting them on the spot without warning.
- Do not make assumptions. A Mexican student might connect with the struggles of working-class immigrants to send money home to family—or the student could be a member of the landowning elite.
- Students should never be asked to explain or defend the actions of the country they came from, as if they were the spokesperson for their entire country.
- Establish a safe and supportive learning environment, where difference is a positive thing and where laughing at mistakes (such as mispronouncing a word) is unacceptable.

When MLEs feel comfortable and safe speaking in front of their peers and sharing their experiences, everyone benefits.

Barriers That May Affect Multilingual Learners of English in Social Studies

The barriers facing MLEs are many and varied. We have organized them here by factors related to students' languages, cultures, and backgrounds, but there is some overlap. More important than the categories is that MLEs might be affected by a wide range of factors, and each student's situation is unique.

Linguistic Barriers

Most teachers are aware that school is difficult for students who are learning English. In the following sections, we go into more depth on how language background affects learning, discussing how aspects of language, such as unevenly developing proficiency, vocabulary challenges, and psychological factors, can affect MLEs.

Imbalanced English Proficiency

The level of English proficiency among MLEs varies. Some learners may have developed advanced skills in using English, but many others still need lots of support. It is also common for MLEs to show imbalanced proficiency levels across the four basic domains of language: listening, speaking, writing, and reading. Some students can understand quite a bit of what they hear and read but struggle to produce written or spoken English on their own. Other students are confident speakers and have excellent listening comprehension, but their reading and writing lags far behind.

Additionally, language learners almost always master informal social language much more quickly than they learn academic language. Language acquisition researcher Cummins (2000) found that basic interpersonal communication skills (BICS) are generally developed within 1 to 2 years of language learning; however, the more formal academic language, which he referred to as cognitive academic language proficiency (CALP), can take 5 to 7 years (or more) to master. A student who has acquired BICS may seem, when they are interacting with peers and adults, to be a fluent speaker of English who does not need any support, but when faced with understanding and producing more complex academic language, the learner may still need help. Teachers who are not aware of this distinction might assume the student is lazy, when in fact the student is showing a very typical pattern of language growth.

Conventions and Vocabulary Challenges of the English Language

Compared to many other languages, English is thought to be relatively easy to learn. However, specific aspects of the language can be challenging for MLEs, especially for those who use a different writing system. Consider the following:

- Arabic is read from right to left, is written in a cursive script, and makes no distinction between uppercase and lowercase letters.
- Ukrainian has inflected verbs, changing form based on person, number, or gender.
- The grammar in Chinese does not address time through the verb tenses but uses time specific words in the sentence, such as *Yesterday I eat pork*.
- Vietnamese is a tonal language in which the pitch of a word can change the meaning.
- In Spanish, nouns, adjectives, determiners, and pronouns are assigned a gender.

On top of dealing with the new conventions of English, MLEs are also learning a language with the largest vocabulary. For example, Merriam-Webster (n.d.-b) has 470,000 entries in *Webster's Third*

New International Dictionary, although some argue that there may be more than a million when including slang, compound words, industry lingo, and verb tenses. Compare this amount to the 135,000 in German, 93,000 in Spanish, and 85,568 in Chinese (Andrews, 2024). MLEs are also challenged by the fact that English may have the largest number of synonyms; for instance, there are 205 synonyms and antonyms of *say* (Merriam-Webster, n.d.-c), not to mention the myriad of multiple meaning words with *run*, running up a total of 645 definitions (Winchester, 2011), including the following:

- Flashlights *run* on batteries.
- A fence *runs* around my yard.
- I want to *run* an idea by you.
- I hope to *run* into you at the game.
- Great idea! Let's *run* with it.

Idioms, a type of figurative language with meanings that cannot be derived from the individual words, number at 25,000. Their usage is common in everyday English (e.g., *think outside the box*) as well as more academic and formal contexts (e.g., the president asking a political party to *reach across the aisle*). Similarly, phrasal verbs, phrases consisting of a verb with a preposition, adverb, or both, can be daunting to master as their meaning is different from each separate part. In common usage, there are more than 600 phrasal verbs: *come* has at least 37 (UsingEnglish.com, n.d.), including these:

- Please *come up* with your answer by tomorrow.
- He hasn't *come down* from the excitement of the party.
- We haven't *come to* a decision.
- *Come back* when you're finished.
- She *comes by* her talent naturally.
- Take off your shoes before you *come in*.
- She *comes off* as a shy person.

As teachers, we can ease these challenges by being culturally sensitive, creating a welcoming classroom setting, providing encouragement, and differentiating vocabulary instruction to MLEs' proficiency levels.

Academic Vocabulary

In social studies classrooms, MLEs are not only challenged by the conventions of English and the types of words previously mentioned, but they also encounter texts with academic vocabulary full of abstract concepts. These vocabularies are different from everyday words they use in daily conversations; instead, these words are often associated with discipline- and culture-specific references. Also, a certain group of vocabulary can represent U.S.-specific definitions rather than the familiar ones in their home countries (e.g., *democracy*). Compared with their non-MLE peers, MLEs usually require additional effort and time to familiarize themselves with these vocabularies so that they can better follow instructors in class.

For example, in an American history class discussing the U.S. foreign policy system, MLEs may struggle to keep up because they are unfamiliar with terms like *intervention* or *sanctions*. The language barrier can prevent them from fully participating in the discussion, speaking about their own experiences, or expressing their opinions. To help MLEs participate more effectively, the teacher must teach basic political vocabulary in advance and use visual aids, such as charts and images.

The Effects of Anxiety on the Brain

Anxiety can have a profound effect on students' participation and learning. Many MLEs may refuse to speak in classroom discussions or read aloud in class because they are worried about making mistakes or embarrassed about their accents. The fear of being laughed at or judged by non-MLE peers not only reduces students' opportunities to practice English but also affects their brains' ability to learn language.

The affective filter hypothesis, incorporated into second language acquisition by Krashen (1982), describes a psychological barrier that impedes language input. This barrier, created by negative emotions such as anxiety and lack of motivation, can block the language learning process.

The classroom environment, along with the attitudes of the instructor and other students, can raise or lower the students' affective filter. For example, when the classroom exhibits an inclusive environment and when the teachers and peers are welcoming to MLEs, the affective filter can be lowered. This can result in a student's overall feeling of well-being and allow the student to better learn the new language. Teachers should therefore create a supportive environment where students feel welcome and safe to participate in class activities and take risks in using the English language.

Motivation

Another factor language acquisition researchers have identified that contributes to differences between students in language learning speed is motivation (Gardner, 2001). Countless factors affect MLEs' motivation to learn English, and each individual student may respond to these factors differently. Some MLEs are self-driven to overcome the challenges in comprehension and improve their English proficiencies as needed; however, others may feel discouraged and even question their self-worth when they experience challenges related to their English proficiencies. Gradually, students with high motivation can find themselves successfully achieving their learning outcomes and building confidence in further studies, but students with low motivation may be left behind and experience emotional stress and anxiety. A student's family and community can also have an effect on their motivation; some MLEs' families have very high academic expectations, which could either increase or decrease students' motivation for language learning (Vera et al., 2012). Other students' families or communities may have a different perspective, seeing other endeavors as more important than education; this too could either spur a student to achieve more despite the opposition of their family or reduce their motivation to learn English because it is not aligned with their family's values or priorities.

Cultural Barriers

In addition to exploring the linguistic barriers facing MLEs, it is also necessary that teachers understand how culture shapes MLEs' experiences in social studies classes. Like language, MLEs' cultural backgrounds can impact how they approach school and curriculum and how they interact with teachers and peers. Understanding MLEs' cultural backgrounds is essential for more inclusive classrooms where all students feel comfortable participating.

Cultural Patterns of Interaction

Culture affects all of our interactions with others, often in ways of which we are not even aware. Some behaviors that teachers may perceive as disrespectful are in fact just different cultural ways of showing respect.

- **Eye Contact**. In white middle-class American culture, making eye contact while talking with someone is a way of showing respect and interest in them. When teachers from this culture are talking to students who are in trouble, they interpret eye contact as the student showing respect and taking their behavior seriously, while a student who is avoiding eye contact is perceived to be disrespectfully blowing off the discussion. However, in many cultures—including many Asian cultures and African American culture—making eye contact in such a situation would be a show of defiance, and the best way to show respect for elders during a scolding is to humbly not meet their eyes.

- **Punctuality**. "On time is late, and early is on time!"—or at least, it is according to many European and American cultures. From this cultural perspective, a student walking into class late is disrespecting the teacher and showing a disregard for their education. However, in many other cultures, including Latine culture, relationships are prioritized above schedules, and being on time is not really important. A Cuban student might genuinely not understand why his teacher is frustrated when he lingers in the hallway chatting with friends after the bell.

- **Gender Lines**. For many middle school teachers, making groups is complicated by the fact that many middle schoolers are resistant to working in groups with classmates of another gender. In most cases, this is based on childish "boys/girls have cooties" attitudes, and teachers are likely to just tell students to cut out the silliness and get to work. However, some Muslim and Arab students may refuse to work with peers of another gender, not because they are squeamish or prejudiced about them, but because it is a culturally important behavior expectation. A teacher might interpret a Muslim girl's refusal to sit next to a boy as defiance when in fact she is trying *not* to defy her parents' instructions.

These and other culturally motivated behaviors and interactions can cause friction between

MLEs and their teachers when the teacher does not understand the source of the behavior. It is important to understand the specific cultural norms of the communities our students come from—and to keep an open mind when they act in ways that clash with our own cultural expectations.

Cultural Assumptions About Teaching and Learning

Approaches to education vary widely among cultures. Social studies education in the United States is increasingly moving away from memorizing dates and events to constructing historical arguments, sourcing and corroborating documents, and fostering civic values and responsibility. Some MLEs come from countries with similar approaches to social studies, while others come from settings where being a good student of history means memorizing what the textbook says happened. For example, Nepali culture views education as a process of an expert giving students the answers, which the students are expected to memorize and reproduce exactly. A student from Nepal may struggle in an inquiry-based social studies classroom, where students are constructing their own understandings rather than memorizing those received from an expert.

Another area where approaches to education vary among cultures is the line between collaboration and cheating. In the United States, it is generally assumed that copying an answer from a friend is cheating because the educational focus in this cultural setting is on developing original thought and on making sure students understand *how* they get to the correct answer. In other settings, such as in many parts of Asia, the emphasis in education is on working together and on making sure students know the correct information, as determined by experts. It is quite common for students to copy each other's work in these cultures, and it is seen as proper collaboration, not cheating. Just as an American student who did not write down the homework assignment might copy the details from a classmate, copying a friend's answers is seen as a responsible move students can take in order to make sure they are working with the correct information. Similarly, a teacher from a Western cultural background might consider an essay composed almost entirely of quotations from other sources to be pushing the line of plagiarism because, in these cultures, it is important for students to show that they understand the sources they draw on. In other cultures, putting experts' words into your own words could be seen as arrogant, as if you were claiming to know better than them. Educators whose students come from different cultural backgrounds such as these will need to teach them the conventions of academic work in Western culture and in the meantime to interpret their actions as honest attempts to be the best students they can.

Interactions With Curriculum

When discussing sensitive topics like human rights throughout history, different cultural norms, values, and beliefs might lead to misconceptions. Social studies textbooks frequently exclude detailed information regarding minorities and controversial topics (Romanowski, 2009) or represent cultural ideas in ways that do not align with students' understanding. Many times, teachers base instruction on cultural assumptions—the values and priorities that form the foundation of every culture—without realizing it. For example, many teachers present capitalism as an obviously better system than communism, based on an assumption that individual success is everyone's highest priority. For a student who comes from a more collective culture that values cooperation for the common good over individualism, this argument might be very confusing.

Isolation in Group Activities

MLEs may feel isolated in collaborative learning due to cultural differences or language barriers (García & Kleyn, 2016). Teachers often intentionally group MLEs together for logistical reasons: It is easier to provide modified materials or for a language teacher to provide support to a single group. Or teachers might put MLEs in a group together so that they can help translate for each other or because the students may feel more comfortable speaking in front of other language learners. These are all valid reasons to group MLEs together, and such groupings are often appropriate. But *always* grouping MLEs with each other and never with their non-MLE peers contributes to isolation within the classroom and to a perception that MLEs are not really part of the learning community. When MLEs work together with non-MLEs, both groups of students have the opportunity to learn from each other.

Reflect on the group structure in your classroom:
- Are all students valuable members of the classroom community?
- How can you tailor group activities to encourage participation from all students, regardless of language proficiency? For specific strategies to support collaborative learning for all students, see Chapter 2.

Barriers Resulting From Backgrounds of Multilingual Learners of English

Although every student who comes into our classrooms has a unique set of background knowledge and experiences, the background MLEs bring can often differ from that of their peers in surprising ways. Sometimes, those differences are gaps: Some MLEs may not know who George Washington was or that not all countries have a president. Some may have never attended school. This section explores how MLEs' backgrounds can create learning challenges.

Interruptions in Education

Nearly all learners who find themselves studying social studies in a new country have experienced some interruptions in their education. In the most extreme cases, students have significant gaps in their education or no prior formal education at all; these students are commonly referred to as students with interrupted formal education (SIFE or, alternatively, students with limited or interrupted formal education [SLIFE]). Most commonly, those identified as SIFE are refugees; others come from places where school may have been available, but they were not able to attend for economic or safety reasons.

- Hawa is a Somali girl who was born in a refugee camp in Kenya. From ages 7 to 11, she attended school in the camp sporadically, learning to recite a few passages from the Quran. The school only occasionally had access to supplies like books or pencils, so Hawa was not able to learn to read or write. She is now in the seventh grade, cannot write her own name, has never touched a computer, and believes that the sun goes around the Earth. On the other hand, her experiences living in a camp among people from many different places have helped her develop excellent interpersonal and communication skills; Hawa fluently speaks four languages and is quickly picking up spoken English.

- Illia went to school in Ukraine from first grade (age 6) to eighth grade (age 13). When Russia's full-scale invasion of the country began, Illia was unable to attend school. He finished his eighth-grade year doing online schooling, but he did not really understand the material presented in the recorded lessons and did not have a teacher to ask for help. Partway through Illia's ninth-grade year, his family fled to Poland, where they spent 6 months before moving to the United States. When Illia finally got registered in a U.S. school, he was placed in 11th grade. He has a solid foundational education and excellent study skills, but he is lost in his trigonometry class because he was never able to grasp algebra.

- Paw Htoo is a Burmese girl from the Karen ethnic group whose family lived as refugees in Thailand. Although there was a school nearby that some children attended, Paw Htoo never went. With her father killed in the violence that pushed the family out of the country, Paw Htoo has to care for her younger siblings while her mother works to put food on the table. Even if she were an only child, however, Paw Htoo probably would not go to school: She has known too many girls who have disappeared on the 4-mile hike through the mountains to and from school, kidnapped to become sex workers in Bangkok.

- Carlos has attended school in the United States ever since kindergarten. However, because his parents are migrant farm workers, every one of Carlos's school years has been pieced together: a few months in New York for apples and grapes, then to Florida for the citrus harvest in the late fall, then back home to Mexico to spend a few weeks with Carlos's grandparents, then to Georgia for onions in the spring, and on to North Carolina before the end of the school year for the summer vegetables. Not only does each move involve time out of school, but each state has its own curriculum and scope and sequence. In his sixth-grade year, Carlos learned about ancient Egypt four separate times but always missed out on Ancient Mesopotamia, China, and India.

Absence of Assumed Common Knowledge

SIFE experience significant challenges when they encounter a school system that assumes that all children have had several years of continuous education. Some students enter high school unable to hold a pencil or with no understanding of sound–symbol correspondence. Many facts that are assumed to be common knowledge are new to them (e.g., the moon goes around the Earth, but the Earth goes around the sun; Black people were enslaved and deprived of their rights by white people in the Americas for decades). SIFE of all ages often find the unspoken expectations of a traditional classroom bewildering and arbitrary (e.g., stay in your chair even if your legs are uncomfortable; raise your hand if you want to talk; success means making the correct marks on a paper, but if you look at your friend's paper to see what the correct answer is, you get in trouble).

Lack of First-Language Literacy

Learning to read and write is an especially significant challenge for students who never acquired literacy in their first language or languages. These students sometimes bewilder their general education teachers, as they may acquire fluent speaking and listening skills relatively quickly. They often have an excellent memory for everything they hear and can explain concepts or historical events fluidly and in great detail. But when the structure of school requires them to read or write for learning or to demonstrate their understanding, they are suddenly unable to do the work. Some teachers might interpret this as laziness when, in fact, it is a logical effect of the students' background.

Gaps in Education

It is important to remember that even students who do not have extreme interruptions in education like SIFE may still have gaps. The political and economic upheavals that force families to leave their countries and move to a new community frequently also result in some missed school, as does the long process of an international move with all the appointments and red tape involved. Finally, the effects of the global COVID-19 pandemic led to interruptions in the education of students all around the world. Even in schools that pivoted quickly to virtual schooling, the education students received in the spring of 2020 was anything but normal. While situations such as these may not be recognized as official interruptions in education, we still need to be aware of their effects on students.

Differences in Background Knowledge

Even if students' education was never interrupted, they may have different background knowledge than their non-MLE peers. The obvious example is U.S. history. Children in the United States grow up learning about the country's history from kindergarten; in some states, students take U.S. history almost every year with maybe 1 or 2 years of world history. By the time they get to high school, the typical U.S. student knows quite a bit about U.S. history. As a result, high school social studies teachers often skip over or barely touch on the basics, rightly opting to go deeper and cover topics students are not as familiar with. This benefits most students; however, it is important to be conscious of MLEs in the classroom who cannot reasonably be expected to know, for example, who Abraham Lincoln was or why the U.S. Civil War was fought, and to provide clarification and opportunities for them to fill in those gaps.

Even when MLEs have studied the same historical topics as their peers, there is no guarantee that they learned about them in the same way (or even that they learned the same facts). For example, a high school student from China will doubtless have already studied the Great Leap Forward, but it is quite likely they learned a very different story from the one presented in history classrooms and textbooks in the United States. This disconnect could be confusing or emotionally challenging for students, especially if the teacher asks the Chinese student about this without preparation, as if speaking for their whole country, or uses the situation as an opportunity to preach about governments lying to their people. But this situation is also a priceless opportunity for everyone in the classroom, if handled carefully and empathetically, to learn about how a source's perspective affects the way history is presented.

Trauma

Many MLEs—like their non-MLE peers—have background experiences that include traumatic events. Families rarely pick up and move to a new country because everything is going great. Some MLEs carry with them memories of war or gang violence, while others are dealing with more personal experiences of family-related trauma. Others experience generational trauma, carrying in their genes the physical and psychological effects of devastating events that happened to their parents and grandparents; this is particularly common with Indigenous students and with refugee students who may have been born in camps and whose families are still displaced years after the inciting events. Research has shown that trauma, whether direct or generational, can have a profound effect on the brain's ability to learn (e.g., Jensen, 2009; Mulligan et al., 2025).

The effects of trauma may be especially pronounced in the social studies classroom, where the content may connect to students' traumatic prior experiences. While war, genocide, and human rights violations are inescapable parts of our curriculum, it is always important to approach these topics carefully, avoiding graphic images and depictions that could trigger bad memories for students with related experiences. Keep in mind that students may not feel comfortable sharing these experiences right away, so they may have traumas you are not aware of. If you are not sure, err on the side of caution when presenting difficult content.

Another way trauma can affect MLEs is in political expression. MLEs who come from countries where political expression is restricted may be hesitant to participate in discussions on political issues. If a student has been taught for 15 years that saying anything critical of the government is dangerous, it can be difficult for them to shed that mindset. For example, a Cuban student may be afraid to make a post about the freedom of speech to a shared class blog because they fear that expressing their views could lead to repercussions for their family back home. Rather than brushing off the student's concerns, the teacher can offer a less public way to participate, such as writing a reflection paper instead of posting online.

Different Life Experiences

Finally, MLEs' experiences of everyday life may differ in significant ways from those of other students in the classroom. Teachers understand the importance of drawing on students' experiences, connecting the content with their everyday lives. However, in applying this understanding, we sometimes make assumptions about students' experiences that do not apply to our MLE students.

For example, as a high school world history teacher, Kaedmon was used to engaging students in learning about urbanization during the Industrial Revolution by using photographs and texts that emphasize some of the most challenging aspects of tenement life. As they presented this lesson to a group of MLEs, however, they found themself looking at a room full of blankly polite faces, rather than the shock and disgust that they usually see as signs of engagement with this content. Only after class ended did Kaedmon remember that, just a week earlier, one of their students from Eritrea had described the living conditions he experienced in a refugee camp in Ethiopia: He had shared a dirt-floored plastic tent with 12 other boys. No wonder he wasn't impressed by the accounts of up to eight people living in the same apartment!

Conclusion: Every Student Is an Individual

When considering the ways MLEs' linguistic, cultural, and personal backgrounds can serve as barriers and assets, it is important to remember above all that MLEs are individuals. Their backgrounds—and the ways those backgrounds affect their learning—vary as much as those of any other group of students. Some Arabic speakers struggle to learn and use the English alphabet; some have no trouble with it. Some students from collective-focused cultures are collaborative and sociable; others are independent souls who prefer to work alone. Some refugee students are extremely well educated; others do not know how to write their own names. Even two students from the same country may have vast differences in background knowledge and experiences. Each student is first and foremost a unique person, and we need to connect with them as individuals.

As you get to know your students, use the information in this chapter as a guide, not for what specific conclusions you can draw about your MLEs, but for what kind of *questions* you should ask. And remember that few people feel comfortable sharing everything about themselves right up front. Getting to know your students and understanding how their language, culture, and experiences affect them is an ongoing process—one that is absolutely critical for providing quality instruction to MLEs.

Classroom Connections

In the next pages, you will meet the five focus students that we will follow throughout the rest of this book. As we introduce the students, we have highlighted how the factors discussed in this chapter serve as assets and barriers for them. The student identity cards include AI-generated images created for educational use. They represent fictional characters and do not depict any real individual.

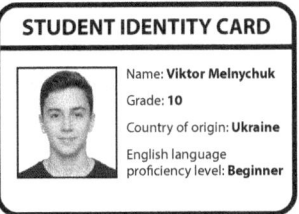

STUDENT IDENTITY CARD

Name: **Viktor Melnychuk**
Grade: **10**
Country of origin: **Ukraine**
English language proficiency level: **Beginner**

Viktor used to love school. All his friends were there, he was top of his class in everything except math, and his football (American soccer) club made it to regional finals. Now, he walks with his head down through the halls, noisy with conversations and inside jokes he does not understand, and struggles to express even simple ideas in English. He misses being competent. He misses knowing what is going on. He misses Ukraine.

Some days are especially hard. This morning, he had a history test on the breakup of the Soviet Union, something he knows all about: both from learning about it in school in Ukraine and from his grandpa's stories. Political changes the American students struggle to keep track of are things that he was familiar with when he was 10 years old. He could ace this test.

Except, during the period before the test, an oven malfunctioned in the cafeteria, and the school had an unplanned evacuation. The blaring alarm, the frantic exit into the blowing snow, the sirens and flashing lights of the fire trucks that responded—it all was too similar to the air raids he experienced in Kherson before he and his family got out. Viktor spends the entire test period halfway to a panic attack, staring at the questions without seeing them, and finally circles answers at random with 2 minutes before the bell.

Traumatic experiences like Viktor's can have a profound effect on a student's ability to learn. Creating a safe, welcoming learning environment, as discussed in Chapter 4, will help students like Viktor to feel comfortable in school and to continue their learning.

Viktor also faces linguistic challenges. While Ukrainian shares a few letters with English, there are many that do not overlap—and some of the ones that do have completely different sounds. What looks like a /y/ sound to Viktor now has to be pronounced /n/, /n/ is now /h/, and /r/ is now /p/; sometimes he thinks it would be easier just to start over with a whole new alphabet. As a result, reading and writing remain difficult for Viktor, even as he starts to pick up spoken English.

Despite all the barriers stacked up against Viktor, he also brings some very valuable assets. First, Viktor has a high level of education, especially in European history, which he knows more about than most of his classmates (and many of his teachers). Because he is already familiar with many of the topics he is studying in school, Viktor has an easier time learning the vocabulary associated with them. Instead of learning new concepts and new words at the same time, he just has to match the new words with the concepts he already knows.

Viktor also has strong reading and writing skills in his first language. Not only does his Ukrainian literacy allow him to benefit from translated materials and get right into learning the content even while he is still working on English, but his grasp of the fundamentals of reading will make learning to read a new language easier than if he did not yet have print literacy. Although the letters are a little mixed up to him, he knows how to sound out a word, how to check his understanding as he reads, and how to use context clues to determine the meanings of unfamiliar words—because he has been doing it in Ukrainian for years.

Additionally, Viktor's experiences in the war, while creating a heavy load of trauma, have also given him a valuable perspective on the relevance of world events. Unlike some of his classmates, who frequently whine, "Whyyyyy do we have to learn this? It's never going to be important!" Viktor understands that abstract-seeming topics like militarism, alliances, imperialism, and nationalism can all too suddenly become very relevant indeed. He has a deep desire to understand how his country got into such a precarious situation and how other past dictators were stopped. Once he is able to focus on school and understand his classes, he becomes a deeply engaged, thoughtful student of history.

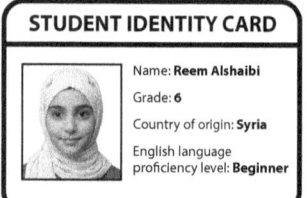

STUDENT IDENTITY CARD

Name: **Reem Alshaibi**

Grade: **6**

Country of origin: **Syria**

English language proficiency level: **Beginner**

Reem is so tiny and adorable, with her big brown eyes and the little sparkly butterfly clips she always wears on her hijab, that people forget that she has lived through more challenges than many adults. She was born into a country at war with itself, and she was just 6 when her family finally got the money together to flee Syria for Europe. They moved from place to place for a while, finally ending up in a refugee camp in Turkey, where they stayed until their resettlement in the United States was approved. Now, after 3 years in the United States, she is beginning to be comfortable speaking the language and is slowly working toward reading and writing proficiency.

A major barrier facing Reem is the enormous gaps in her education. Between the turmoil caused by the Syrian civil war, the time her family spent moving from place to place, and the lack of resources in their camp in Turkey, Reem barely went to school at all before she came to the United States. Even now, after 3 years in the country, there are huge gaps in her background knowledge. She has never heard of Hitler, she does not know that the United States is barely 200 years old, and she cannot find her home state on a map.

Language differences also act as a barrier for Reem. Although her prior education was very inconsistent, she reads a little Arabic, which has helped her as she learned to read English. But the languages are very different—both in their grammar and in their writing systems. Reading from left to right still feels unnatural for Reem, and she is always forgetting to write down the vowel sounds, not just the consonants, when she spells words in English. Reem also has a harder time with English vocabulary than students who speak a first language more closely related to English. While some words like algebra and geography sound very similar to words she knows in Arabic, she does not have as much of a head start on the vocabulary as her Spanish-speaking classmates, who seem to get half the dictionary for free.

Reem also brings a barrier of trauma with her. Although she was young when she left Syria and remembers very little of the war itself, Reem went through a lot of difficult experiences during her family's journey to Turkey and their time in the refugee camp. In addition, the older members of her family, who do remember the war and the horrible things they experienced before leaving Syria, are affected by that trauma—which indirectly affects Reem as well. Growing up surrounded by adults staggering under their own trauma is a kind of trauma of its own.

As much as her experiences have left their marks on Reem in the form of trauma, they also have imbued her with a wide range of strengths. Unlike many of her American classmates, Reem has lived in multilingual and multicultural settings for as long as she can remember; as a result, she arrived in the US speaking Arabic, Turkish, Dari, and a little Kurdish. Learning all those languages has primed her brain to subconsciously analyze new language, make connections to grammatical structures she already knows, and fluently use the limited vocabulary she knows to make herself understood. Learning a third language is almost always easier than a second, and a fourth is easier than a third. Now on her fifth additional language, Reem will find that English proficiency comes quickly to her, bolstered by the deep linguistic awareness and practical communication strategies she has already acquired.

In addition, because her path has brought her into contact with people from many different linguistic and cultural groups, Reem is able to navigate differences and communicate across cultural barriers with ease. She is used to considering perspectives different from her own, and she has a sophisticated, if subconscious, understanding of how people from different cultural backgrounds see the world. Not only will this understanding support Reem's communication and learning in her new school, but it will also benefit her classmates as Reem shares her perspective and experiences.

The greatest asset Reem brings to the classroom is her resilience, born of years of hardship. Remember, Reem is a survivor of a civil war, a grueling and dangerous journey to safety, and years of struggle in a resource-poor refugee camp. The worries and dramas of the seventh-grade hallways are nothing to her. Learn a whole new language? No problem, she has already learned four! Big math test on Friday? She has seen bombs and mobs; she is not scared of numbers. Although there are still big challenges facing Reem, after everything she has overcome just to be here, she is confident that she can get through this as well.

STUDENT IDENTITY CARD

Name: **Nyandeng Atong**
Grade: **9**
Country of origin:
South Sudan
English language
proficiency level:
Intermediate

Nyandeng is a puzzle to many of her teachers. A bright, friendly girl from South Sudan, she has incredible people skills and excellent spoken English. She actively participates in every classroom discussion; she can recall details the class learned way back in September; and she is always ready to volunteer an answer, even if she is not sure about it. And then she fails every single quiz. Her essays are random quotations from documents (and sometimes the instructions) strung together with no rhyme or reason. Nyandeng's social studies teacher is starting to wonder if she is just lazy—willing to participate when it is just talking but not caring enough to put in the hard work on written assignments. After all, it is not her English that is the problem: She speaks and understands just fine!

In fact, Nyandeng's English language development is the barrier preventing her from succeeding in school—even though her learning is progressing entirely typically. In Nyandeng's home community, safety concerns prevented her from attending the underresourced local school, and nobody in her family was able to teach her at home. As a result, Nyandeng only started learning to read a few years ago. Like most people who do not have literacy in any language and who grew up in a multilingual setting, Nyandeng is a quick learner of spoken languages and has an excellent memory for what she hears. And, equally typically, she is still struggling to read first-grade texts, even after a few years of instruction. Nyandeng's language development, while completely normal, will be a barrier to her learning without the proper supports.

As a student with limited formal education, Nyandeng has gaps in her background knowledge. Nyandeng will need support from her teachers to fill in those gaps in background knowledge in ways that are accessible to her (e.g., videos, audiobooks) while she is still building her foundational reading ability.

However, Nyandeng also brings significant assets to the classroom. In part because she is learning to read so late in the game, Nyandeng has excellent interpersonal communication and listening skills. She has an amazing memory for anything she hears; if you cannot write down a grocery list on paper, you learn how to keep a dozen items in your brain until you get to the shop. In addition, Nyandeng has excellent people skills. She is confident, funny, and outgoing, assertive when she needs to be, charming when that is what will play best. She knows how to navigate a multicultural world and advocate to get her needs met, and she has the drive to do it. These abilities allow Nyandeng to excel at collaborative learning and make her an invaluable group member when students are working on projects together.

STUDENT IDENTITY CARD

Name: **Minh Nguyen**
Grade: **11**
Country of origin:
Vietnam
English language
proficiency level:
Advanced

*Teachers are amazed that **Minh** only arrived in the United States 2 years ago: Her English is already excellent, thanks to years of classes back home in Vietnam. On top of that, she has excellent study skills, a thorough prior education, and a strict house rule of "no YouTube before homework" that keeps her on track. Her essays are meticulously organized and full of detail; her multiple-choice test scores are always in the high 90s. Minh's teachers are encouraging her to take AP courses next year.*

Then a teacher runs her paper on the Watergate scandal through a plagiarism checker. Minh is called into the office, her father has to leave work to meet with the principal, and her teachers are angry and disappointed. They expected better from her. They thought she was an honest girl.

Minh feels humiliated—and confused. She wrote the essay exactly the way she was taught to, the way she has written dozens of essays before. All Minh's extensive prior education has been in a system based on a different philosophy of what learning means and how it happens. In Minh's culture, to learn something means to find out what the experts have determined to be true about it, to memorize that information, and to be able to produce it when prompted. Minh copied the language her sources used because, as she has been taught, it would be arrogant to think she could explain it better than the experts did. In this scenario, Minh is prevented from successfully participating in American schools by barriers resulting from cultural differences.

While Minh has the study skills to acquire new vocabulary and grammatical structures independently, she still needs support with the conventions of academic writing in the United States—some of which, like the definition of original work, blur the lines between linguistic and cultural factors. For example, Minh knows how to organize her writing, but the assumptions of what good organization looks like differ between Vietnam and the United States. Similarly, there are some classroom activities—especially inquiry activities where students must work together to construct new knowledge on their own, rather than receiving it from an expert source—where Minh will need extra support to understand how the assumptions about learning in the United States differ from those she is used to.

Of course, Minh also brings a range of assets to the classroom. For example, because she grew up reading extensively in her first language, reading in English comes easily to her. She can now use texts in both her languages to build her knowledge. Minh also brings an asset that can benefit the entire class: She grew up and was educated in a very different culture from that of the United States. By highlighting Minh's unique perspective, Minh's teacher can help both her and her classmates benefit from the cultural exchange.

STUDENT IDENTITY CARD

Name:
Yadiel Ayala Gonzalez
Grade: **8**
Country of origin: **Cuba**
English language
proficiency: **Advanced**

Many of **Yadiel**'s teachers are surprised when they learn he receives English language services. He speaks English easily and with hardly a trace of an accent and is overheard in the hallways speaking English with his friends much more often than Spanish. Because of this, many teachers assume that Yadiel is fully fluent in English and that his academic struggles are due to laziness or apathy.

In fact, Yadiel is still learning English. While he has a solid foundation in basic interpersonal communication—the informal, talking-with-friends English—he is still building his competence in academic English, which can take 7 or more years to acquire. Yadiel's educational background is a barrier for him here. Because he left Cuba when he was fairly young, he never had the opportunity to learn academic Spanish. Now he is trying to acquire an academic language in his second language without a first-language foundation.

Another barrier confronting Yadiel is his cultural style of learning and communicating. In Yadiel's community, learning is a group activity, accomplished through lots of (loud) talking and back-and-forth communication. Unfortunately, the largely white, middle-class teachers in Yadiel's school come from a cultural background where learning is something you do independently, by quietly reading books or by taking notes as the teacher lectures. Yadiel is not able to pinpoint the cultural divide; he just knows that sitting in a classroom feels like suffocating.

However, Yadiel's community and culture also provide him with a lot of support. That support might not come in a form school staff can easily recognize—his parents cannot attend parent-teacher conferences because they work nights, and nobody at home understands algebra well enough to help him with his homework. Nevertheless, Yadiel's mom and dad place a high value on education and are always impressing upon him the importance of working hard in school and earning his diploma. His parents also have a wealth of real-world knowledge and experience. In a family history project, when other students are interviewing their parents about what they remember of watching 9/11 on television, Yadiel can ask his parents about how the fall of the Soviet Union affected Cuba politically and economically. In addition, Yadiel is involved in a local Latine advocacy group, which supports Latine students in school and career and promotes pride in their rich history and culture. Yadiel's community is certainly an asset.

Another asset Yadiel brings to the classroom is his bilingualism. Although he does not have academic Spanish, he is still a fluent speaker with years of experience translating for his parents and other relatives. He can fluidly switch between languages, whether interpreting for a classmate or selecting the best words to make his point with a bilingual peer. Similarly, his experience moving between cultural worlds has given him a deep understanding of culture and its effect on how we communicate and see the world. These assets not only make Yadiel stronger cognitively but can also be leveraged in the classroom to position Yadiel as an expert who can help both his MLE and non-MLE peers.

Chapter 2. Supporting Multilingual Learners of English at the Lesson-Planning Level

STUDENT IDENTITY CARD

Name:
Yadiel Ayala Gonzalez
Grade: **8**
Country of origin: **Cuba**
English language
proficiency: **Advanced**

*It is not a mystery to anyone why **Yadiel** cannot pass the state's standardized exams. Like many of the students (both MLEs and students whose first language is English) in his underresourced urban school, he does not read at grade level. He can understand and use information from texts at a fourth- or fifth-grade level, but when faced with a text at a high school level, he is not able to understand it well enough to answer questions about it. In addition, Yadiel admits that he gets confused and frustrated by a lot of the words in the questions. After his teacher clarifies that "explain the historical circumstances that led to the event depicted in the document" just means "explain what caused the event in the picture," he sighs, "Why can't they just ask it like a normal person?"*

It is clear that while Yadiel is proficient in everyday English, he still needs to develop his academic language. But his teachers are not sure how to help him do that. After all, he has been exposed to this kind of language in the social studies classroom since kindergarten, and he still has not grasped it. So, what more do his teachers need to do?

STUDENT IDENTITY CARD

Name: **Minh Nguyen**
Grade: **11**
Country of origin:
Vietnam
English language
proficiency level:
Advanced

***Minh** has really been struggling in her American history class. The problem is not the workload; honestly, it is less homework than she had in Vietnam. The problem is also not the difficulty of the primary sources. The language is old, but she is good with a dictionary; if she takes her time, she can eventually work out the meaning. The problem is that she cannot seem to locate any answers.*

It is like what happened last week with the Andrew Jackson lesson. She carefully studied the assigned textbook chapter about the seventh president's accomplishments and came into class ready to discuss the importance of the changes he made. And then the teacher passed out a whole new set of texts about Jackson—but instead of adding more details to the story she already knew, they were saying completely different things! Some of them presented a picture of a racist bully who ignored the law and did whatever he wanted; others argued that Jackson ended the domination of the presidency by a small elite and made the office truly effective by expanding its power. It was like she was reading about three or four different people.

At the end of class, Minh went up to her teacher: "Which one is true?" she demanded, holding up the packet of confusing and sometimes contradictory sources. The teacher just smiled, said that history is about choosing how to tell a story, and started talking about the importance of interrogating sources and constructing your own knowledge. Minh does not understand. She just wants to know the right answer so she can be successful!

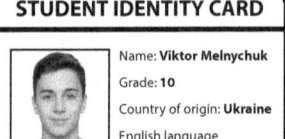

STUDENT IDENTITY CARD

Name: **Viktor Melnychuk**
Grade: **10**
Country of origin: **Ukraine**
English language
proficiency level: **Beginner**

Viktor hates tests. He used to be so good at them, but now he just stares at a paper full of words he does not know, with no pictures or maps to hint at what the questions might be asking. He has access to a dictionary, but even a 10-question multiple-choice test has hundreds of different words, and he does not even know where to start looking them up. He spends 50 minutes painstakingly translating the first question word by word and then 5 minutes frantically filling in bubbles at random to finish the test in time.

The worst part is that he knows he knows this material. The class is learning about World War I, a topic Viktor already studied back in Ukraine. In seventh grade, he and his best friend did a presentation about the assassination of Archduke Franz Ferdinand. They talked about Serbian nationalism and even used Google Maps to locate the street where Gavrilo Princip got his lucky shot at the Archduke. He knows more about this topic than most of his classmates, but his test still comes back with a big red 20%.

In this chapter:
- Integrating content and language objectives
- Disciplinary literacy
- Collaborative learning
- Supporting MLEs in assessments

Creating instruction that makes deep social studies learning accessible to multilingual learners of English (MLEs) starts with lesson planning. To support both language and content learning, educators can design lessons that integrate language objectives with content goals, advancing students' language proficiency alongside academic understanding. Key to selecting appropriate language objectives is an understanding of the disciplinary literacy practices of social studies: the ways in which professionals and informed citizens employ social studies in the real world. Another factor of instructional design that can bring academic learning into better alignment with how humans naturally learn is collaborative learning, in which students work together to build their understanding as members of a community rather than in isolation. Finally, planning instruction also includes planning assessments: determining how students will demonstrate their understanding of what they have learned. Traditional assessments, with their heavy reliance on reading and writing academic English, can be a huge barrier to MLEs' success in school—but they can also be modified to be accessible and can even be replaced by authentic assessments that give students a flexible, relevant method to show their understanding. By applying all these principles in instructional planning, educators not only build language and academic skills for MLEs but also nurture all students' critical thinking and global awareness, preparing them to thrive in and contribute to a diverse and interconnected world.

Integrating Language Learning Objectives With Social Studies Standards

Integrating language learning objectives with social studies standards is essential for ensuring that MLEs have equitable access to academic content while simultaneously improving their language proficiency. As a teacher, this approach allows you to support your students in gaining content knowledge and developing their academic language skills in tandem. It also provides a framework to meet the diverse needs of MLEs, enabling them to better understand complex topics while strengthening their ability to communicate effectively in both their first language and English. You may be asking yourself, "This is great, but how do I fit one more thing into my planning?" This section outlines practical strategies for embedding language learning goals within social studies instruction.

The Intersection of Language and Content Learning

For MLEs, effective instruction requires a dual focus: mastering content and developing language. As a teacher, you recognize the importance of aligning both language and content objectives in your lessons. By identifying the linguistic demands of social studies content—such as explaining, comparing, and arguing—you can help your students better grasp the academic language they need to succeed. This allows you to teach the specialized vocabulary and language structures that are essential for MLEs' academic success. In their book, *Long-Term Success for Experienced Multilinguals*, Huynh and Skelton (2023) emphasize the importance of combining the content objective with the language objective: "When an objective makes the academic language expectation clear, every lesson moves the students one step closer to becoming content experts" (p. 95). Students begin to see the lesson objective as a guide with specific direction rather than an abstract expectation. As educators, we are expected to know and understand the expectations of standards, but if we write our lesson objectives in standard educational terminology, we are communicating with other educators and not our students. When you bridge the gap between the content standard objective and the language objective, you are creating meaning for students.

For teachers, the content objective demonstrates knowledge of what they are teaching, and the language objective is how the student will show their mastery of the content. Students do not always know what it means to analyze, examine, or even understand, but when given direction to use cause-and-effect statements or comparative language, we are giving them the *how* and not just the *what*.

Example: Understanding Historical Events (American Revolution)

- Content Objective: Analyze the causes and effects of the American Revolution.
- Language Objective: Use cause-and-effect language structures (e.g., *because, due to, as a result*) to explain how key events contributed to the American Revolution.

Start by defining a clear objective for both content and language. You may already have the content or language objective, but you may need to partner with a content teacher or English language teacher to define the other area.

The content objective (the what) comes from your standards or district guides and focuses on what students should know or be able to do regarding the subject matter.

- Example: Students will explain the causes and effects of the American Revolution.

The language objective (the how) focuses on the language skills students need to achieve the content objective. Often, the best way to identify a specific language objective is to look at the assessment: How are students being asked to demonstrate their understanding of the content? What specific words, language patterns, or skills will they need to use to be successful? For example, if students will be showing their understanding of the causes of the American Revolution by answering multiple-choice questions, then reading and understanding vocabulary in context will be essential to their success. However, if they are showing their understanding by writing a paragraph about how various events led to the American Revolution, then the most important language structure is cause-and-effect words: because, as a result, due to, etc.

- Example: Students will use transition words (e.g., because, therefore) to connect causes and effects in a paragraph.

Now put the two objectives together.

- *Students will explain the causes and effects of the American Revolution by using transition words to connect causes and effects in their writing.*

This intentionality creates a cohesive understanding of what students will be doing in class as well as support in the evaluation. This strategy is effective not only for MLEs but for all students. If they know what and how they are demonstrating their understanding, they can then focus on the content being taught instead of trying to determine what information they need to remember for the assessment. Language objectives provide a structured approach to help students build proficiency in both content knowledge and academic language, ultimately leading to greater success in social studies and beyond. This approach fosters an inclusive, supportive classroom environment in which all students can thrive and contribute meaningfully to discussions and learning activities.

Clarity in the *what*, *how*, and *why* of teaching, not only for the teacher but also for the students, will help guide the lessons and clarify the needs for specific support in each lesson, as you will see in the rest of this chapter.

Disciplinary Literacy: Reading and Writing in Social Studies

Social studies is more than just memorizing names and dates. In fact, many social studies teachers would say the names and dates are the *least* important part of social studies! Instead, social studies is about understanding *why* changes happen in our world and *how* different people's accounts of those changes are shaped by the tellers' own context and perspective. These bigger understandings and the high-level thinking, reading, and writing skills that underlie them are the real core of social studies education.

Many English language teachers come to the field from an English (literature or language arts) or language (linguistics, second language acquisition) background and later on find themselves coteaching in a social studies classroom. If that sounds like you, then this section of the book will be especially helpful. In the following pages, we give a brief overview of what English language specialists need to know about the special reading and writing skills that are fundamental to social studies education. In addition, we argue that the foundational literacy strategies you may be familiar with from English language arts (ELA) and other content areas, while helpful, are not sufficient to help MLEs overcome the unique challenges of reading and writing in social studies. In the following sections, we offer strategies and approaches you can add to your practice to meet these demands.

What Is Disciplinary Literacy?

Disciplinary literacy, as defined by Shanahan and Shanahan (2012), is "the unique tools that experts in a discipline use to engage in the work of that discipline" (p. 8). It is essentially the idea that a one-size-fits-all approach to reading just does not match up with how people read in real life. The way you read a recipe blog is different from the way you read a text message from a friend, which is different from the way you read an online news story, which is different from the way you read—or do not read—the terms and conditions for your phone's latest update.

In the same way, experts in different disciplines read in different ways and for different purposes. A historian reading a recently released book about former U.S. President Reagan is going to look first at who wrote the book and what their perspective is; however, in Shanahan and Shanahan's (2012) study on the practices of expert readers, the mathematics experts declared "almost stridently, that thinking about [the] author would only be a distraction" (p. 11) when reading an academic text in their field. Similarly, a scientist writing a paper does not really focus on whether the words sound pretty, as long as they communicate the findings clearly, but a poet writing a poem might agonize for days over the difference between *glimmer* and *glint*.

These differences in reading and writing by disciplinary experts trickle down into secondary school. As students move beyond "learning to read" in the early grades, through "reading to learn" in late elementary school, and onward into middle and high school, the differences between their classes widen. By late high school, the kind of writing a student is asked to do in their social studies class is totally different from the kind of writing their ELA teacher is looking for. These differences can be obvious—reading poems versus reading primary source accounts of trench warfare—or they can be subtle. Many teachers are not even aware that when a social studies teacher and an ELA teacher ask a student to "analyze" textual evidence, they are asking for different things.

It is especially important for English language teachers to be aware of the specific literacy practices central to social studies because our usual "bag of tricks" will not get our students where they need to be. Monte-Sano (2010), in an analysis of 11th graders' historical writing, found that many of the students followed the so-called rules they learned in ELA class about making evidence-based arguments, but because they were using evidence like English professors and not like historians, their work was not successful in their history class. She concludes that "although generic argumentation is a necessary component of historical writing, it alone is not sufficient" (p. 560). To empower our students to succeed in their social studies classes—and as adults, whether as professionals in the education field or as active and informed citizens—we need to do better. General literacy strategies are helpful, but we need to add specific instruction in the disciplinary literacies of social studies.

Reading in Social Studies

The main way in which reading in social studies differs from reading in other content areas is the focus on a text's source. In other academic contexts, students are used to reading for information, with the simple goal of understanding and remembering what the text tells them. Social studies emphasizes another layer of meaning in every text, a layer that is only accessible when students look beyond the words themselves to the source and context of the original document (Wineburg, 1991).

Shanahan and Shanahan (2012) identify sourcing, contextualization, and corroboration as the key practices historians engage in when reading in the discipline.

- *Sourcing* refers to analyzing the author's perspective (based on their positionality and relationship to the events discussed in the text) and their purpose in writing the text.
- *Contextualization* is an analysis of the context in which the document was written, including recent events, sociocultural climate, and the specific use and audience of the document.
- *Corroboration* means making connections between multiple documents and perspectives, noting and interpreting the similarities and differences in the way they present events and ideas.

Dimension 3 of the National Council for the Social Studies (2013) C3 Framework reflects this focus on using documents and evidence with their source and context in mind. The first standard of Dimension 3 describes students engaging in work such as using "the origin, authority, structure, context, and corroborative value" (D3.1.6–8 and D3.1.9–12) of various sources to decide which sources to use to support historical arguments, evaluating the credibility of their sources, and drawing evidence from multiple sources to construct defensible claims. These practices are rarely found in the other core disciplines, so teachers of social studies need to explicitly teach them.

Disciplinary Literacy in Practice: Reading a Primary Source

Let us look at an example of what reading in history looks like in practice and how a general, one-size-fits-all literacy approach falls short. Students in a 10th-grade world history class were asked to analyze a speech by Maximilien Robespierre in order to identify his point of view regarding the Reign of Terror.

Maximilien Robespierre was one of the leaders of the new French government. He gave this speech to other leaders on February 5, 1794:

> Outside France, all the tyrants surround you; inside France, all the friends of tyranny conspire against you …. We must suffocate the internal and external enemies of the Republic [the new French government] or perish with her. In this situation, the first rule of politics is to guide the people with reason [logic] and the enemies of the people with terror ….
>
> The protection of society is only for peaceful citizens; there are no citizens in the Republic other than the supporters of the Republic. The royalists and conspirators are nothing but strangers—or better yet, enemies …. Are not the internal enemies the allies of the external enemies? The assassins that tear us apart from within; the schemers who buy the consciences of the people's representatives; the traitors who sell them … are any of these people less guilty or less dangerous than the tyrants they serve? (Adapted from Robespierre, 1794)

General Literacy Strategies

If we simply apply our general literacy strategies to this document, we might pay attention to frequently repeated words (*tyrants, internal, external*). We might notice that many of the words in this document are very negative (*enemies, tyranny, assassins, schemers, traitors*). We would conclude that the Reign of Terror was important because France was in big trouble. We understand the main idea of the document, but we are far from understanding it like a historian.

These general literacy strategies, while they may be helpful for basic reading comprehension, are not sufficient for understanding a document historically—and they may even lead us astray. Instead, we need to approach this document as a historian would.

Disciplinary Literacy

A historical approach to the document involves sourcing, contextualizing, and corroborating it.

- **Sourcing:** We notice that this speech was made by a leader of the new revolutionary government. This means that this source can help us understand Robespierre's motivations for beginning the Reign of Terror. It may *not* be a reliable source of information on how the Reign of Terror actually played out, but it *is* a reliable source for why revolutionary leaders chose to start the Reign of Terror.

- **Contextualization:** We know from our prior learning about the French Revolution that Robespierre's government has recently executed King Louis XVI and that all the other monarchs in Europe were terrified of what would happen to them. This helps us understand Robespierre's references to *external enemies* of France: He is afraid because all the other European countries are lining up to fight France.

- **Corroboration:** In order to do this, we need to bring in another document. Since we decided that Robespierre's speech would not be a reliable source of information about the effects of the Reign of Terror, we read an eyewitness account. This second source tells us that most of the people who were arrested during this time period had done nothing wrong. We compare this to Robespierre's talk of spies and traitors inside France and call into question his claim that France was actually full of internal enemies.

Using the disciplinary skills of sourcing, contextualization, and corroboration, we have gained a stronger (and more historically accurate) understanding of this primary source and what it can teach us about the French Revolution's ending and about the ways political leaders may spin facts and play on people's fears to win support for their policies.

Writing in Social Studies

In the area of writing, there is both good news and bad news for the teacher transitioning from an ELA approach to a social studies approach. The good news is that the *types* of writing students are asked to do in social studies are often quite similar to the writing they do in other classes. As seen in Dimension 4 of the C3 Framework, students communicate their understandings in social studies by making arguments. Similarly, in ELA, students are primarily asked to make arguments about literature and informational texts rather than simply recount what the text said. The specific types of claims will vary, but in this case, social studies and English are more closely aligned than one might expect. In social studies, we are never simply retelling what happened; we are making *arguments* about how and why past events unfolded.

Social studies differs from ELA in the way arguments can be supported. Both fields rely on evidence to support claims. However, what that looks like on paper can be quite different.

History writing, which centers around analysis of primary and secondary sources, reflects the reading side of social studies literacy: sourcing, contextualization, and corroboration (Monte-Sano, 2010). To successfully use evidence from documents in social studies, students must not only explain what the evidence says but also explain what they infer about the source, connect the document to the context in which it was written, and corroborate it with evidence from other sources.

In contrast, when students write about literature, they often are expected to concentrate primarily on the text itself. The author's background might be mentioned, but the main focus is the text. This approach will fall short in a social studies context, in which students are expected to analyze not only what the text says but also how its source and context may have affected the text.

Clearly explaining how social studies writing differs from ELA writing makes both types of writing less confusing and more accessible for students, especially those with emerging language proficiency.

Challenges and Strategies for Multilingual Learners of English

The literacy practices central to social studies present both challenges and opportunities for MLEs.

Double Literacy Work

Sourcing, contextualizing, and corroborating are more complex than simply reading a text for comprehension. For students who are struggling with merely understanding what a text says (or even with decoding the words themselves), adding *another* level of thinking to the task can be very daunting. Now, not only do students need to work out unfamiliar words and gain an understanding of what the text of the document says, but they also need to extrapolate beyond the document.

What To Do: Multiple Reads of Less Text

All this reading is too much to do all at once. MLEs may need to make multiple passes through the document, first focusing on comprehension, then working on sourcing, contextualizing, and corroborating the text. Because this will take more time, teachers can cut down the amount of work—requiring MLEs to analyze fewer documents, reducing the length of each document, or providing documents at a lower reading level.

Cultural Assumptions About Education

This approach to reading and learning can be challenging for students who are used to a model of education where the role of the student is not to construct new knowledge but simply to receive knowledge from experts (such as in many East Asian cultures; see Chapter 1 for more on how MLEs' cultural backgrounds can serve as both barriers and opportunities in the classroom). For a student who has been taught to view the texts in school as sources of truth (or at least of the correct answers), it can be disorienting and frustrating to be told that, *actually*, the texts they are reading are not always correct and that it is the student's job to use the texts to figure out what is true. From these students' point of view, to question the reliability of a text provided by an instructor could be a show of disrespect toward the instructor; to claim a more accurate understanding of historical events than the author of a document could be seen as an arrogant position for a student to take.

What To Do: Teach About Cultural Differences

Be explicit about what students are being asked to do and why. Acknowledging a student's discomfort and explaining how educational practices differ among cultures can help students get past their worry about trespassing boundaries. Plus, it is always good to be transparent about the purpose of learning activities; this allows students to take ownership of their learning.

Need for Deep Vocabulary Knowledge

Reading like a historian requires students to understand more vocabulary beyond what is required to simply read for information. In particular, many cases of bias that are obvious to fluent English speakers rely on the author's choice of a particular word among the many similar but not identical options available. These shades of meaning may be very challenging for MLEs to grasp if they only know one word for a given meaning or if these subtle differences do not carry over in translation. For example, an author's choice to describe the Black Lives Matter movement as either a *rebellion* or a *revolution* reveals something about their perspective on the movement; however, the definitions a beginning MLE gets for the two words might be nearly identical.

What To Do: Teach Bias by Comparing Information

A more accessible way to work with bias in documents is to focus on the information the author chose to include or omit rather than their word choices. Instead of depending on subtle differences in connotation, this approach requires students to have only a basic comprehension of the text. A classic example of this type of work is the common U.S. history activity in which students compare two eyewitness accounts of the Boston Massacre. The students can easily notice that a British officer's account includes the claim that the colonists were shouting insults at the British but omits the detail that one of the British soldiers was brandishing a large sword. In the colonists' account in the *Boston Gazette*, students can notice that the account describes the sword but does not say anything about the colonists shouting. A very fruitful (and often easy to create) variation on this activity is to compare textbook accounts or Wikipedia articles from different countries about a historical event. For example, the descriptions in a Japanese textbook and a Chinese textbook of the Nanjing Massacre read like completely different events. These activities allow MLEs to participate fully in higher order thinking and analysis alongside their non-MLE peers.

In addition to the preceding specific strategies, all the general strategies discussed in the next section of this chapter can help make disciplinary literacy more accessible to MLEs. Providing primary sources at a lower reading level, having students work more frequently with images (e.g., political cartoons) rather than texts, and reducing the lengths of passages are all valid strategies for reducing language barriers so that MLEs can practice the skills of engaging with texts like historians. Rather than "watering down" the curriculum, these modifications give MLEs a more academically rigorous learning experience—one that is faithful to the way experts in the discipline actually work in the field.

Is All This Really Necessary?

Teachers of MLEs face the temptation to just skip the extra steps that disciplinary literacy entails. It takes so much more time, and it is hard to do higher order thinking when our students are struggling to sound out words. Can we just give MLEs the need-to-know facts to memorize and leave it to the general education students to wrestle those facts out of primary sources?

It is essential that we do not do this. Rather than being an extension for accelerated students or even an optional addition to the content, the literacy practices discussed in this section are the *heart* of the discipline of social studies. To omit them for MLEs in favor of spending more time on reading comprehension or acquiring factual knowledge is to trade social studies class for reading class or a trivia competition. Our MLEs have the right to learn this part of the curriculum just like their non-MLE peers.

In addition, the disciplinary literacy of social studies offers an opportunity to show the relevance of social studies and of learning English for students' lives in the real world. Many students struggle to see the relevance of what they are studying in school, and this applies to MLEs as well—especially long-term MLEs who have been learning English for years but are unable to show proficiency as measured by standardized assessments. While most MLEs recognize the importance of basic English as opening opportunities in life and career in the modern world, they do not always see why academic English matters. Why should they work so hard to interpret poetry; they are never going to read and analyze a poem after they graduate high school. Why do they need to memorize all the archaic vocabulary found in the Declaration of Independence when nobody uses those words anymore?

In contrast to academic tasks in which the practical importance can be difficult to see, it is easy to tie sourcing, contextualization, and corroboration to real-world situations that young people care about. These skills are about knowing who and what to believe, and our students will use them any time they are trying to investigate the truth of a social media rumor, detect false and misleading claims from political candidates, or figure out whether the threatening email they just received from *irs.com* is a scam. (Of course, finding time to make these connections will always be a challenge, and so will convincing any 13-year-old student that they could ever *possibly* be the victim of a scam. But the connections are there.) Disciplinary literacy is not only at the core of social studies as an area of study but also the answer to the age-old question, "Why do we have to learn this anyway?"

Collaborative Learning

In a 12th-grade American History class during a lesson on child labor in the Industrial Revolution, the teacher begins with a simple explanation, showing images and using clear language. Students work in mixed-proficiency groups, rotating through a gallery walk of primary sources like political cartoons and Lewis Hine photographs. Guiding questions are provided in English and students' home languages to ensure accessibility. In each group, MLEs collaborate with peers to analyze the sources. Group members rephrase ideas and encourage participation while MLEs contribute observations using prompts like "What do you see?" They record findings using graphic organizers, supported by sentence starters and word banks. After the gallery walk, groups present their findings, with MLEs sharing insights with peer support. For example, Viktor, an MLE, describes an image by saying, "kids working … no school." His group helps expand the idea: "They're sad because they have to work." The teacher facilitates, scaffolding their language and connecting ideas to broader social themes.

This scenario demonstrates how collaboration empowers MLEs to engage with challenging content. Working in groups allows MLEs to

- share ideas in a low-pressure setting,
- build confidence through peer support and rephrased contributions, and
- develop critical thinking by exploring multiple perspectives.

What Is Collaborative Learning?

Collaborative learning means students working together to achieve shared goals, and peer support emphasizes mutual support to enhance learning and emotional well-being. These approaches are particularly beneficial for MLEs in navigating language and content challenges by fostering language skills and critical thinking through peer interactions and scaffolded tools (Langan & Lawrence, 2021).

Challenges of Collaborative Learning for Teachers

Although the benefits are clear, teachers often face specific challenges when working with MLEs:

- **mixed proficiency levels**: MLEs often have varying language abilities, which can hinder equal participation and understanding in group work.
- **resistance to collaboration**: Cultural or personality differences may lead to

reluctance in collaborating because some students may feel uncomfortable or unfamiliar with group dynamics.

Benefits of Collaborative Learning for Multilingual Learners of English

When these challenges are overcome through strategic planning and appropriate supports, collaborative learning leads to a wide range of academic and social-emotional benefits for MLEs.

1. **Academic Growth**
   - transitioning from informal to academic literacy
   - enhancing content understanding through cross-linguistic resources
   - leveraging students' home languages and cultural backgrounds
   - building confidence in using academic English through interactive discussions and projects
   - taking an active role in the learning process through dialogue and problem-solving

2. **Social and Emotional Development**
   - building a sense of belonging
   - building trusting relationships that support risk-taking in a safe, collaborative environment
   - encouraging empathy and cultural exchange through collaborative activities

3. **Critical Thinking**
   - developing problem-solving and analytical skills
   - encouraging students to challenge stereotypes and explore diverse perspectives
   - supporting cognitive development through peer interaction and collaboration

4. **Motivation and Engagement**
   - reducing anxiety and creating a safe space for learning
   - promoting active participation and respect among peers
   - framing mistakes as opportunities for growth
   - valuing all voices and fostering an inclusive environment

---

What Is the Teacher's Role in Collaborative Learning?

The teacher's role should be limited to facilitating and monitoring during collaborative learning, which means creating a positive environment that sets clear expectations for group work, emphasizing respect and encouraging students to participate, and ensuring that group activities reflect diverse perspectives to ensure full participation. Especially for complex projects, teachers must also provide support for MLEs who face language barriers or difficulties with group dynamics.

It is also essential to evaluate collaborative learning by offering MLEs opportunities to share and present their work to recognize their efforts. Providing feedback and highlighting group success and personal progress help MLEs improve academically.

Strategies for Implementing Collaborative Learning

It is important that teachers provide proactive strategies to ensure all students can succeed in collaborative settings.

Group and Pair Work Activities

The following activities promote both content learning and language practice, encouraging collaborative engagement among MLEs:

- **Group Research Projects**: MLEs collaborate on topics, such as the history and impact of colonization. This allows them to practice language skills while exploring complex historical content.
- **Role-Playing Historical Events**: Simulating historical scenarios, such as taxation or voting systems during the French Revolution, helps MLEs practice language in context while gaining a deeper understanding of historical events.
- **Peer Review Sessions**: MLEs review each other's work on topics, such as the effects of industrialization. This allows them to practice reading, writing, and providing constructive feedback in English.
- **Concept Mapping**: Students create visual representations of key concepts, relationships, or historical events, which helps MLEs organize and understand complex content.
- **Peer Teaching**: MLEs teach each other specific topics or sections of the material, reinforcing their knowledge and building communication skills.
- **Debates**: Engaging in structured debates on historical or social justice issues (e.g., should colonization be forgiven?) helps students articulate their ideas in English and practice critical thinking.

Roles and Responsibilities

Assigning specific roles within group activities ensures active participation and the development of essential skills:

- **Group Leader:** MLEs with stronger language skills can facilitate discussions and keep the group focused.
- **Note-Taker:** This role can be assigned to MLEs developing writing skills, allowing them to practice summarizing group discussions.
- **Presenter:** MLEs can present the group's findings, which helps build confidence in speaking skills.
- **Timekeeper:** This role provides a way for MLEs with more beginning English proficiency to contribute to the group's work, ensuring the group stays on task.

Group Discussion Protocols and Activities

These strategies support all students, but especially MLEs, by providing structure to guide academic language while promoting cooperative learning:

- **Think-Pair-Share (TPS)**: MLEs first think about a question related to a topic (e.g., social justice), discuss it with a partner, and then share their ideas with the class. This strategy provides structured opportunities for speaking and listening practice.
- **Jigsaw**: MLEs specialize in different topics (e.g., causes of World War I) and then teach their group members, deepening understanding while practicing English.
- **Numbered Heads Together**: Students work in small groups, with each member assigned a number. Before anyone shares an answer, the group makes sure every member understands the material. After the group agrees, the teacher calls a number, and the student with that number shares the group's answer.
- **Socratic Seminars**: Students engage in group discussions based on a reading or topic, using critical thinking to answer questions and respond to each other's ideas. This promotes deeper engagement with academic language.
- **Gallery Walks**: Students post their work around the room and engage in discussion with peers, offering and receiving feedback. This activity helps students visualize ideas and enhances comprehension.
- **Fishbowl Discussions**: A small group discusses a topic while others observe, providing feedback afterward. This encourages active listening and critical thinking.
- **World Café**: Students rotate through different discussion stations, sharing and developing ideas on social studies topics. This promotes collaboration and ensures every student participates.

Supporting Multilingual Learners of English in Assessments

In many regions, teachers face restrictions for curriculum and assessments, often being required to use standardized tests that may not fully reflect the abilities and knowledge of their students. Although these standardized assessments are necessary in some contexts, they often fail to accommodate the unique needs of MLEs. To support all learners effectively, it is crucial to acknowledge these limitations while advocating for teachers to develop their own assessments whenever possible. Teacher-created assessments allow for a better understanding of student progress, align more closely with classroom instruction, and can be tailored to students' language proficiency levels.

Standardized vs. Teacher-Created Assessments

The key difference between teacher-created and standardized assessments is flexibility. Teacher-created assessments can be adapted to meet students where they are in their language development, integrating scaffolds like visuals, simplified language, or bilingual support. These assessments ensure that the focus remains on assessing student learning and growth in a way that is meaningful and accessible. They can include oral presentations, open-ended questions, or hands-on projects that align with students' strengths.

Standardized assessments, on the other hand, are often rigid, with vocabulary and language structures that may pose additional challenges for MLEs, potentially skewing the results to reflect their language skills rather than their content knowledge. However, even within the confines of standardized testing, we can teach MLEs strategies to help them demonstrate their knowledge effectively.

Teach Students to Focus on What They Know

When a reading passage in a test is packed with unfamiliar vocabulary, it can be overwhelming. Students often fixate or get stuck on the words they do not know, especially when trying to apply the annotation strategies they usually use in ELA, such as marking unfamiliar words. Instead, encourage students to highlight all the words they understand. This helps them focus on what they *do* know, which is often enough to piece together the main idea of the passage.

Show Students How to Make Their Own Tools

Students who are accustomed to graphic organizers, word banks, and other supports may feel lost when they have to write in a testing situation without those supports. To overcome this barrier, teach students how to create their own simple organizers as they take the test. The specifics depend on the format of the particular test, but these tools could be as simple as writing a checklist in the margin for the parts of an essay or paragraph or brainstorming a self-created word bank of vocabulary words related to a topic before starting to write.

Explicitly Teach Students to Wrap the Question Into Their Answers

For answers of one or two sentences (such as the document-based short-answer questions often seen on history tests), restating the question is a very helpful support for MLEs. Students can learn a systematic formula for using the question to create their own sentence starter, enabling them to write their answer as a complete sentence.

- For the typical question beginning *who, what, where, when, why,* or *how,* the formula is usually to cut the question right after the word *do* or its variants, change the verb to past tense, and then add *because* or *by* to answer why and how.
- Given the question "Why did the British want to trade with China?" the answer becomes "The British want**ed** to trade with China **because** ...."

Standardized assessments will always make it challenging for MLEs to fully show their understanding of content. However, by teaching strategies like these, we can give our MLEs the best chance possible.

Modify Traditional Assessments

Many teachers still use traditional assessments, such as multiple-choice tests and document-based essays, in the social studies classroom for a variety of reasons. These assessments are usually more familiar to both students and teachers. There are also many assessment items in these formats already available, making them much easier and faster for teachers to create. Most importantly, students (and sometimes teachers) are often assessed at the end of the school year with a district, state, or national standardized test, and teachers believe that they need to model their classroom assessments after "the big test" in order to properly prepare students.

For all these reasons, it is unlikely that traditional assessment formats are ever going to go away. Therefore, it is important that teachers modify these tests to provide a more accurate assessment of what MLEs know and are able to do.

Dual-Language Assessments

The ideal support for MLEs is to provide the assessment in the language they are most proficient in. When possible, giving MLEs a translated version of the assessment to use *alongside* the English one is an excellent support. It is important to give students both versions: They may need to refer to the English version if there is a translation error (especially if the assessment was made using machine translation such as Google Translate, which has inconsistent accuracy). In addition, students may not know the academic vocabulary in their home language. For example, an 11th grader who moved to the United States from Vietnam at 8 years old will likely not understand *giải trừ vũ khí hạt nhân* because they only learned *nuclear disarmament* in English. They may still benefit from the Vietnamese translation of the exam, but they will need to use the two versions side by side.

Simplifying Language

Typically, multiple-choice questions on social studies tests use high-level academic vocabulary that can prevent MLEs from understanding what the question is actually asking. When a student gets the question wrong, the teacher does not know whether this is because the student did not know the content or because they did not understand the wording of the question. Content vocabulary (Tier 3 words) should be kept in the questions, but the other words that link the content vocabulary (Tier 2 words) should be made as simple as possible. See Chapter 3 for more on vocabulary tiers.

Modifying Documents

Many traditional assessments, such as stimulus-based multiple-choice questions and document-based essays, ask students to read and analyze primary sources. If these sources are kept at their original length and language (usually at or above grade level), the only information these assessments will provide is that most MLEs do not read at grade level. If you want to assess higher order skills such as analyzing the point of view of a document or contextualizing a source, you must use documents that the students understand. Using visual documents such as political cartoons, reducing the length of textual documents, and simplifying the vocabulary and sentence structures in the sources will increase the accuracy of the assessment data.

Example: A Traditional Question Set—Before and After

A 10th-grade history teacher has always used the following stimulus-based question set (based on standardized tests commonly used in his state) to assess his students' understanding of the Industrial Revolution and their ability to identify point of view in a primary source document.

Question Set 1: Original

I was married at 23 and went into a colliery when I was married. I used to weave when about 12 years old and can neither read nor write. I work to Andrew Knowles, of Little Bolton, and make sometimes about 7s. a week, sometimes not so much. I am a drawer, and work from six o'clock in the morning to six at night. stop about an hour at noon to eat my dinner: I have bread and butter for dinner; I get no drink. I have two children, but they are too young to work. I worked at drawing when I was in the family way. I know a woman who has gone home and washed herself, taken to her bed, been delivered of a child, and gone to work again under a week. I have a belt round my waist, and a chain passing between my legs, and I go on my hands and feet. The road is very steep, and we have to hold the rope; and, where there is no rope, by anything we can catch hold of. There are six women and about six boys and girls in the pit I work in; it is very hard work for a woman. The pit is very wet where I work, and the water comes over the clog-tops always, and I have seen it up to my thighs: it rains in at the roof terribly; my clothes were wet through almost all day long. I never was ill in my life

---

but when I was lying-in. My cousin looks after the children in the day-time, I am very tired when I get home at night; I fall asleep sometimes before I get washed. I am not so strong as I was, and cannot stand my work so well as I used to do. I have drawn till I have had the skin off me: the belt and chain is worse when we are in the family way. My feller [husband] has beaten me many a time for not being ready. I were not used to it at first, and he had little patience: I have known many a man beat his drawer. I have known men take liberties with the drawers, and some of the women have bastards. I think it would be better if we were paid once a week instead of once a month, for then I would buy victuals with ready money. It is bad to live on 7s., and rent 1s. 6d. (Great Britain, 1842)

1. Based on the excerpt, what is the author's point of view concerning working conditions in the mines?
    a) The competitive wages justified the challenging conditions.
    b) Colliery labor was an appropriate occupation for female laborers.
    c) Labor conditions in coal mining were appalling and inhumane.
    d) Drawing was distinguished labor because it contributed to industrial growth.

2. Which historical development contributed to the conditions described in the document?
    a) Communist leaders' drive to industrialize resulted in unrealistic five-year plans.
    b) Europeans sought to exploit native populations in Africa and Asia in order to extract natural resources.
    c) An abundant food supply caused a population boom in Britain, leading to mass migration from the countryside to urban areas in search of employment.
    d) The rise of international trade agreements led to multinational corporations relocating production to nations with more lax labor regulations.

Realizing that the only data this test item would yield was that the MLE students could not read documents and questions at this reading level (something he already knew!), the teacher decided to rewrite the test item, so that it would actually tell him whether his students understood the content and the disciplinary skill of determining point of view.

The teacher made the following changes to the primary source used in this stimulus-based question:
- He reduced the length of the passage so that students did not waste their time struggling through irrelevant text.
- He modernized the language (e.g., *had a baby* instead of *been delivered of a child; tops of*

my shoes instead of *clog-tops*).

- He simplified the sentence structure (e.g., breaking up long sentences, adding phrases for clarity).
- He added definitions for words and phrases that are challenging or used in technical ways (e.g., *in the family way; pit*).
- He divided the long paragraph into several short paragraphs, each about a different topic.

He also rewrote the answer options for the multiple-choice questions, removing most of the academic language so that the questions used simple, everyday language. However, he kept the question stems, a common wording on state assessments that he had already taught the students. He also kept the specific academic vocabulary that the students had practiced in the Industrial Revolution unit (e.g., *conditions, wages, factories, population, increase*).

The teacher feels confident that this revised test item and new question set will provide more accurate data about what his students understand about the Industrial Revolution and about point of view. The revised test item is as follows:

Question Set 2: Revision

I work from six o'clock in the morning to six at night. I stop about an hour at noon to eat my dinner. I have bread and butter for dinner; I get nothing to drink.

I worked in the coal mine when I was in the family way [pregnant]. I know a woman who has gone home, had a baby, and gone back to work again under a week.

The road in the mine is very steep. There are six women and about six boys and girls in the pit I work in; it is very hard work for a woman. The pit [section of the mine] is very wet where I work, and the water always comes over the tops of my shoes. I have seen it up to my thighs.

I am very tired when I get home at night; I fall asleep sometimes before I get washed. (Adapted from Great Britain, 1842)

1. Based on the excerpt, what is the author's point of view concerning working conditions in the mines?

   a) The high wages made the bad conditions okay.

   b) Working in coal mines was good for women.

   c) The working conditions in the coal mines were very bad.

   d) Working in coal mines was important because it helped factories.

2. Which historical development contributed to the conditions described in the document?

   a) Communist leaders who wanted to build factories set five-year goals that were

b) Europeans made African and Asian people work for them so they could take their natural resources.

c) Extra food caused a population increase in Britain, leading to many people moving from farms to cities to find work.

d) After countries made trade agreements, companies moved their factories to places with no laws to protect workers.

Use Alternative Assessments

Alternative assessments are informal assessments that allow students to integrate what they know in a nontraditional, meaningful way rather than simply recalling information. They are especially suited to MLEs because they can show a rounded picture of a students' abilities and can be adapted to different situations, learning styles, and language proficiencies. These assessments can include the following:

- **Nonverbal Assessments**: Students point, use gestures, or physically match images with definitions.
- **Pictorial Assessments**: Students draw or make collages, concept maps, infographics, or cartoon panels of a historical event.
- **Performance Assessments**: Students role-play, conduct an interview, create a music video of a song, or give a class presentation.
- **Written Projects**: Students construct response journals, poems, dialogues, skits, letters, brochures, social media profiles, or advertisements.

In a world history class, consider assigning a brochure on ancient Egypt, highlighting the social structure, religion, and important achievements. In an American History class, students might write a letter home in the voice of a soldier in the trenches of WWI or a child employed in a factory during the Industrial Revolution. For an American government class, students can write acrostic poems about the platforms of the Democratic and Republican parties or create an infographic on the three branches of government. These types of alternative assessments serve as fun, engaging activities that can track students' progress over time, unlike standardized tests, which only measure a student at a particular time during the year. Alternative assessments can be helpful in tracing a students' strengths and weaknesses and informing further instruction. The same strategies that are essential for making instruction accessible for MLEs—providing visuals, vocabulary supports, sentence frames, and so on—are key to modifying alternative assessments for MLEs.

Make Authentic Assessments Accessible for Multilingual Learners of English

Assessment is an integral element of teaching and learning. In practice, teachers design different assessment tasks to inform and adjust their teaching, understand students' achievement of course learning outcomes or curriculum standards, and provide feedback on students' learning progress. One underlying issue among many existing assessments (e.g., cloze tests), however, is that they have over focused on testing students' mastery of content knowledge (i.e., the specific facts, concepts, and ideas students learned in different units). Although students need to and should master content knowledge, such assessment tasks are often "trivial, contrived, and meaningless." This approach "breeds low engagement in schoolwork and inhibits transfer of school learning to issues and problems faced out of school" (Newmann, 1996, p. 362). To make learning meaningful, authentic assessments have been increasingly introduced and applied in classrooms recently because they can help students use and apply knowledge in real-life situations and prepare students to be capable citizens.

While authentic assessments are commonly posited to be useful and valuable, the additional challenges behind them should be underscored. First, designing authentic assessments can be demanding for teachers. Besides the common considerations of reliability, validity, and practicality, teachers should also consider students' background knowledge to tailor the assessment task for students to a certain extent. In addition, teachers may have difficulty predicting the real-life situations that students may encounter. Furthermore, completing authentic assessments can be challenging for students. They may feel anxious about their abilities to finish the task or encounter trouble in accessing resources. More critically, the perception of "authenticity" differs among stakeholders. For instance, students may feel a gap between the authenticity instructors aim to preserve and the applicability of current abilities to future real-life practices.

Despite these challenges, instructors can thrive in creating authentic assessment tasks. To begin, instructors should make it clear to students that authenticity is a subjective concept (Ajjawi et al., 2024). Although it may be impossible to achieve the intended authenticity, students will still make progress and acquire knowledge throughout the task. Instructors can also invite students to share feedback and propose suggestions, which can highlight students' ownership in assessments, motivate students to learn and participate, and help instructors build an environment of feedback and dialogue. In addition to developing a new mindset, instructors can create authentic assessment tasks while referencing Mueller's (2010) *Authentic Assessment Toolbox* and the following questions suggested by Wootton (2021):

- What is a typical "real-world" scenario? What skills does this require? How can this be turned into an assessment?
- What are the required skills that you want to measure? What do you want your students to gain as a result of the module?
- What activities can you give the students to prepare for the assessment? … How can they aid the "real-world" simulation?
- What skills and knowledge need to be directly taught to the students? How does this fit around your planned activities? (p. 77)

Example: United Nations Proposal Project

A world history teacher has, for many years, concluded her unit on modern global conflicts with a standard essay exam. However, she is dissatisfied with the way this assessment converts a relevant and important real-world issue into yet another list of facts to be memorized. She decides to develop an authentic assessment. (The following example is inspired by curriculum materials developed by Shoman, 2024.)

The teacher thinks to herself: What do real-world experts in global conflicts actually do with their understanding? Well, they try to make peace. Although peace-making happens through many methods and in many settings, the teacher focuses her assessment on one major venue for peace-making efforts: the United Nations (UN).

In the assessment description, the students are positioned as members of a special committee to Palestine (similar to the committee that proposed UN Resolution 181, or the Partition Plan, in 1947), tasked with investigating the occupation there and proposing a solution. The students must come up with a plan for resolving the occupation and present their plan to the "General Assembly" (i.e., their classmates).

The new assessment is engaging, allowing students to write for a real audience other than their teacher and to role-play as world leaders and imagine themselves in that position someday. It is also academically rigorous: For a successful peace proposal, students must summarize the history of the region, explain how their plan would address five important issues that play into the ongoing occupation, and take into account the goals and perspectives of several key stakeholders on both sides of the colonial rule. It involves historical thinking, as students consider varying points of view, make predictions about how various actions will play out based on past events, and write not just a summary of facts but a historical argument about interactions among nations and groups. It also involves so-called "soft skills" that are important not only for students considering a career in international relations but for all active citizens: speaking and writing for clear communication and persuasion, identifying and interpreting bias in sources of information, working together in a group, and finding solutions to complex problems.

In the end, the students and the teacher found that the authentic assessment was not only much more interesting than the traditional essay exam, but the students were also able to demonstrate a much deeper understanding of modern conflicts and the challenges involved in resolving them. It took much more time and preparation than the old assessment, but it was worth it for the high-quality learning it produced.

Providing Feedback to Multilingual Learners of English

Feedback is crucial to MLEs' academic and linguistic growth, and teachers need to engage students in the process so they can see if they are mastering the skills they are learning.

Feeling the autonomy of their learning success through constructive feedback helps students see progress and areas for improvement in each assignment. For instance, before providing feedback, teachers could ask their students to identify one strength and one area of improvement. Explicit feedback also reinforces learning by addressing gaps in real time, not just at the end of a project. Moreover, it builds confidence when students know they are on the right track in small, everyday activities (Allman, 2019).

Strategies for Making Feedback Comprehensible
- Use **simple, specific language:** Avoid jargon.
- Offer **actionable steps:** "Add two more examples from the text."
- Pair feedback with **visuals** or **examples:** Show a model response for comparison by highlighting key differences.
- Provide **audio or written feedback** for flexibility.
- Encourage **self-reflection:** "What would you add to your answer?"

Feedback That Leads to Growth

Constructive feedback helps all students learn by showing what they have done well and what they need to improve. It motivates growth by turning errors into learning opportunities. For teachers, feedback shows student progress, guides instruction, and can be provided in different settings: ongoing feedback to improve language skills, feedback during and after assessments, and reflective feedback. Constructive feedback should have the following characteristics:

- **targeted:** Connect feedback to clear goals or objectives. Use rubrics and assessments to make expectations and progress measurable.
- **specific:** Provide actionable, understandable, and nonjudgmental guidance.
- **timely:** Give feedback during learning rather than after.

In addition to these elements of constructive feedback, MLEs require a more balanced, differentiated, scaffolded, and supportive feedback that is tailored to their language level and developmental needs. These elements of feedback are important for MLEs because they emphasize growth over perfection, helping students gain confidence and competence in language use.

- **balanced:** Focus on both form (grammar) and meaning (clarity). For example, "Your sentence structure is correct, but clarify the main idea to make it easier to understand."
- **differentiated:** Recognize individual progress and patterns in errors. For instance, for a beginner, focus on basic word order; for an advanced learner, refine complex sentences.
- **scaffolded:** Focus on one specific skill before addressing other skills.

- **supportive**: Encourage risk-taking and learning from mistakes. For example, instead of correcting every grammatical mistake, acknowledge effort and suggest one key improvement area.

Table 2.1 *Example Rubric With Accessible Language and Visuals*

Criterion	Great (4)	Good (3)	Needs Work (2)	Missing (1)
Answering the Question ?	Answers the question completely and clearly.	Answers most of the question clearly.	Partially answers the question but misses some parts.	Does not answer the question.
Using Evidence	Includes 3+ details from the documents.	Includes 2 details from the documents.	Includes 1 detail from the documents.	Does not include details from the documents.
Organizing Ideas	Essay has a clear beginning, middle, and end.	Essay is mostly organized but has some confusion.	Essay is hard to understand.	Essay is not organized.
Language Use	Sentences are clear, with few grammar mistakes.	Sentences are mostly clear but have some mistakes.	Sentences are hard to understand.	Sentences do not make sense.

Creating Accessible Rubrics for Multilingual Learners of English

Rubrics help clarify expectations and guide student performance. To make them more accessible for MLEs, teachers can implement the following strategies:

- **Use clear, simple language:** Avoid jargon or complex sentence structures. For example, instead of *demonstrates critical analysis*, use *shows clear thinking and good reasons*.
- **Add Visuals:** Add icons, diagrams, or color-coded sections to represent rubric components visually.

Examples:

Question icon (?): for answering the question

Document icon (📄): for using evidence

Structure icon (🔧): for organizing ideas

Speech bubble icon (💬): for language use

Star Icon (✩): for including your own opinion.

- **Provide examples:** Include annotated models of work at each performance level.

Examples:

A high intermediate MLE says or writes, "The author thinks teamwork is important because it helps people solve problems. For example, in the story, the characters build a house together." *Feedback: This is a strong answer because it includes an idea and an example.*

A low intermediate MLE says or writes, "Teamwork is good." *Feedback: Add more details and examples from the story.*

- **Translate key terms:** If possible, offer translations or definitions of critical vocabulary in the students' home languages.
- **Use color-coded levels:** green for *great*, yellow for *needs work*, and red for *missing*.
- **Use a checklist format:** This is a helpful format for a rubric for beginner students, as it has minimal text to read and focuses on the most important goals.

Writing Checklist
- Did I write a topic sentence?
- Did I add two pieces of evidence from the text?
- Did I use my own words?
- Did I check my spelling?

Application Beyond Assessments

Accessible rubrics should apply to all student work—not just formal assessments. This includes homework, classwork, projects, and participation. Clear expectations help MLEs build confidence and understand how to succeed in every task.

Conclusion: Planning for Success

By beginning with clear content and language goals aligned with the practices of reading and writing that are central to the discipline of social studies, educators can create lessons that target the most important learning for MLEs. From this starting point, educators can thoughtfully incorporate collaborative learning strategies and design assessments that use accessible and authentic methods to accurately assess what MLEs have learned. In addition to these broad strokes of designing lessons for MLEs, teachers need to use a wide variety of scaffolding strategies to make content accessible for MLEs and allow them to participate alongside their peers. These strategies are the topic of Chapter 3.

Classroom Connections

STUDENT IDENTITY CARD

Name:
Yadiel Ayala Gonzalez
Grade: **8**
Country of origin: **Cuba**
English language
proficiency: **Advanced**

*As **Yadiel**'s teachers begin identifying specific language objectives to teach alongside their content objectives, they start to see a shift in Yadiel's performance on assessments. While just being exposed to academic vocabulary in class was not enough for him to pick it up, when Yadiel works with a specific, targeted list of words, woven into instruction and assessments in intentional ways, he starts to gain traction with academic vocabulary. Similarly, with explicit instruction about how to use transition words in his writing to express complex relationships, Yadiel becomes better able to explain his reasoning and construct a grade-appropriate historical argument. He still has more to learn—developing proficiency in academic language takes time! But the student who spent years stalled out at almost-but-not-quite is now making progress.*

STUDENT IDENTITY CARD

Name: **Minh Nguyen**
Grade: **11**
Country of origin:
Vietnam
English language
proficiency level:
Advanced

*As **Minh** is discovering, social studies is not just about knowing what happened in the past and why; equally important is studying the different accounts that people tell about history and the ways each source's unique context and perspective shapes the story it tells. These disciplinary literacy practices are especially challenging for students like Minh, who come from educational systems where a good student memorizes the answers supplied by the experts. Minh's teachers can support her (and all her classmates) by explicitly showing how reading and writing in social studies differ from reading in other classes. Minh may also need scaffolds, like simpler or shorter texts, so that she can focus her energy on this new way of thinking rather than on reading comprehension.*

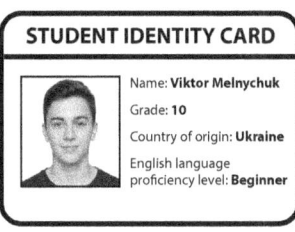

STUDENT IDENTITY CARD

Name: **Viktor Melnychuk**
Grade: **10**
Country of origin: **Ukraine**
English language
proficiency level: **Beginner**

Viktor's teacher knows that Viktor understands more than he is able to show through standardized tests and begins exploring creative assessment options. The teacher starts by simplifying the language in multiple-choice tests so that the questions are measuring what Viktor knows about the content rather than how many words he knows. Even this makes a difference, but it is not until she suggests that Viktor draw his answers rather than write them that she realizes just how much Viktor actually knows about world history.

Inspired by these results, the teacher tries out an authentic assessment for the unit on the Cold War. Working together, the class creates a virtual museum exhibit about daily life in the Soviet Union. The images and other visuals Viktor selects for his portion of the exhibit show a clear understanding of the content, but it is his writing that really shines in this new format. Given the opportunity to use the language supports available in the real world and to revise his writing for clarity, Viktor is able to show a sophisticated understanding of how economic systems affect daily life.

Chapter 3. Supporting Multilingual Learners of English at the Lesson-Delivery Level: Teaching Strategies and Activities

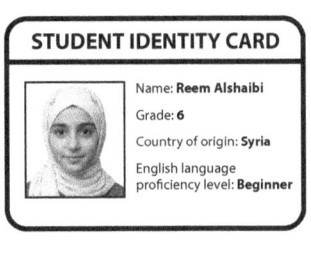

Reem is doing her best to follow along in her world history class. She writes down what the teacher writes on the board, very carefully copying the shapes of the unfamiliar letters, so different from the Arabic script she is used to. She listens for the phrases that she recognizes: "Turn the page," "Do questions two and three on your own," "The homework is …." She does not understand questions 2 and 3, but when the teacher goes over them with the class, she copies down the correct answers. She dutifully makes a note of the homework assignment in her planner.

At the end of class, the teacher passes out an exit ticket in which the students have to write a short paragraph response. Reem knows that she needs three sentences to make a paragraph, but she does not understand the question: "If you were a trader on the Silk Road what would you bring to help you overcome the challenges of the journey?" Unsure of how to answer, she resorts to pulling evidence from the papers the class used today and turns in the following paragraph:

> The Silk Road was a major trade route between China. Base your answer on the information from Document A. 100 CE Buddhism spreads along the Silk Road and reaches China.

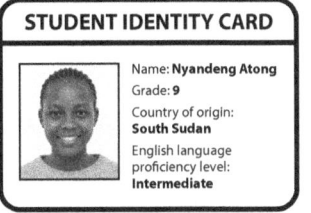

*Throughout a lesson on the American Revolution, **Nyandeng** seems confused. She follows along, trying to answer questions and participating in a jigsaw activity with her peers, but she is having trouble keeping track of the patriots and the loyalists, despite lots of images on the lesson slides and a vocabulary guide that she frequently checks.*

It is not until the end of class, when Nyandeng asks, "Wait, why are they fighting Britain? Britain and USA are friends, no?" that her teachers realize the source of the confusion: Nyandeng has no idea that Britain used to control the United States. What they had assumed was common knowledge is something Nyandeng never learned.

Minh's social studies teacher is not sure how to help her. The problem is not that her English is limited—the teacher has experience supporting beginning language learners. It is that Minh's language is already so advanced. She already knows all the words on the vocabulary lists the teacher usually gives multilingual learners of English (MLEs), and her test scores show that her reading comprehension is almost at grade level.

Minh also has excellent study skills, taking detailed notes and highlighting key information. The teacher understands that Minh is not yet proficient in English and needs some extra help—he is just not sure what that help should look like.

In this chapter:
- Building and activating background knowledge
- Incorporating visuals and multimedia
- Simplifying language
- Teaching vocabulary
- Building academic skills
- Supporting writing

We teachers have a plateful. Crafting lesson plans to reach benchmarks and state standards, writing personal growth plans, filling out state teacher assessment documents, taking required courses on the science of reading and dyslexia, completing workplace training on blood-borne pathogens and fire safety, incorporating social-emotional learning into lessons, differentiating for gifted students and those with special needs, not to mention managing general student behavior when many students would rather have detention than put away their cell phones.

And now you are faced with students who may not know the English language and may not be able to read or write in their first language due to gaps in their education. If you are an English language teacher, you may thrive on the challenges. But if you are a social studies teacher, you may be thinking, "My job is to teach the content standards, not the English language."

But keep in mind, all teachers, to an extent, are teachers of English. If you were a biology teacher, you would not allow students into a lab without giving them tools and training on how to use the lab equipment. And you would not allow students into the lab without providing and explaining the terminology you will be using during the experiment. As social studies teachers, your tools are the English language. As social studies teachers, you are the experts in the language of your content.

In the past, teaching English to MLEs was seen as the responsibility of only English language teachers. However, due to the requirements of the Every Student Succeeds Act (ESSA), increasing immigrant populations, and limited resources, an extensive, collaborative approach is essential.

In fact, as Mohamed (2024) commented, "When language and content teachers can collaborate to meet the linguistic needs of students, it helps to strengthen students' communicative language development, promote critical thinking, and increase levels of cognitive engagement" (para. 5).

But here is the good news. MLEs bring a wealth of diversity to your social studies classes, and based on the students' proficiency levels, you are free to differentiate your content to meet their needs. As in special education, this may involve changing the expectations of what they will be learning.

Change the expectations? We teachers are required to hold all students to high academic standards. Yes. But all students may not meet those standards at the same rate, or they may show their understanding in different ways. While we need to ensure MLEs are exposed to high standards and full engagement in our classes, we must also be realistic.

Research shows that it may take MLEs 5 to 7 years to develop academic language skills. Many students can speak well in a social situation, which often masks their low academic language. They may *sound* fluent. But when they read content texts and encounter words such as *nation*, *compromise*, or *troops*, they are often at a loss.

Considering this, how can an immigrant or refugee with emerging English proficiency be expected to perform the same tasks as her grade-level peers, at the same speed, to the same level of complexity? She cannot. This is why you will have to modify your instruction to match her level. The sheer amount of vocabulary, the complexities of a variety of texts, and the new information and concepts can be overwhelming for MLEs at any level. The sink-or-swim approach is not only ineffective, but it can raise students' *affective filters*—the term in language acquisition research to describe how intense anxiety can limit or even shut down the brain's ability to learn (Krashen, 1982).

So, what do we do? *Focus on the big ideas.*

Have you ever seen those person-on-the-street interviews on late-night talk shows? An interviewer stops a random person walking by to ask a question such as, "How many states are there in the US?" Then you, sitting on your sofa eating popcorn, and most of the audience in the studio cringe when someone says 52.

Think about those interviews and ask yourself: "What do I want my students to know and to remember once they leave the classroom?"

Do they really need to know the words *latitude* and *longitude* when they do not yet know the words *continent* or *ocean*? Do they need to know the Tennis Court Oath or the Declaration of the Rights of Man, or is it enough to understand that the French Revolution challenged the societal order and created a system based on equality? Do they need to know the specific differences between the Federalists and Antifederalists, or is it okay that they learn that power is divided between the federal government and the states?

Taking time to distinguish what your MLEs *need to know* versus what is nice to know helps them to gain essential meaning while building a strong foundation in the language.

While it is natural to be concerned about student performance on standardized tests and the reality that those could bring down your teacher evaluation, think of why you got into teaching in the first place. Regardless of test scores, you will want your students to walk out of your classroom armed with the knowledge and skills that allow them to be informed citizens.

The Tennis Court Oath may not appear on this year's test, but the idea that the French Revolution challenged the social order will. By focusing on the *need to know*, the big ideas, we cut through the clutter and zero in on the knowledge we want students to have and not the language proficiency. Furthermore, focusing on the big ideas—and focusing on depth, not breadth—*is* the best way to prepare MLEs for high-stakes tests. This is achieved by simplifying your expectations and your language.

Do not stress out over this. Give yourself permission to be imperfect. Start small and build as you go. Understand that there is a learning curve for you as well. The more you differentiate, the better you will get at it. The longer students are in your class, the more proficient they will become. Not only will this benefit your MLEs, but it may also benefit your students with learning challenges and those with emerging reading skills. Be sure to save everything. Save all versions of documents that you create for MLEs so that you can begin building a library for future use.

Build and Activate Background Knowledge

Consider the following passage:

> Having crumbled to 214 all out, with Jonathan Trott's 84 not out the glue across an otherwise brittle English innings, the tourists were back in the contest when Paul Collingwood's brace had the hosts wobbling at 100 for five at the turn of the 21st over. (Walsh, 2013, para. 1)

If asked to summarize this passage, how would you do it? Would you ace it or struggle? This passage, an announcement from a cricket match, exemplifies the importance of background knowledge in reading comprehension.

Build Background Knowledge

We cannot assume every MLE will know that Britain used to control the United States, who Hitler is, or that one cannot drive a car from the United States to Spain. In the well-known 1988 baseball study by Recht and Leslie, researchers gave two groups of students a passage about baseball and asked them to depict the actions in the text on a replica field. The lower ability readers with knowledge of baseball outperformed the high-ability readers with little knowledge of the sport (Recht & Leslie, 1988). Since then, dozens of studies on the links between background knowledge and reading comprehension have consistently found that students with more background knowledge are better able to comprehend texts. In short, both MLEs and non-MLEs will all benefit from the building of background knowledge.

For example, in high school U.S. History teacher Peggie's district, American History usually starts with Reconstruction. During a unit on Jim Crow laws, she informally assessed what her students knew about the Civil War. After a brief chat with her students, she learned they had no idea about the Civil War in the United States or even what slavery was. For MLEs to gain the most out of the unit, she knew she had to teach the basics of the Civil War. She could have students watch a simplified video, such as those by Brainpop or Simple History, or have an AI-powered website such as Diffit create a passage at an appropriate reading level in Farsi and Arabic. Because she wanted to ensure her students understood both essential Tier 2 and Tier 3 vocabulary, she chose to create the following summary for her students:

The Civil War and Reconstruction

Between 1861 and 1865, the United States had a **Civil War**. The southern part of the country (the **South**) fought (fight) against the **North**. One of the main reasons for the war was **slavery**. The South wanted slaves to work on their farms or large **plantations**. The North wanted to end slavery. In 1863, President Abraham Lincoln stated (said) that all slaves were **free**. In 1865, the North won the war shortly after President **Lincoln** was **assassinated** (murdered). The country then began **reconstruction** (to build again).

After the war ended, the states ratified (voted) the **13th Amendment** to end slavery. However, many people in the South did not want the slaves to be free. States created **Black Codes** to control the former slaves. These laws said Black people must have jobs, that bosses could beat their Black workers, and also that Black people could not own **land**. Because of these laws, there were **protests** and fighting. President Johnson sent army **troops** to help control the problems in the South.

By deliberately exposing her MLEs to background on the Civil War, Peggie created a knowledge base upon which to build future lessons on Reconstruction and Civil Rights.

Activate Background Knowledge

As essential as building background knowledge is, so is the activation of prior knowledge. Learning is never built on nothing. Educational psychologists believe that all people learn by adding new information and experiences to preexisting schemas or mental frameworks (see Hammond, 2015, for more information). For example, as children we might learn about zebras not by memorizing information about it, but by recognizing that it is something like a horse and from there identifying the ways in which it is similar to and different from the animal we already know about. The teacher's role in this process is to identify the background knowledge that students *do* bring to the classroom and to activate it so that students are ready to add to their understanding.

Activating this prior knowledge helps all students learn, but it is especially important to MLEs, whose job of learning the content and language at the same time is much easier if they can attach new words to the concepts and understandings they already know. Sometimes, we can connect new learning to content the students have already studied, either in their prior school or earlier in the year. More often, activating background knowledge means drawing on general, everyday student experiences and connecting them to the new content.

Examples of Drawing on Prior Knowledge

- As bellwork for their first lesson on the French Revolution, a middle school World History teacher asks students the following question: "Should older brothers and sisters have to do more chores around the house than young brothers and sisters? Why or why not?" *The teacher is drawing on students' experiences about being treated differently from others and feelings of resentment over unfair conditions.*
- A high school U.S. History teacher opens a unit on the Industrial Revolution with a gallery walk activity where students make observations about images of living and working conditions during this period. *The teacher is prompting students to recall any prior learning they may have about industrialization as well as drawing out key vocabulary that the students will need to use in this unit by having them use words they already know* (e.g., work, factory, pollution, injured) *to describe what they see.*
- In his first lesson on Indigenous peoples of the Southwest, a middle school U.S. History teacher shows an image of a Pueblo village and asks students to reflect on how this community is similar to and different from the community they live in now. *The teacher is activating students' background knowledge about the things all people need and how we organize our communities to provide these needs.*

In activities meant to wake up students' prior knowledge, it is important to avoid assumptions about universal experiences or prior learning. Some of the experiences and knowledge that are common for students from your particular context may be totally unfamiliar to MLEs. Please consult Chapter 1 for an in-depth discussion of the varied backgrounds MLEs bring to the classroom.

Incorporate Visuals and Multimedia

Images are a direct way of communicating meaning. Social studies covers complex themes through disciplines such as history, geography, civics, and economics, often requiring abstract and critical thinking. Visual aids and multimedia tools can bridge language barriers and make these abstract concepts more tangible and comprehensible (Cummins, 2000; Echevarria et al., 2017). Incorporating visuals—photographs, drawings, maps, timelines, symbols, videos, and diagrams—is one of the most important strategies to make content comprehensible for MLEs. (Visuals have the bonus of usually making the lesson more engaging for everyone else as well.) Images and other visuals can show the meanings of challenging words, help MLEs recognize when they are studying a topic they have already learned, and deliver new content in an accessible way (see Table 3.1 for explanations and ideas).

Recent research shows the enormous benefits of visual aids in improving learning outcomes, particularly for MLEs. Hsu (2014) demonstrated how visual aids such as multimedia presentations and infographics promote vocabulary retention and comprehension in English for MLEs. At the same time, Kristina and Nagara (2023) indicated that visuals improve motivation and engagement. Visual aids can also help students understand complex concepts by organizing information using timelines or maps (Mayer, 2009), engaging them with dynamic content like interactive maps and simulations (Fadel, 2008), and promoting inclusivity by representing diverse cultures and perspectives, fostering equity and validation of students' experiences (Gay, 2010).

Select Appropriate Visuals and Multimedia

Visuals must be chosen carefully to ensure that they clearly show the concept you actually want students to learn. Corporate clipart for concepts like *leader*, *organization*, or *resources*—often the first items to show up in an image search—sometimes uses some very opaque metaphors. It is also important to verify the accuracy of the visuals you use.

Another important detail makes a big difference: Make sure that the visuals you use represent people of diverse races, genders, and ages. If every person shown in your lesson slides is white, it sends a quiet but strong message about the kind of people who belong in school and the kind of people whose stories are worth discussing. Additionally, visuals should not perpetuate stereotypes and should portray all people respectfully and accurately.

Support Understanding of Videos for Multilingual Learners of English

Social studies teachers often use documentaries and other videos in the classroom. These resources can be highly engaging, and they can support all students' learning by providing memorable, easy-to-understand visuals. Like other ways of incorporating visuals, videos of all kinds can be a valuable support for MLEs' understanding. However, videos can also present unique challenges for MLEs. The following strategies suggest ways to combat these challenges.

Preview the Video With Multilingual Learners of English in Mind

It is important to remember that not all video resources are created equal. YouTube and other video hosting websites have millions of options, and while some are fantastic resources that use animations, still images, and historical footage in meaningful ways to help students grasp the content, others are just a voiceover paired with pictures that do not always show the most important elements of the story. A good way to assess the value of a video for MLEs is to watch it with the sound off; if you can more or less follow the story from just what you see, then it is relatively accessible for students who are learning English.

Avoid Fast-Paced Resources

Some videos may be excellent but not well suited to MLEs' needs. For example, the CrashCourse series by popular vloggers and authors John and Hank Green is an engaging, high-energy resource for fluent speakers of English, but John's frenetic speaking pace and low-context, disjointed style of humor make the series a poor resource for beginning or intermediate learners of English. See Chapter 6 for specific suggestions of YouTube channels that produce videos that can be helpful for MLEs.

Turn on the Subtitles

The value of subtitles when available in a student's first language is obvious, but even English subtitles (for when a class includes students from many different language backgrounds) can be a huge boost to MLEs' comprehension. One important warning: When using YouTube or another service with automatically

Table 3.1 *Strategies and Practical Applications of Visuals and Multimedia in Social Studies*

Visuals and multimedia	Strategies for social studies instruction	Practical applications
Graphic organizers for historical events and processes	Use tools like Venn diagrams, cause-and-effect charts, and flowcharts to organize and simplify historical events and social processes (Marzano et al., 2001).	Examine the American Revolution through an interactive timeline and troop movement maps.
Interactive maps and geographic tools	Leverage GIS tools like Google Earth to teach geography, explore regions, and connect them to historical and cultural contexts (Brophy & Alleman, 2007).	Compare the Sahara Desert and the Amazon Rainforest to discuss environmental impacts on human activities.
Multimedia presentations on historical and current events	Incorporate videos, animations, and audio from platforms like YouTube and PBS LearningMedia for engaging content delivery (Paivio, 1990).	Watch an animation on the legislative process and role-play as Congress members debating a bill.
Primary source analysis with visual aids	Integrate historical photographs, maps, and documents to analyze context, perspective, and significance (Wineburg, 2001).	Analyze Civil Rights Movement images and cartoons to understand challenges and public sentiment.
Virtual field trips to historical and cultural sites	Utilize virtual reality (VR) and augmented reality (AR) for immersive visits to historical sites, museums, and landmarks (Fadel, 2008).	Take students on virtual trips to places like ancient Rome or WWII battlefields for an engaging historical experience.
Infographics and data visualization for social studies topics	Present data visually to help students interpret patterns and understand complex topics (Kress & van Leeuwen, 2006).	Students create an infographic comparing cultural traditions across different regions.

generated subtitles, it is important to preview them. Sometimes this technology works quite well, and other times it produces garbled nonsense. If the latter is the case, it is best to look for a different resource.

Pause for Processing Breaks

Even expert readers frequently pause to check their understanding or clarify the meaning of a word. Taking a break can help listeners understand what they are hearing in videos as well. Although the

---

Strategies

1. Connect to Prior Knowledge

- Compare maps, graphs, or timelines from students' home countries with local examples to foster relevance and deeper understanding.
- Invite students to share personal stories, traditions, or historical events from their backgrounds that relate to the topic, encouraging connections between their lived experiences and new content.

2. Preteach Vocabulary

- Introduce key terms (e.g., *latitude, legend, increase*) with visuals and bilingual glossaries.
- Use interactive activities such as word sorts, realia (real-world objects), or sentence frames to reinforce understanding and encourage contextual usage.

3. Simplify and Scaffold

- Use clear imagery, minimal text, and visual aids.
- Break down components like symbols, titles, and axes into manageable parts.

4. Hands-On Practice

- Create maps, graphs, or timelines collaboratively, incorporating students' home language(s) and English.
- Use manipulatives or digital tools for interactive learning so students can make visuals and connections through the process.

5. Layered Questioning

- Start with basic *what* or *where* questions and progress to deeper analysis (e.g., "How does this affect climate?"). This creates a process for inputting information.
- Incorporate wait time and sentence starters to support language development and allow all learners, especially MLEs, to process and respond thoughtfully.

6. Cultural Context and Comparisons

- Discuss culturally relevant examples and provide explicit explanations of idioms, symbols, or events.
- Encourage students to compare similar practices or beliefs from their own cultures, fostering mutual respect and deeper understanding of diverse perspectives.

---

images may be easy to understand, the voiceovers in documentaries can often use complex academic language, especially if they include readings of historical documents. While MLEs especially benefit from the teacher pausing the video every few minutes to clarify the information, highlight important points, or answer questions, all students will benefit from this scaffold. Teachers can also implement this modification in videos that students watch independently for homework, using EdPuzzle or a similar educational video platform that allows teachers to insert check-for-understanding questions right into the video.

Explicitly Teach Maps, Political Cartoons, Timelines, and Graphs

Teaching how to use visual tools like maps, political cartoons, timelines, and graphs is a vital skill for MLEs to enhance their critical thinking, content comprehension, and language acquisition. These tools serve as bridges to understanding primary sources, such as historical maps or archival cartoons, and secondary sources, like textbook timelines or data interpretations, allowing students to engage deeply with content across contexts. These strategies aim to bridge language barriers and develop students' analytical and interpretive skills.

Maps, political cartoons, timelines, and graphs can be challenging for MLEs due to cultural assumptions and unfamiliar conventions. Teachers can address this by explicitly teaching visual symbols, providing context, and integrating language supports. This helps students interpret visual information while building language and cultural understanding.

By blending these strategies, visual tools can enhance learning, bridge cultural gaps, and support academic confidence for MLEs.

Simplify Language

Even when a student understands the basic concepts, the language used to explain and assess them may be a barrier.

Imagine you are an MLE trying to answer the following question in your U.S. History homework: *Identify the contributing factors that made the coal miners' strike of 1902 a challenging issue for Roosevelt to address and evaluate his success in responding to the grievances raised.* The good news: You know all about the coal miners' strike of 1902, having learned about it in class yesterday. The bad news? You have no idea what this question is asking you *about* that event.

For one thing, there is a lot of difficult vocabulary. Not only are there words you do not know like *contributing factors* and *grievances*, but there are familiar words that make no sense here. An *address* is the location where you live, but Roosevelt did not go to anybody's house over the strike. Even more difficult, you cannot find any question words in this supposed question—there is no *who, what, where, when, why,* or *how.*

Now imagine how it would be different if your teacher had just asked the question in plain, simple language (and asked each question on its own instead of jamming two or three questions into one): *Why was the coal miners' strike a difficult problem to solve? (Give 2–3 reasons.) Was Roosevelt successful in helping the miners with their problems? Why or why not?*

Simplifying language is about adjusting the complexity of communication to make sure students understand and can engage without barriers. This is both verbal and written. It involves clear and concise sentences (e.g., avoid slang, idioms) to present information step-by-step, highlight the most important information, and most importantly check for understanding. You should also encourage summarizing the essential information and pausing to give students a chance to ask clarifying questions. The following strategies are for your reference.

Speak as Clearly as Possible

You do not have to slow down to a snail's pace or speak like an *I Can Read* book. But adjusting the pace of your speech just a little bit and making sure you are enunciating clearly can make a big difference in how much your MLEs can understand.

Use Synonyms

Whether you are speaking or writing, simplifying your words is imperative.

- *country* is better than *nation*
- *land* is better than *territory*
- *Look at the picture on page 5* is better than *Focus your attention on the diagram on the adjacent page.*

Avoid Idioms

In particular, avoid idioms (i.e., phrases that do not make sense when you break them down into the definitions of their individual words or that rely on metaphors for their meaning, such as *barking up the wrong tree*) because they are a huge challenge for language learners to understand.

Explain Words With Multiple Meanings

Encountering the word *address* in the coal miners' strike example, the word *arms* when reading the Second Amendment, or *crash* when hearing about the Wall Street Crash of 1929 will no doubt cause confusion for many MLEs. Take a brief moment to explain the various meanings of words and the context in which they are used.

Make Texts Accessible

Many of the texts used in social studies—from primary sources to textbooks to news articles—are very complex. Students struggle to engage in higher order thinking about these texts because they often expend all their energy just trying to understand what the texts say. Teachers can make texts more accessible for MLEs by using leveled texts or by modifying them to be more comprehensible.

However, you can also do it yourself! It is not terribly difficult, once you learn how to do it, and you end up with a document that is perfectly tailored to your students and your purpose. Use the checklist in the sidebar to guide you through the changes that can make a difficult document more accessible.

Checklist for Making Texts Accessible

- Cut down the document to the most important parts.
- Break up long paragraphs.
- Break up long sentences.
- Reword complex or outdated sentence structures.
- Exchange archaic words for more familiar ones.
- Add definitions for important content vocabulary.

Chunking the text is particularly important. In addition to making the organization of the ideas in the text clearer and giving students a chance to process each idea, breaking up big blocks of text makes the task of reading the document feel less overwhelming. It can also be helpful to divide up a reading that has accompanying questions so students can focus on just one question at a time and more easily locate the answers in the text.

Common Sense: Before and After Modifying

The following example shows how a very dense primary source can be modified to be more accessible for MLEs. This text was modified following the steps recommended in the sidebar.

Before

Europe is too thickly planted with kingdoms to be long at peace, and whenever a war breaks out between England and any foreign power, the trade of America goes to ruin, *because of her connection with Britain.* The next war may not turn out like the last, and should it not, the advocates for reconciliation now will be wishing for separation then, because, neutrality in that case, would be a safer convoy than a man of war. Everything that is right or natural pleads for separation. The blood of the slain, the weeping voice of nature cries, 'Tis time to part. Even the distance at which the Almighty hath placed England and America, is a strong and natural proof, that the authority of the one, over the other, was never the design of Heaven. The time likewise at which the continent was discovered, adds weight to the argument, and the manner in which it was populated increases the force of it. The reformation was preceded by the discovery of America, as if the Almighty graciously meant to open a sanctuary to the persecuted in future years, when home should afford neither friendship nor safety. (Paine, 1776)

After

Europe has too many countries to be at peace for long. Whenever a war starts between England and any other country, America's trade goes to ruin, *because of her connection with Britain.*

> The next war may not turn out like the last. If that happens, the people who now want reconciliation [staying with Britain] will then want separation [leaving Britain]. If Britain loses a war, it will be safer to be neutral [not on anyone's side].
>
> Everything that is right or natural pleads for separation. The blood of the dead, the weeping voice of nature cries, IT IS TIME TO GO.
>
> Even the distance between England and America is a strong and natural proof that God never wanted England to control America. (Adapted from Paine, 1776)

Many teachers worry that editing primary sources is "watering down" the content. After all, students have to be able to deal with these kinds of documents on state-mandated final exams, in college courses, or in other situations outside of our control—so giving them easier work now would be failing to properly prepare them. However, keep in mind that students need to be able to practice higher order thinking with documents at their reading level or else all their energy goes into decoding. Far from making the work too easy, by providing modified documents, teachers make it possible for MLEs to be pushed to do more complex and challenging analysis.

It is also important to remember that students will build their reading proficiency by working with increasingly challenging texts over time. Raise that level of challenge too abruptly, and students cannot grow; increase it gradually over the course of a school year or semester, and students can make steady progress toward the proficiency they need to achieve by the end of the year.

Explicitly Teach Vocabulary

While a new language or new content could never be boiled down to just vocabulary, learning vocabulary is essential to being able to learn in English, especially in social studies. All content areas do, of course, have their own specialized vocabulary, but in social studies the pressure to understand, remember, and correctly use academic words is especially heightened due to the importance of historical documents in this field. We cannot get away from old texts: It is where the study of history lives. Therefore, it is important for all social studies teachers who work with MLEs to pay special attention to vocabulary instruction.

Vocabulary Tiers

The first step in effective vocabulary instruction is choosing the right words to teach. Education scholars divide the vocabulary that students encounter into three groups or tiers, originally developed by Beck et al. (1987). Tier 1 vocabulary is the everyday words that students will hear in normal conversation: *house, bus, listen, play, sad, big*. As social studies teachers, we do not need to teach these words; students are exposed to them so often and in such high-context situations that they will pick them up on their own.

At the other end of the spectrum, Tier 3 words are specialized academic words that students only hear in school and in a specific class or content area. In social studies, the Tier 3 vocabulary includes the names of people (e.g., *Harriet Tubman, the Mongols, Deng Xiaoping*), places (e.g., *Rome, the Alamo, the USSR*), and events (e.g., *the Neolithic Revolution, the Progressive Era, the Great Leap Forward, the Holocaust*). Our field's Tier 3 vocabulary also includes many general terms that describe concepts and processes specific to history and economics; words like *alliance, supply and demand, separation of powers*, and *colonize* all fall into this category. Tier 3 words also include words that are used in more than one content area but have different meanings depending on the context. For example, a *product* in mathematics is the result of multiplying two numbers, but in social studies, it is a good manufactured by people.

Social studies teachers are usually already aware of these vocabulary words, which all our students, regardless of their first language, need to learn. The only difference for our MLEs is that they may not be able to learn as many of these words, given all the other words they are trying to learn at the same time (i.e., Tier 2 vocabulary); an appropriate scaffold is to select about half of these words from each unit as the *most* essential for MLEs to know.

The final group of vocabulary words is a little harder to pin down, but it is where teachers of MLEs in social studies classes really need to focus our attention. Tier 2 contains all the academic vocabulary words that are used across multiple content areas. Words like *increase, develop, maintain, primary, decline*, and *contribute* are just a few of these easily overlooked words. Many more examples of Tier 2 words can be found in Coxhead's (2000) *Academic Word List* or Browne et al.'s (2013) *New Academic Word List*. These academic projects analyzed many thousands of academic articles to determine the words most frequently used in this kind of writing. (Because they are based on high-level scholarly articles and are also extremely long, these lists should not be used as is, but they are an excellent starting point for becoming aware of the academic vocabulary commonly used in social studies.)

It is easy for teachers to overlook Tier 2 vocabulary because we are usually comfortable with these words ourselves, and so they fade into the background. Teachers might also assume that as long as students know the "main" words in a sentence or a question, they should be able to piece together the rest of it. However, Tier 2 words are often key to understanding documents or questions.

More importantly, the definitions of many vocabulary words depend on a student's understanding of the words in the definition. For example, here is the definition of *democracy* from Merriam-Webster (n.d.-a): "government by the people: rule of the majority." Seems pretty straightforward, right? Unless you do not know the Tier 2 words *government, rule*, and *majority*. If you are teaching about democracy, you may have to teach these words along with democracy.

Select the Most Essential Vocabulary

Keep in mind it can take a student six–25 encounters to learn a new vocabulary word. If we were to multiply the number of weekly vocabulary words students are expected to learn in social studies, science, mathematics, and other content classes, plus the social language and slang they want to learn, well … that is a lot of vocabulary! Narrow down the few Tier 3 (content-specific) words you want them to know. And include the Tier 2 and Tier 3 words they need to understand them.

There are thousands of academic words that students could encounter in social studies activities and assessments. How is a teacher to know which ones to choose to teach? Start with the end goal: How will students be assessed? What words will they need to understand to complete the assessment? What words will they need to be able to use in their writing? The documents students will use, the questions they will answer, and the types of writing you expect them to produce will likely suggest more Tier 2 vocabulary than you could hope to teach in a year.

From the words you have brainstormed, select some that are most essential to understanding or explaining the content in the unit and some that students will be able to use throughout the school year and in other classes. How many you choose will depend on the ages and proficiency levels of your students, the length of the unit, how much instructional time you have, and many other factors. Ten words is a good starting point.

During her high school U.S. History unit on the Second Industrial Revolution, Peggie thought students should know the Tier 3 words *monopoly* and *sweatshop*. But she knew she also had to include Tier 2 words such as *product, factory,* and *labor*. Later, she added *oil* because she learned her students thought they were talking about olive oil. She made a simple vocabulary guide with images so students could use it for reference during class and later as a study guide for a test (see Table 3.2).

Table 3.2 *Sample Vocabulary Guide With Images*

Word	Tier	Definition	Example	Translation
conditions	2	how it is in the place where you live or work		condiciones conditions ظروف
factory	2	a building where things are made		fábrica usine مصنع
labor (laborers)	2	work (workers)		trabajo (trabajadores) travail (travailleurs) عامل/عمال
monopoly	3	complete (100%) control of a **product** or business by one person or group		monopolio monopole مونوبلي/احتكار
oil (petroleum)	2	black liquid used for heating, lighting lamps, and making cars move		aceite huile نفط/بترول
product	2	a thing that is made		producto produit منتج
sweatshop	3	a shop or **factory** where workers **labor** long hours at low **wages** under unhealthy **conditions**		fábrica con explotación exagerada atelier clandestin مصنع استغلالي
wages	2	pay		salarios salaires رواتب/أجور

Create a Vocabulary-Rich Environment

Once you have a list of target vocabulary words—some Tier 3 and some Tier 2—how do you make sure the students learn them? Research has found that in order to acquire new vocabulary in a second language, students need to have repeated meaningful exposures to them (e.g., McQuillan, 2019). That is, they need to hear or read the word in a context where the meaning is clear, and this needs to happen many times. There is no consensus on an exact number of repetitions needed (and it almost certainly varies by student), but estimates range from six to 25 (McQuillan, 2019). Regardless of the exact number, the teacher's task is clear: Get the target vocabulary in front of students as many times as possible in as many different ways as possible.

Create Meaningful Exposures

If you have selected words that naturally appear in the texts (here, *texts* refers to documents, articles, test questions, videos, and any other words the students see in class) students will be using over the course of a unit, you have several exposures of those words ready to go. You can increase the number of exposures by working your target vocabulary into lesson materials and classroom conversation whenever possible. This is a great opportunity for social studies teachers and English language teachers to collaborate on lessons: One teacher creates the content side of the materials, and the other looks for places to add the target vocabulary.

A teacher trying to create meaningful exposures of the Tier 2 word *sufficient* found the following opportunities:

- Her original bellwork question for Monday's lesson read, "What did you do this weekend? Did you sleep in?" She rewrote it to ask, "What did you did this weekend? Did you get *sufficient* sleep?"
- One of the questions in the review Kahoot she had created about the Paleolithic Era asked why hunter-gatherers always moved from place to place. The old answer read "Because there wasn't enough food in one place"; she changed this to "Because there wasn't *sufficient* food in one place."
- Her slides about the Neolithic Revolution talked about early humans having more food after the introduction of farming. She changed them to say that early humans now had *sufficient* food.
- When students were working in small groups, the teacher wanted to know if she needed to add on some extra time to the activity. She made sure to word her question as follows: "Will two more minutes be *sufficient* time to finish?"

When you start to look for them, you will find opportunities to create meaningful exposures to vocabulary in everything you are already doing in the classroom.

Prompt the Students to Use the Words in Speaking and Writing

Students not only need to see and hear the words; they need to practice using them in speaking or writing. A great way to achieve this is to add a word bank (a box of vocabulary words to choose from) to any written assignment, with the requirement that the students must use a certain number of words from the bank to get full credit. When students have to work a vocabulary word into a sentence, they *have* to think about what it means, making this activity a meaningful exposure to the word.

Challenge Students to Find the Words Outside Your Class

Kaedmon has an ongoing challenge with their students: If they find any of the week's vocabulary words in the reading for another class or in their independent reading book, they can show Kaedmon to earn a hard candy. Not only has this practice greatly increased certain students' engagement in independent reading, but it has made students more aware of the importance of academic vocabulary—and not just in their classes and textbooks. Even the student who refused to read anything other than *Naruto* books would routinely find the target words three or four times a week in his book!

This section is not meant to suggest that there is no place for vocabulary-specific practice activities. However, with the press of high-stakes final exams and curriculum maps that seem to expand every year, it can be difficult to find much time to just work on vocabulary. If our vocabulary instruction is limited to 5 minutes a day or half an hour every other Friday—and it is the easiest thing to eliminate when we fall behind—it will be nowhere near enough to help our MLEs learn all the words they need to know in order to be successful in social studies. For this reason, it is essential that vocabulary instruction be built into *all* of our teaching.

Employ Practice Strategies

When we do have the time to work on vocabulary on its own, there are many excellent methods for explicitly teaching new vocabulary to MLEs. A popular method for introducing or practicing new vocabulary is the Frayer model. This is simply a graphic organizer in which the target word is written in the center, surrounded by four boxes in which students show the word's meaning in different ways: a definition, a picture, an example, a nonexample, a sentence, a translation, and so on. The advantage to this method is that the content of the four boxes can be adjusted based on student levels and interests. For example, students with emerging English proficiency may struggle to use the word in a sentence, and a student who has been learning English for a long time or who does not read or write their first language may not benefit from a translation. The specific items you choose to go in the four boxes do not really matter; the important thing is that each box creates a meaningful exposure to the word.

Figure 3.1 shows two examples of a Frayer model—one that a beginning student might create (*absolute monarchy*) and one that would be good practice for an advanced student (*proponent*).

Figure 3.1 *Frayer Models*

definition	other forms	Related:
a person who supports an idea or plan	to propound	to propose (v.) proposition (n.) proposed (adj.)

proponent

✓synonyms (same meaning)	example sentence
advocate for Champion of supporter partisan opponent adversary ✗ antonyms (opposite meaning)	Proponents of the tax argued that it would fund schools.

definition	picture
a king or queen with 100% power ↑ power	¡Dame dinero!

absolute monarch

my language	effects on people
monarca absoluto (rey o reina)	bad because take money and control people and no derechos

Note. The example at the top shows how a student with advanced English proficiency might use a Frayer model. The example on the bottom shows a version appropriate for a beginner.

Vocabulary Activities to Avoid

Some commonly used vocabulary activities are not the most effective way to learn new words. In the following sections, we explain how you can make these activities more effective.

Flashcards ... Without Teaching Students What to *Do* With Them

Teachers frequently have students make flashcards of new vocabulary words, and then these flashcards are carried around in a backpack for weeks and never used to practice. You can teach students how to *use* flashcards for review, or they can use one of the many flashcard apps that keep track of how often the learner gets them right or wrong and retests them at longer or shorter intervals depending on the learner's success. (The field of available apps is vast and ever-changing. At the time of writing, Anki is one excellent flashcard app, but searching online for "free flashcard app with spaced repetition" will bring up other options.)

Practicing the Definitions ... but not *Using* the Words

Another common mistake in vocabulary instruction is to *only* practice and test connecting the words to one specific set of definitions. Students often get very good at matching the word to the definition provided but are unable to use the word in a sentence, understand it in reading, or even recognize the meaning when it is stated in different words. Students *must* practice actually using the words to understand what they hear and read and to communicate in speaking and listening in order to truly learn them.

Word Walls ... That Go Unused

Many teachers know that having a word wall, where important vocabulary is posted, is a highly regarded practice. However, simply having the words posted on the wall (especially when it includes just the words without definitions or visuals) does very little to benefit students. In order for a word wall to be an effective vocabulary support, teachers need to teach students how to *use* it. Not only can students refer to the word wall when unsure of the meaning of a word, they can also use it as a support for writing, looking at the wall to jog their memories of the key terms they should be mentioning in their answers.

Support Note-Taking and Other Academic Skills

Using guiding notes, graphic organizers, and example paragraphs gives students structure, clarity, and models for success. This helps students process new information and express their understanding more effectively.

Create Guided Notes

Guided notes are partially completed outlines or handouts that help students focus on important information during a lesson. Guided notes help most students stay engaged, show them what to focus on, and make learning easier by organizing key ideas. This common strategy can be an important support for MLEs; however, overly complicated guided notes can actually be a barrier to comprehension for beginning MLEs because they have to spend all their time struggling to copy rather than trying to understand the information. Simplifying the notes allows MLEs to reap these same benefits as their non-MLE peers.

Rachel Schoch, a social studies teacher at Southview high school in Sylvania, Ohio, noticed her MLEs struggling with copying the guided notes she projected in class. They did not know common letter combinations, spelling rules, or abbreviations; some of them spoke languages that used a different alphabet and had to write each English letter by copying its shape. It took them a long time to finish, frustrating their non-MLE peers and using valuable minutes from the lesson. At the end of it all, the students had been working so hard to copy the words that they had not processed any of the material. The teacher began to differentiate the presentation slides so that the non-MLE students filled in the more specific Tier 3 words that were underlined, and the MLEs filled in the general Tier 2 words that were highlighted. She also added synonyms in parentheses for Tier 2 vocabulary such as *nations* and *territory* that she knew her newcomers would struggle with. Making two different hard copy sets required some time at first, but she found that the guided notes she made for MLEs were also useful for her students with Individualized Education Programs as well as some of her general education students who struggled with handwriting stamina. See Figure 3.2 for the original version and modified version of the guided notes activity.

Figure 3.2 *Sample Guided Notes Activity*

Treaty of Versailles notes (original version)	Treaty of Versailles notes (modified version)
• Signed by _____ in 1919 at the Paris Peace Conference • Ended _____ • _____ the map of Europe by creating 9 new nations (countries) out of the territory (land): _____	• Signed by President Wilson in _____ at the Paris Peace Conference • _____ World War I • Redrew the _____ of Europe by creating _____ new nations (countries) out of the territory (land): Austria–Hungary, Russia, and Germany

This modified guided notes activity kept the MLEs engaged in the class and enabled them to copy down words they were most likely familiar with rather than struggling with copying the unfamiliar words their peers were writing.

Similarly, traditional study guides that ask students to review important information by finding it in a textbook force beginning MLEs to focus all their energy on searching for and copying key words, leaving them no time to work on understanding and processing the information. Instead, why not give beginner and intermediate students the notes with the answers already filled in? With advanced students, you can include the page and/or paragraph number of where to find the information.

Use Modified Graphic Organizers

Graphic organizers such as Venn diagrams, T-charts, and timelines are visual tools that help students organize information in an easy-to-understand format. They can be used to collect information while reading or studying historical images or to prepare ideas for writing. Graphic organizers, like the one in Figure 3.3, can be a powerful tool for supporting MLEs' understanding, but they often need to be modified in order for students to take full advantage of them.

- Add pictures to help explain the meanings of the sections.
- Provide sentence starters to help students put their ideas into words.
- Allow students who are not yet ready to write in English to fill in the graphic organizer in their home language or to draw their answers.

Figure 3.3 *See-Think-Wonder Graphic Organizer*

See	Think	Wonder
I observe …	I think …	I want to know …

Note. Emojis and other simple images can make graphic organizers more accessible for beginning MLEs.

These tools break down complex ideas into smaller parts, helping students see relationships and remember information better. This is especially powerful for MLEs as the organization of the information is represented visually instead of being explained in words.

Support Writing

Supporting MLEs in writing tasks within the social studies classroom requires intentional scaffolding to address both content understanding and language development. Writing in this context can be complex, as students must analyze historical events and documents, synthesize information, and articulate their ideas using academic language. In addition, as discussed in Chapter

2, the expectations for writing in social studies differ from those in other content areas. What an ELA teacher means and what a social studies teacher means when they tell students to analyze their evidence may be two very different things.

To ensure success, educators can implement a variety of strategies, such as providing writing frames, using graphic organizers, and modeling writing examples. These approaches help break down the writing process into manageable steps, allowing MLEs to build confidence, organize their thoughts, and develop the academic language needed to express themselves effectively.

Align Your Supports to the Task

Writing instruction—like anything else in teaching—is never a one-size-fits-all endeavor. Whenever considering how best to support students' writing, you should always start with your end goal in mind. The specific type of writing your students are doing, the information they need to understand, and the skills they need to be successful will determine the type of scaffolds and other supports that will be most helpful for them. To illustrate this, let us examine the development of a specific essay organization tool.

In Kaedmon's home state of New York, one of the graduation requirements for all students is passing a standardized history exam. The most challenging element of the exam, for most students, is a document-based essay. This task is so overwhelming that Kaedmon found most of their students tended to panic and forget everything they had practiced in class. Kaedmon and their social studies and special education coteachers knew that they needed to create a simple, consistent writing model that students would remember, even on test day.

They started developing their tool by looking at what they wanted their students to be able to do. First, they created a memorable paragraph model that covered the elements identified on the state rubric to evaluate students' writing about historical events. Then Kaedmon created sentence starters for each part of the paragraph by analyzing examples of successful writing. They studied model essays provided by the state and asked social studies colleagues, "What does really good historical analysis sound like for you?" Including the most frequently used phrases from these models, Kaedmon developed sentence starters that MLEs (and non-MLEs) could use to get started when writing each part of their paragraphs. None of these sentence starters does the work for the students—the actual *thinking* is all their own—but they give a little nudge in the right direction so that students are thinking about the right questions. The final organizer the students use is in Figure 3.4.

Figure 3.4 *Social Studies Writing Support for MLEs*

This year, remember to CHEAT!	
Claim	One example of [issue] is...
Historical circumstances	This happened because...
Evidence	Document...shows...
Analysis	– This was positive/unfair because... – Because of this... – This is similar to...
Tie to claim	This example shows how [issue]...

Break Down the Writing Process

As with reading, a large writing task can be overwhelming for all students, but especially for MLEs for whom writing can be a major challenge. Breaking the task into smaller steps helps make writing manageable. Start by studying a model text to understand structure, brainstorm ideas with peers or teachers, and use a graphic organizer to plan thoughts. Students can then focus on writing one paragraph at a time, such as an introduction, body, or conclusion. This approach prevents overwhelm and builds confidence.

Graphic organizers are essential tools for organizing thoughts before writing. Examples include timelines for sequencing historical events, T-charts for comparing and contrasting, and cause-and-effect diagrams for mapping relationships. A paragraph planner can help students structure ideas into topic sentences, supporting details, and conclusions. These visual aids promote logical structuring and prepare students for more coherent writing.

Support Language Production

Providing model writing examples gives students a clear blueprint. Analyze sample paragraphs or essays together, highlighting elements such as topic sentences, evidence, and analysis. Encourage students to imitate the structure while inserting their ideas. Writing frames and sentence starters, such as "The main cause of _____ was _____" or "One similarity between _____ and _____ is _____," can guide students, reducing cognitive load and allowing them to focus on their content.

Sentence frames not only help students structure sentences but also benefit proficient English speakers who struggle with writing. These tools are invaluable for scaffolding both writing and speaking activities, offering a framework for expressing complex ideas.

Encourage Collaborative Writing and Feedback

Collaborative writing fosters peer learning and builds confidence. Pair or group students to brainstorm and draft together, assigning roles such as brainstormer and writer. This reduces individual pressure and helps students learn from one another.

Frequent and specific feedback is crucial during the writing process. Use checklists for self-assessment, such as "Does my paragraph have a topic sentence?" and provide color-coded or rubric-based feedback for consistency. Mini-conferences to review drafts can offer personalized support, encouraging incremental improvement and stronger writing skills.

Conclusion: Strategies to Enhance Your Lessons

Teaching social studies to MLEs requires a comprehensive approach that prioritizes equitable access to content, fosters cultural inclusivity, and promotes language development. By integrating the strategies discussed in this chapter, educators can create a classroom environment where all students are able to learn and demonstrate their understanding. This holistic approach not only enhances academic achievement but also prepares students to navigate and contribute meaningfully to a diverse and interconnected world.

Reflection Questions

1. How can you incorporate Tier 2 academic vocabulary into your existing classroom routines?

2. What scaffolding techniques could you implement to help students engage with primary and secondary sources?

3. How can visual aids and graphic organizers enhance MLEs' comprehension of social studies materials?

4. What kind of writing are students expected to produce in your class, and what supports might MLEs need to be able to meet the standard?

5. What is one lingering question you have after reading this chapter, and where can you go to find the answer?

Classroom Connections

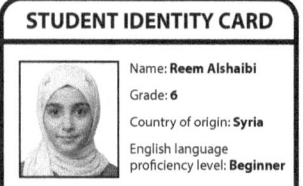

STUDENT IDENTITY CARD

Name: **Reem Alshaibi**
Grade: **6**
Country of origin: **Syria**
English language proficiency level: **Beginner**

When **Reem**'s teachers look at her exit ticket of randomly selected copied sentences about the Silk Road, they realize that her careful compliance with the expectations of school mask a deep lack of understanding. Together, the social studies teacher and English language teacher brainstorm ways to make their class more accessible to her. For their next lesson, the English language teacher creates a vocabulary guide with the most important Tier 2 and Tier 3 words from the lesson, explained in simple English and illustrated with pictures, and the social studies teacher makes sure that all those words appear in the day's slides or in the questions the students will be answering.

As the class works with documents about the Silk Road, Reem works in a small group with other MLEs. Their group has just two documents, and both have been simplified and reduced to the most essential parts. At the end of class, when the exit ticket (How did the Silk Road contribute to cultural diffusion?) is passed out, Reem uses a sentence starter from the board to put her thinking into a complete sentence, using the vocabulary guide she received at the beginning of class to help her with spelling. Her finished exit ticket, which—while not perfect—shows a solid understanding of the fundamentals of the lesson, reads: The Silk Road contributed to cultural diffusion because spread religion ideas. Because Buddhism religion from India. Buddhism religion go China.

STUDENT IDENTITY CARD

Name: **Nyandeng Atong**
Grade: **9**
Country of origin:
South Sudan
English language
proficiency level:
Intermediate

While teachers always need to consider students' background knowledge, this is especially important with students with interrupted formal education like **Nyandeng**. By talking with Nyandeng about a visual timeline they had in the classroom, her teachers become aware that her gaps extended far beyond just British colonization in the Americas. There are so many things that they just assumed all ninth graders know that Nyandeng has never had the opportunity to learn. After this conversation, the teachers decide to start every new unit with a fill-in-the-gaps activity, in which Nyandeng and other students who missed some foundational learning can get ready for the new unit, while students who already have the necessary background can deepen their understanding with an enrichment activity.

At the same time, Nyandeng does have a lot of background knowledge—she has not spent the past 14 years asleep! It is just that her background knowledge is different from that of most of her peers. Nyandeng's teachers learn as much as possible about her experiences so that they can make those connections: Though Nyandeng does not know about the American Revolution, she has spent her whole life listening to adults talk about the civil war in which South Sudan split away from the North. She has a deep, real-world understanding of the political, cultural, and economic factors that can cause one part of a country to declare independence from another part. Once she makes that connection, suddenly the patriots and loyalists become real to Nyandeng.

STUDENT IDENTITY CARD

Name: **Minh Nguyen**
Grade: **11**
Country of origin:
Vietnam
English language
proficiency level:
Advanced

Students with advanced English proficiency like **Minh** still benefit from many of the strategies identified in this chapter. For example, though Minh has little trouble understanding her teacher and other students when they speak to her, the faster pace and unfamiliar speech patterns of the voiceovers in historical documentaries can be challenging for her; because of this, she always understands better when her teachers turn on the subtitles in videos. She no longer needs subtitles translated into Vietnamese, but having the English subtitles to refer to helps her understand the audio better.

Two key areas of focus for Minh are building academic vocabulary (especially the often-overlooked Tier 2 words that will benefit her in all her classes) and support for writing. At the beginning of each unit, Minh's teacher identifies about a dozen general academic words that appear most frequently in assessment items and primary source documents; he then makes sure to build in exposures to these words throughout the unit. It takes some time for this vocabulary work to show results, but slowly Minh becomes better able to understand grade-level academic texts. In addition, Minh benefits from a range of writing support: Although she is able to write sentences on her own, she still needs to build her skills for writing longer texts, especially in connecting her ideas. With explicit instruction in how to use transition words and phrases to show the logical connections between ideas, Minh learns how to express her ideas more clearly—a skill that will help her not only in social studies class but also in life beyond school.

Chapter 4. Supporting Multilingual Learners of English in Our Classrooms: Equity and Inclusion in Social Studies

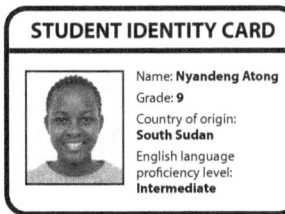

STUDENT IDENTITY CARD

Name: **Nyandeng Atong**
Grade: **9**
Country of origin: **South Sudan**
English language proficiency level: **Intermediate**

Nyandeng is in world history class in the middle of a fascinating discussion of how the Neolithic Revolution led to other changes in how people lived, when a careless comment stops her short.

"Before the beginning of civilization," her teacher says, "humans lived as hunter-gatherers. This meant they had to be nomadic, always moving from place to place. Of course, people don't live like that now. Why do you think we stopped living this way?"

Nyandeng's hand shoots up. "I don't think humans did stop living like that. In Sudan, there's lots of people who still move from place to place with their animals."

Instead of welcoming the correction, the teacher frowns. "Of course, in some parts of the world, there are tribes of people who still follow primitive ways of life. But ever since the dawn of civilization, more than 10,000 years ago, the vast majority of humans live in permanent settlements, where they can have a much higher standard of living." She turns her attention to the rest of the class. "So, who can tell us why humans wanted to change from nomadic living to permanent settlements?"

Face burning, Nyandeng slumps down in her seat, glad that she had not added that some of those people who live as nomads in Sudan are her own grandparents, uncles, aunts, and cousins.

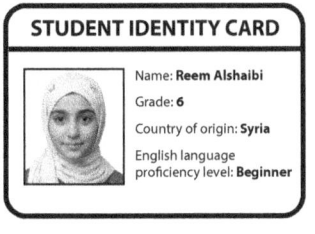

STUDENT IDENTITY CARD

Name: **Reem Alshaibi**
Grade: **6**
Country of origin: **Syria**
English language proficiency level: **Beginner**

Reem can count on one hand the number of times Islam has been mentioned in her world history class: They have covered Atatürk's plan to modernize Turkey by rejecting religious laws, the Iranian Revolution and its establishment of an Islamic government, and the oppression of women by the Taliban in Afghanistan. In all the stories, the people who look like her are portrayed either as helpless victims who are oppressed by her religion or as foolish (at best) opponents of modernization and freedom.

And every time, she can hear whispers behind her, feel eyes on the back of her hijab.

Reem's baba always says that their people have a glorious history, that her homeland was the birthplace of civilization, that Islamic scholars preserved the world's knowledge when the West was in flames. But she never got to learn any of that back home in Syria; the war started before she went to school. And now she is wondering if it is just fairy tales.

Yadiel's school makes a big deal about Hispanic Heritage Month: Pledge of Allegiance in Spanish, posters on the bulletin boards, "This Day in Hispanic History" on the morning show. The school chorus sings at least one Spanish-language song every year, and many of the new books in the library feature Latine kids on the covers. The school has put a lot of effort into making sure that students like Yadiel see themselves represented in the holidays and heroes that are celebrated in the school. (They have also spent a lot of money on the posters and other decorations.)

STUDENT IDENTITY CARD

Name:
Yadiel Ayala Gonzalez
Grade: **8**
Country of origin: **Cuba**
English language
proficiency: **Advanced**

None of that stops Yadiel from feeling like the real him is not welcome.

Yadiel is not consciously aware of it. Even if he stopped to think about it, he probably could not name all the little ways in which the school culture is different from the culture at home—assumptions about how people learn, how we interact, how we show respect and disrespect, how we show interest and boredom. He just knows that walking into some of his classrooms feels like putting on a mask, covering up the real him.

In this chapter:
- Language justice in education
- Culturally responsive teaching
- The cultural iceberg
- Revising curriculum to represent your students
- Diversifying learning activities

All teachers would agree with the fundamental principle of ethics in education: that all students deserve the chance to learn. What we may not be aware of is the subtle ways that some students may be sidelined from learning. In the preceding example, Nyandeng's teacher did not want to make her feel unwelcome in the classroom, but her lack of reflection about the implications of her words resulted in just that. And students who feel that they or their cultures are not welcome in the classroom are not likely to learn much there.

Equity is particularly important in social studies, a field which promotes students' development into active, conscious citizens. When only a subset of people participates in public life in a democratic society, the government is likely to address only the needs of those people. When we promote participation in social studies learning for a wider range of students, we are promoting a more inclusive society, where everyone can have a voice in setting our priorities and policies.

An important part of making learning accessible and welcoming to all students is confronting injustice and bias in our teaching practices and curriculum. In particular, it is essential that we recognize the unconscious ways in which practices that have been going on for years actually sideline groups of students and that we take steps to make our classrooms and schools more welcoming for these groups. This chapter addresses ways in which educators at all levels can promote inclusion for multilingual learners of English (MLEs), from policy efforts that support bilingual and multilingual education to curriculum revisions that ensure a range of voices are elevated in our teaching materials to practices for reducing unconscious bias on an individual level.

Equity is not only the right thing to do; it is *essential* for students to be able to learn. When students feel anxious or lack self-confidence, their affective filter increases, coming between them and the language they are trying to learn. To learn, students must feel comfortable and respected, and equitable policies and teaching practices are key to this effort.

This factor plays a key role in social-emotional learning, which seeks to help students grow as full people, not only academically. Students cannot engage in the challenging work of developing self-awareness, managing relationships, and resolving conflicts in a classroom where they are not full members of the learning community. Policies, curriculum, and teaching practices that sideline MLEs and other student groups are a fundamental block to students' social-emotional learning as well as to their learning of social studies content and the English language.

Language Justice in Education

Language justice in education means that every student, regardless of their home language, has the right to access and participate in a way that respects and values their home language. It is based on the idea that language is a fundamental means of communication and expression of culture and identity. Especially in the case of MLEs, language justice involves recognizing and valuing their linguistic identities as assets rather than seeing them as barriers to learning. Therefore, when education systems prioritize one language—usually English—over others, we risk marginalizing students whose primary language is not English. As a result, these students' academic performance and sense of belonging may be negatively affected, leading to alienation or isolation from the learning process (Menken & García, 2010). Knowing the deeper implications of language justice is essential for teachers to cultivate nuanced, equitable learning because it involves more than just linguistic adaptation; it requires actively integrating students' languages and cultures into the classroom (Alim et al., 2016).

Barriers to Language Justice

Given that many districts and schools have English-only policies, it is important to understand that several barriers may hinder implementing language justice in education. These policies often stem from a "monolingual mindset," which presents proficiency in English as the only way to success or as the main indicator of academic achievement. Forcing students to give up their first language in favor of English means perpetuating inequality and ignoring the linguistic assets that MLEs bring to the classroom (Flores & Rosa, 2015).

Another barrier is the need for more resources for bilingual education programs. Despite evidence that bilingual education can enhance the academic outcomes of MLEs (Thomas & Collier,

2002), many schools lack support to implement such programs due to limited funding, inadequate teacher training, and a shortage of bilingual teachers. In addition, instructional materials may not be readily available in less widely spoken languages (e.g., Swahili, Pashto, or Tigrinya).

Moreover, emphasizing standardized testing in many education systems can undermine language justice. Standardized tests are often designed with proficient English speakers in mind, leaving MLEs at a disadvantage. Vocabulary and question formats are too complicated, meaning that test scores reflect a student's reading proficiency in English rather than comprehension of the content. In addition, examples and references in test passages and questions are often drawn from the everyday experiences of middle-class people of European descent, which MLE students may not be familiar with. Furthermore, prioritizing test scores might result in curricula that are too focused on test preparation rather than providing meaningful, culturally responsive instruction that values students' linguistic diversity (Valenzuela, 1999).

Therefore, because of these barriers, schools find it challenging to provide the linguistically inclusive education that language justice demands.

One of the most significant barriers to equitable education is working with organizations whose structures contradict language justice principles. Most public schools adopt programs or curriculum resources from outside organizations, assuming these materials support all learners. For example, organizations such as the Institute of Curriculum Services and the Anti-Defamation League define their work as promoting educational equity and language justice. Yet, an analysis of their practices reveals that they perpetuate approaches that limit curriculum diversity and exclude marginalized voices, silencing Indigenous peoples, immigrants, Muslims, Palestinians, and LGBTQ+ communities (Murad, 2024). Therefore, no organization that selectively advocates for students' rights can be trusted to lead efforts toward equitable education.

Classroom teachers, including social studies teachers, play a key role in resisting this pattern. Instead of relying on prepackaged educational programs, teachers can examine resources, center student identities in curricula, and advocate for local initiatives that reflect marginalized students' experiences, including those of MLEs. Advocating for language justice is something teachers can do in their school districts by urging investment in partnerships with other organizations that fully support all students, including MLEs and other marginalized students. Addressing these structural issues requires educators at all levels to review policies, funding priorities, and partnerships to ensure that every decision aligns with language justice and equity.

Strategies for Promoting Language Justice

Language justice should be intentionally supported in social studies classes. To guarantee that students' linguistic and cultural identities are acknowledged and valued, one effective strategy is providing a comprehensive curriculum incorporating different languages and opinions. For example, social studies teachers can include primary source documents in students' home languages, allowing MLEs to engage with historical content in a linguistically accessible way (García et al., 2016).

Programs for bilingual and multilingual education are also critical to advancing linguistic justice. Through these programs, MLEs can develop their literacy and content knowledge in both English and their home language. Research has shown that students in dual-language programs often perform better academically and linguistically than their peers in English-only programs (Thomas & Collier, 2002). By supporting bilingual programs, schools may foster a more equal learning environment where MLEs' linguistic skills are seen as learning resources rather than as deficiencies.

To illustrate the impact of language justice, consider the example of the International High Schools in New York City, which serve newly arrived immigrant students from diverse linguistic backgrounds. These schools have successfully implemented an education model that prioritizes bilingualism and biliteracy. Teachers actively incorporate students' home languages as learning resources and design the curriculum to be culturally and linguistically responsive. As a result, students at these schools have higher graduation rates, and they are more likely to pursue post-secondary education than their peers in traditional schools (DeCapua & Marshall, 2011).

Empowering students to speak their home language in the classroom is another essential component of language justice. Social studies teachers may do this by encouraging their MLEs to work collaboratively on projects, show their work in different languages, and discuss challenging topics in their first language. According to Cummins (2000), this method increases students' cognitive engagement and fosters a sense of belonging and validation in the classroom.

Role of Educators in Language Justice

Educators are central to advocating for language justice within their schools and communities. They can push for policy changes that support linguistically diverse students by supporting bilingual

---

A Story of Language Empowerment in the Classroom

In Ms. Brown's diverse 11th-grade U.S. History classroom, most of the students were having a spirited and productive discussion about the Civil Rights Movement. Ms. Brown noticed, however, that her MLEs seemed hesitant to participate. She theorized that language barriers made it difficult for some of them to express their thoughts confidently. She also worried that the students might not see the relevance of the content.

In response, Ms. Brown modified the culminating activity of the unit, a project that explored the theme of continuity and change by asking students to compare the Civil Rights Movement and the Black Lives Matter protests of 2020. She made three major changes to her plan for the project: First, she dropped the mixed-level groups she had originally set up and instead organized the students into small groups based on shared first languages. Second, she invited all the groups (both MLEs and non-MLEs) to compare the Civil Rights Movement with any event in U.S. or world history with similar goals and themes. She suggested a few examples to the class, including some from the countries her MLEs came from. Finally, she let the MLE groups know that they were not only *allowed* to present their project bilingually but that she would really love to see that approach. Ms. Brown encouraged translanguaging by allowing students to use both English and their home languages throughout the project, including in drafts, discussions, and final presentations. She assessed their historical thinking and use of evidence, not just language accuracy, and asked students to include brief English explanations or captions to support understanding.

As the students worked on the project, Ms. Brown saw a transformation in her MLEs. Students who usually sat on the sidelines in group work, silently copying whatever their group members wrote down, became active participants in the work when able to research and discuss in their first languages. A student who usually spent class trying to surreptitiously watch soccer videos on his Chromebook became invested in working on his group's presentation, excited about the opportunity to inform his classmates about the Ukrainian Maidan revolution. A group of Arabic-speaking students presenting on the parallels between the Civil Rights Movement and Palestinian struggles against imperialism asked to take their poster home so they could get together over the weekend to work on it.

The classroom buzzed with lively, multilingual discussions, and the final presentations were richer and more nuanced, showcasing diverse perspectives. The non-MLE students were fascinated by the bilingual presentations, and those taking Spanish as their high school language paid especially close attention to the group presenting on Indigenous rights groups in Latin America, trying to catch words they knew. All the students—MLEs and non-MLEs alike—gained a deeper understanding of the struggles for equal rights in U.S. history and worldwide through these connections.

In the weeks following the experiment, Ms. Brown continued to notice a shift in the way her MLEs participated in classroom discussions. Now that people had started talking, she frequently observed students using their first language to discuss with peers when working in small groups. In whole-group discussions, students who once hesitated began speaking up, even those who made frequent mistakes in English. The increased participation showed that the students felt more comfortable taking risks, knowing that the classroom was a safe place for language learners. Some students even volunteered answers in whole-class discussion in their first languages, with peers jumping in seamlessly to translate, just as they had in the bilingual presentations. By creating a space where students could draw on their linguistic and cultural assets, the teacher had transformed the classroom into a community of learning and belonging.

education programs or adopting culturally and linguistically relevant teaching methods that benefit students from various language backgrounds. Additionally, educators can seek professional development opportunities to deepen their understanding of language justice and learn strategies for effectively teaching MLEs (Lucas & Villegas, 2013).

One of the most important strategies for advancing linguistic justice is culturally responsive teaching. This method uses the students' language and cultural backgrounds as a foundation for learning. MLEs can observe how their personal experiences are represented in the curriculum when a social studies teacher, for instance, includes the students' family histories in an immigration lesson. These methods improve academic engagement and achievement while validating students' identities (Gay, 2010).

> **Language Justice in Action**
> *Strategy*: Language Stations
> - Set up discussion stations with prompts in multiple languages.
> - Students rotate, responding in their preferred language and synthesizing key English points.

As educators, we play a vital role in advancing language justice by honoring and building upon our students' linguistic diversity. This begins in the classroom through the use of instructional strategies that value multilingualism, participation in professional development focused on bilingual education, and implementation of assessment practices that are equitable and responsive to students' language backgrounds. Beyond instruction, teachers also have the power to influence school and district policies that support MLEs. One example is advocating for the Seal of Biliteracy, a recognition awarded to students who demonstrate proficiency in two or more languages. While some states have adopted the Seal of Biliteracy, not all districts have implemented it. Teachers can lead the way by initiating conversations with school leaders about the value of acknowledging multilingualism and its positive impact on student identity and achievement. By collecting data on language use, collaborating with world language and English language colleagues, reviewing state guidelines, and engaging families and communities, teachers can help develop a strong proposal for district adoption. Celebrating students' linguistic accomplishments through initiatives like the Seal of Biliteracy promotes equity, affirms cultural identity, and reinforces the value of multilingualism as an asset in our schools and society (Heineke & Davin, 2020).

While federal policies like the Every Student Succeeds Act (ESSA) include provisions to support MLEs, educators can play a key role in making sure these policies are implemented in meaningful ways at the school level. Title III of ESSA provides funding specifically for language instruction for MLEs and immigrant students, but how that funding is used can vary widely. Schools can promote language justice by using these funds strategically—for example, by investing in high-quality bilingual or dual-language programs, providing sustained professional development for teachers working with MLEs, and ensuring that instructional materials reflect students' home languages and cultures. Title III funds can also support family engagement efforts, such as offering translation services, multilingual workshops, or cultural events that welcome and affirm families' identities. When teachers are aware of how these funds work and collaborate with school leaders on their use, they help ensure that resources are used to advance equity and meaningful access to learning for all students (Menken & Solorza, 2014). By changing materials, practices, and supports, teachers can influence the policies that affect students on a daily basis.

California provides another example of adopting policy to support language justice by repealing its English-only education mandate through Proposition 58, restoring schools' option to offer bilingual education. This policy change has allowed many schools to reinstate or expand bilingual programs, providing more equitable opportunities for MLEs to succeed academically (Callahan & Gándara, 2014).

Actionable Strategies for Teachers
- Provide Bilingual and Multilingual Materials.
  - Use primary sources, news articles, and literature in students' home languages alongside English versions to improve comprehension and engagement.
  - Provide translated summaries of key social studies concepts (e.g., *democracy, revolution*) in students' home languages.
  - Create dual-language glossaries with student input (e.g., *government, gobierno* [Spanish], *chính phủ* [Vietnamese]).
- Use Translanguaging Practices.
  - Allow students to use their full linguistic repertoire in the classroom.
  - Encourage brainstorming, note-taking, discussions, and written responses in multiple languages before transitioning to English.
  - Use apps like Microsoft Translator for real-time translation during class discussions.
- Pair Students for Peer Language Support.
  - Implement structured peer support in which proficient bilingual students assist in translating or explaining content to emerging MLEs.
  - Create a "buddy system" where emerging MLEs are paired with bilingual peers during collaborative projects or group discussions to foster natural language development.
- Nurture Community Partnerships.
  - Invite bilingual family members or community leaders to coteach lessons (e.g., a Haitian elder discussing the revolution).
  - Partner with local cultural organizations to provide after-school language clubs or heritage language classes, reinforcing students' home languages while building community connections.
- Advocate for Policy Changes.
  - Encourage teachers to push for bilingual education programs, access to interpreters, and language-access policies in school districts.
  - Encourage teachers to advocate for the Seal of Biliteracy by starting conversations with school and district leaders about its benefits and aligning it with existing language programs. Teachers can also collaborate with colleagues to gather student data, review state requirements, and draft a proposal showing how the Seal of Biliteracy supports equity and recognizes multilingual achievement.

Future Directions

Our advocacy for language justice in schools must continue. Teachers, administrators, and policymakers must collaborate to create inclusive and linguistically equitable learning environments. This can be accomplished through innovative bilingual and multilingual teaching strategies that respect students' home languages and cultural identities, state and federal policy changes, the removal of systemic barriers, and an increase and effective use of professional development funds. Thus, schools can protect the rights of MLEs—that all students deserve the chance to learn—and enable all students to succeed academically and socially.

Culturally Responsive Teaching

In launching the "Being Bilingual is a Superpower" initiative, Miguel Cardona, the former U.S. Secretary of Education, shared, "Make no mistake: Multilingualism is a superpower. Knowing more than one language, acquiring a new language through school, or learning new languages later in life can provide tangible academic, cognitive, economic, and sociocultural advantages" (U.S. Department of Education, 2023). In line with the former secretary's vision, teachers should be aware of cultural differences and shoulder the responsibility to help students develop cultural competencies in linguistically and culturally diverse classrooms. To this end, adopting a culturally responsive teaching approach is essential.

Culturally responsive teaching, according to Gay (2002), refers to "using the cultural characteristics, experiences, and perspectives of ethnically diverse students as conduits for teaching them more effectively" (p. 106). It emphasizes achieving academic success while maintaining students' cultural identities and integrities (Ladson-Billings, 1995) and promotes the idea that students could make academic progress in an easier and more meaningful manner if they were taught through their own cultures (Gay, 2000).

Central to culturally responsive teaching is acknowledging the cultural diversity and rich resources that students bring to the classroom to promote their academic achievements. As Richards et al. (2007) noted, effective culturally responsive teaching and learning depends on "culturally supported, learner-centered contexts" (p. 64). Three dimensions—*institutional, personal, and instructional*—are critical in implementing culturally responsive teaching. In short, the *institutional* dimension necessitates the efforts that school administrators devote to fostering a diverse, inclusive, and equal learning environment and promoting culture-oriented and equity-emphasized school policies. The *personal* dimension requires teachers to know themselves through ongoing self-reflection and exploration, such as what they will and will not teach and how their biases may influence the teaching process. The *instructional* dimension concerns activities, materials, and strategies that are used in the teaching process. This chapter focuses on the personal and instructional dimensions. It is important to note that culturally responsive teaching is fluid, complex, and multifaceted. Teachers, therefore, should be cautious when adopting the culturally responsive teaching practices shared in this chapter and take into consideration the consistently evolving and unique cultural contexts of different classrooms (Gunn et al., 2021). Specifically, culturally responsive teaching includes six critical elements:

1. Deepen your understanding of cultural diversity.
2. Reflect on your own culture and how it affects your teaching.
3. Revise curriculum and materials to be more representative of many cultures.
4. Build a caring and safe learning community for all cultures and perspectives.
5. Diversify your learning activities to invite learning in a variety of ways.
6. Know your students as individuals—not just as representatives of a culture.

It is helpful to approach the first two elements from two complementary perspectives: outward-looking and inward-looking.

Deepen Your Understanding of Cultural Diversity

The first element of culturally responsive teaching is an outward-looking perspective that focuses on understanding students' diverse cultural backgrounds and exploring how their cultures shape their learning experiences and engagement with social studies content.

What does culture have to do with teaching and learning? Culture is the foundation for understanding complex historical and social themes in social studies classrooms, particularly for MLEs. Recognizing cultural diversity in the classroom allows teachers to understand better how students perceive and interact with the curriculum. By exploring and incorporating cultural perspectives into lessons, teachers can create a more thriving and inclusive learning classroom that reflects the diversity of MLEs and the world in which they live (Banks & Banks, 2019).

To understand their students' cultural backgrounds, teachers must explore how students' own cultural norms, beliefs, values, and experiences impact their learning (Rizzuto, 2017). Teachers must ask themselves questions like "How do my students' cultures shape their worldviews?" to adapt their teaching strategies to resonate with MLEs' cultural background and respect their identities while encouraging deeper ties to the content. Students from different cultural backgrounds can view historical events through different lenses influenced by their own history. Therefore, the teacher is responsible for creating lessons that integrate cultural experiences into their academic content using inclusive pedagogy and addressing stereotypes to encourage MLEs to express their thoughts, share their opinions, and improve their academics (Sleeter, 2018). This approach supports MLEs' identities and enhances classroom conversations, encouraging critical thinking and empathy as students learn from one another's perspectives (Banks, 2019). For example, in teaching about colonialism, teachers may enrich the curriculum by strengthening a standard text with oral histories or multimedia interviews that emphasize personal perspectives of colonialism's effects. By doing so, students get a broader understanding of history, including the perspectives of those marginalized in traditional curricula. Discussions about how colonialism links with students' cultural histories can further deepen engagement. Resources from the Zinn Education Project and Rethinking Schools provide access to such materials, including lesson plans, primary sources, and narratives that help teachers center marginalized voices and make history more relevant for MLEs.

Reflect on Your Own Culture: The Cultural Iceberg Model

Now that we understand the outward, let us talk about the inward-looking perspective that emphasizes self-reflection by examining teachers' cultural identities, values, and biases and the ways these influence their teaching practices. But first, we need to learn about the theoretical framework behind it.

Using the visual analogy of an iceberg, the "Cultural Iceberg" model (Hall, 1976) suggests that the surface aspects of culture—such as language, traditions, and customs—represent a tiny portion of a person's identity (see Figure 4.1). Below the surface are the deeper aspects like values, beliefs, and thought patterns, which often operate unconsciously but significantly shape interactions and decision-making in the classroom. Reflecting on unconscious cultural aspects allows teachers to uncover how their upbringing and values influence their teaching practices, from the narratives they prioritize to their approaches to classroom management (Gay, 2018).

So, how do we explore our personal cultural iceberg?

Teachers must practice self-reflection to uncover how their own cultural background shapes their teaching. For example, teachers' beliefs about authority influence how they manage the classroom, and their attitudes about time and communication shape their expectations for student participation. Reflecting on what influences reactions enables teachers to realize their own biases and prejudices, making them more conscious when adapting their strategies to support MLEs. Being aware of such connections is crucial when interacting with MLEs, whose cultural norms may differ significantly from those of their teachers.

Figure 4.1 *Cultural Iceberg*

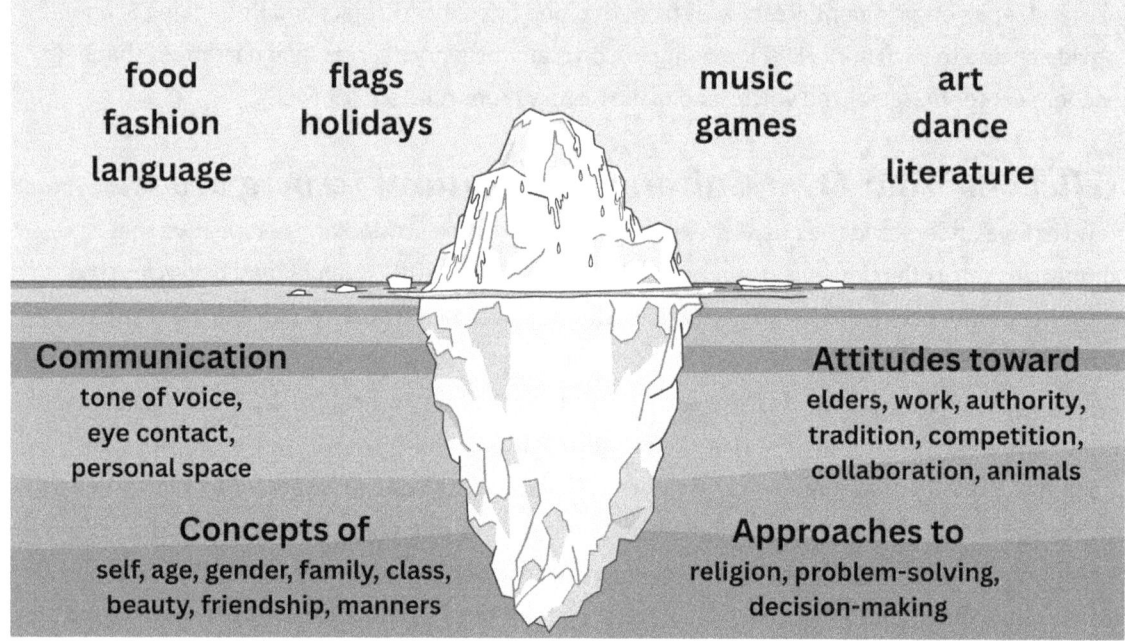

food
fashion
language

flags
holidays

music
games

art
dance
literature

Communication
tone of voice,
eye contact,
personal space

Attitudes toward
elders, work, authority,
tradition, competition,
collaboration, animals

Concepts of
self, age, gender, family, class,
beauty, friendship, manners

Approaches to
religion, problem-solving,
decision-making

Reflection Exercise

Let us practice reflecting on and unpacking our personal cultural icebergs. Take a moment to think about the following questions and write down your thoughts. Use Figure 4.1 to help guide your answers. This exercise will help you uncover the deeper aspects of your culture that influence your teaching practices and interactions with MLEs.

Above the Surface:

- What are three visible aspects of your culture (e.g., language, traditions, customs)?
- How do these surface aspects influence your teaching style and interactions with MLEs in your social studies classroom? Can you think of specific examples in which these aspects shaped a lesson or discussion?

Below the Surface:

- What are three core values or beliefs that guide your behavior and decisions? How do these influence your approach to teaching social studies? Have you noticed these values playing a role in how you handle sensitive topics or classroom discussions?
- Consider your attitudes toward authority, time, and communication. How might these profound cultural aspects affect your expectations of MLEs and your interpretation of their academic performance?
- Reflect on any assumptions or beliefs you hold that may affect how you see others, especially those from different cultural or linguistic backgrounds. How might these

beliefs shape how you engage with your MLEs during a discussion of U.S. or world history? What steps can you take to notice these patterns in yourself and respond in a more thoughtful and equitable way?

Connection to Teaching

Cultural self-awareness significantly influences how teachers provide narratives, design discussions, and evaluate student behavior. Consider the following questions:

1. How does your deep culture influence the way you present social studies content, such as narratives in U.S. history or perspectives in world history? Are there ways to ensure your teaching is more accurate and inclusive of diverse perspectives?

2. What strategies can you integrate to become more aware of the cultural influences shaping your teaching, particularly when addressing complex social issues or diverse historical perspectives? How can you better adjust your approach to serve all students, including MLEs?

Revise Curriculum and Materials to Be More Representative of Many Cultures

Much of the traditional curriculum and teaching materials used in schools in the United States today approach history from a Eurocentric perspective. When classrooms predominantly reflect a singular narrative or perspective, they can unintentionally marginalize students who see the world from another point of view, leading to a feeling of exclusion. For example, a teacher's "Age of Revolutions" unit in World History covers standards on the French Revolution and the Haitian Revolution, but she ends up spending 12 days on the French Revolution and only 2 days on the Haitian Revolution. The message that this sends—without the teacher intending it—is that the things French people did are more important than the things that enslaved Africans in Haiti did. This is a terrible message for any of her students to receive, but it is even worse for her Haitian, African, and African American students.

In addition to imbalanced coverage of different areas of the world, teaching materials often reflect political and cultural biases that can create an environment where MLEs feel misunderstood or undervalued. For instance, many social studies textbooks frame the Middle East primarily through the lens of conflict and terrorism. This narrow portrayal not only reinforces negative stereotypes but can also make students with Middle Eastern backgrounds wonder if their teachers and classmates also see them that way—as nothing but violent terrorists or helpless victims of oppressive regimes. These students naturally may be reluctant to participate in discussion in a classroom where the teacher does nothing to address or challenge the negative stereotypes in the textbook.

On a broad scale, teachers of MLEs have a responsibility to advocate for the adoption of more inclusive standards and curriculum. Districts and schools should regularly evaluate the curriculum materials and textbooks they use for representation and bias, actively search for more inclusive resources and alternative materials, and always ask, "What can we do better?"

Of course, many teachers do not make decisions about the curriculum, textbooks, and other teaching materials. But even when our hands are tied by Eurocentric standards and a textbook someone else chose, we can still find space to work with what we are given in the most responsible and respectful manner possible. We can question the way we have always taught things: Is the French Revolution really *six times* as important as the Haitian Revolution (i.e., the only example in history of enslaved people in the Americas overthrowing their enslavers and establishing a permanent, free nation)? If the standards say that students need to understand how people in the 1800s were inspired by Enlightenment ideas to protest social and economic inequality, why could we not use the example of the Haitian Revolution to teach this standard, just as much as the French Revolution?

While most teachers cannot throw away a biased textbook, they can work with and around the textbook to challenge biases. The teacher with a textbook that only portrays the Middle East as an area of conflict could supplement the information in the textbook with a variety of resources that showcase the rich cultural, scientific, and historical contributions of the region. The textbook itself can be used to teach how bias can creep insidiously into even the most seemingly neutral source. Discovering biased and unjust representations in their own textbook is one of the most effective ways to educate MLEs to be critical thinkers! And when their teacher explicitly calls out the negative stereotypes in the textbook, the Middle Eastern MLEs in the classroom may feel more comfortable sharing their personal experiences and perspectives, enriching the classroom discourse and transforming the learning experience into one that celebrates diversity rather than marginalizes it.

Build a Caring and Safe Learning Community for All Cultures and Perspectives

In addition, culturally responsive teaching has recently played an important role in addressing issues of diversity, inclusiveness, and equity in educational settings. The recognition of students' cultural diversity as pedagogical assets can promote cross-cultural communication, foster "senses of belonging," and advocate for an open and respectful attitude toward cultures in classrooms. These cultural-oriented pedagogies are designed to "cultivate students' voices, entrepreneurial inclinations, and inventive spirits" and "open up worlds of possibilities for each student to bring his or her whole self into the classroom and into the world" (Ladson-Billings, 2021, p. 353). In particular, engaging students in these cultural-oriented pedagogies can build trust between students and teachers. By designing culturally responsive learning activities, teachers show strong interest and willingness to learn from students. In addition, students will feel a strong sense that their home cultures are appreciated and welcomed in their classrooms. In doing so, a community of care and trust is built. Such a community can not only assist teachers in navigating the multicultural landscape formed by MLEs in their classrooms but also motivate students to proactively share their voices and opinions.

Culturally Responsive Teaching in Action
Example: Teach the Industrial Revolution through the lens of immigrant labor. Pair a novel like *The Jungle* with oral histories from local migrant workers to highlight the connections to today's world.

Diversify Your Learning Activities to Invite Learning in a Variety of Ways

Most teachers are familiar with the concept of individual learning styles: Some students need to write information down for it to "stick," others need to hear it, and still others need to see it in visual form. Different cultures also have preferred ways of teaching and learning new information. When people with European cultural backgrounds think of learning, they might imagine a person sitting with a book or taking careful, organized notes on a lecture. If this is your cultural background, this kind of learning may work well for you—and that is okay! But for cultures with a more collective perspective on the world, this kind of individualist approach to learning misses the mark. The best way to learn for people from these cultures may be to talk things out with a group of people by working through a topic in discussion until the group reaches a consensus. There are many variations on this theme: People whose cultural groups have a long history of writing may be those learners who do not feel like something is real until they have it written down, whereas people from groups with long, rich oral traditions may need to repeat a new piece of information out loud in order to remember it.

There are no hard and fast rules for what kind of learning experiences are "best" for a particular culture, nor is there any requirement to change the way you teach or to create 10 different lesson plans for a class with students from 10 different cultures. However, just as the students in your classroom represent a wide range of diverse cultures and experiences and learning styles, your instruction and learning activities should also contain a wide variety of activities so that each student has an opportunity to learn in the way that is more natural to them. Instead of always working independently, students should sometimes work in small groups, sometimes in pairs, and sometimes alone. Instead of always processing new information through writing, students should sometimes discuss with peers, sometimes represent their understanding visually through a mind map or by drawing, and yes, sometimes write. Many of the strategies discussed throughout this book can be used to add variety and opportunities for different kinds of learning to your lessons.

Know Your Students as Individuals—Not as Representatives of a Culture

Although learning about your students' culture is essential for understanding them and for showing respect and value for their backgrounds, it is not enough to just research their countries and cultures. You also need to get to know your students as people, know their individual beliefs and values, likes and dislikes, goals and fears.

This is especially important because all cultural information is, to some extent, generalization. For example, it is a fact that baseball and football are quite important in American culture; however, there are still thousands of Americans who have no interest in these sports. Similarly, Chinese cultural values include respect for tradition, but there are plenty of Chinese people who love to challenge traditions. In addition, no country is completely composed of one culture; every country has regional, ethnic, or social subcultures that could be as different from each other as the cultures of two countries on opposite sides of the world. For an American example, consider the difference between the typical lifestyles and cultures of people living in Los Angeles , California, and Appalachia, in the eastern United States.

Many well-meaning teachers, wanting to show their students that they know about their culture and background, will make assumptions. When meeting a Cuban student for the first time, a teacher might ask, "So, you're a great baseball player, right?" Or a teacher might ask a Thai student to speak about Buddhism, not considering that the student might be one of the 4% of Thai people who are Muslim. Rather than making students feel welcomed, these experiences can make students feel embarrassed and uncomfortable. Getting to know your students as individuals, rather than as representatives of their culture, can prevent these uncomfortable situations and let your students know that they have a place in your classroom community exactly as they are.

Addressing Bias and Stereotypes in Curriculum and Instruction

Among the culturally responsive practices that can help students feel welcome in the classroom and promote better cross-cultural understanding for all students is addressing bias and stereotypes. This principle is particularly relevant to social studies teachers, given the importance of culture and perspective in our content.

Bias refers to "a prejudice in favor of or against one thing, person, or group compared with another, usually in a way that's considered to be unfair" (Santa Monica College, 2025, para. 1). *Stereotypes* are oversimplified ideas about a group of people that can be positive or negative but often lead to unfair generalizations (Dovidio et al., 2005). In educational settings, bias and stereotypes can influence how subjects are taught and how students perceive themselves and others. For example, a history teacher might describe Indigenous resistance to European settlers as unjustified or disorganized. This portrayal reinforces negative stereotypes about Indigenous peoples. It minimizes the significance of their resistance, which distorts students' understanding of Indigenous history (Gillborn, 2005) and justifies the ethnic cleansing of 56 million indigenous people over about 100 years in South, Central, and North America by European settlers (Callison, 2020, p. 135). For MLEs, these biases may relate to race, language proficiency, immigration status, and cultural practices (Banks, 2015), which can negatively impact their learning experiences and sense of belonging.

Explicit bias is any conscious action or attitude that reflects a stereotype or discrimination against any group, such as MLEs. For example, a history teacher might openly express that certain cultures are "less advanced," which could directly influence how they present those cultures in lessons.

Implicit bias refers to any unconscious assumptions or stereotypes that influence the actions or attitudes toward any group, such as MLEs. These biases can be harder to identify but are equally impactful. For example, teachers call on MLEs less frequently, assuming they struggle or do not know the answer.

Educators must understand both types of bias, be aware of their own biases, and make an effort to cover their influence in the classroom to create an equitable learning environment.

Addressing Bias and Stereotypes in Educational Materials and Teaching Practices

Textbooks might present historical events from a single perspective, marginalizing other viewpoints. Illustrations and examples can perpetuate gender, racial, and cultural stereotypes. For example, most world history textbooks in the United States teach that European colonization in Africa was in the best interest of the people and brought them benefits such as technological advancement. However, the textbooks often omit the significant harm that Indigenous peoples suffered, such as the over 132-year French colonization of Algeria in which nearly one million Algerians were killed and slaughtered, including approximately 45,000 in a single day. This biased view reinforces stereotypes that portray African societies as uncivilized before European invasion, distorting the historical record and erasing entire civilizations that were once culturally and scientifically advanced (Lewin, 2007).

Teachers' unconscious biases can affect their expectations and interactions with students, potentially leading to favoritism or discrimination (Sadker & Zittleman, 2009). For example, a teacher might expect MLEs to be less knowledgeable than non-MLEs on any topic just because their English proficiency is low. The teacher might assume that they do not know the terms and concepts in English to share answers in class.

Bias can also influence groupings, classroom discussions, and questions directed at students (Banks & Banks, 2019). For example, in group projects, a teacher might consistently pair students of similar racial or cultural backgrounds, which can reinforce segregation and limit cross-cultural interaction, perpetuating stereotypes.

Addressing Bias and Stereotypes in Curriculum

When evaluating social studies materials, it is important to identify biases that might be limited to one-sided narratives. For example, textbooks may portray immigrants as a problem, overlooking their intellectual, cultural, and economic contributions to society (Sleeter, 2017).

Content Analysis

Examine the representation of different groups in textbooks and other resources. Look for inclusivity regarding race, gender, socioeconomic status, and other dimensions of diversity. Teachers should address potential biases in traditional resources that may prioritize one narrative over another when teaching about the Middle East, for example. Textbooks in the United States often state that after the Oslo Accord of 1993, Palestine and Israel coexisted as two autonomous states. The reality is that Palestine is still under occupation; according to Human Rights Watch (2021), "while Palestinians have a limited degree of self-rule … Israel retains primary control over borders, airspace, the movement of people and goods, security, and the registry of the entire population" (para. 3). Such omissions can make MLEs hesitant to share their stories simply because primary sources, maps, and narratives from the perspective of the Palestinian are not represented, which leads to feeling that their cultural and historical backgrounds are treated unfairly, dishonestly, and disrespectfully.

Teachers must, thus, offer both perspectives to support MLEs' academic growth, encouraging critical thinking and engagement. They should also promote equity by challenging stereotypes and fostering a more nuanced understanding of global issues among all students.

Perspective and Balance

Check if different points of view are included, especially in social studies and history, and make sure the voices of the marginalized are represented. Look for common signs of bias, such as the lack of representation of specific groups, stereotyped representations, or unquestioned assumptions about social norms. For example, while teaching about the Vietnam War in a U.S. History class, a teacher might explore the theme of truth and the responsibility of individuals when they discover hidden truths. Teachers might use Daniel Ellsberg's shifting role in the Vietnam War as an example of moving from ignorance to truth. The class might discuss the responsibility of those who "see the light," asking whether individuals should act to help others see the truth, as Ellsberg did, or remain silent on today's atrocities, such as genocide in Sudan, Burma, Gaza, Rohhina, and Rowanda.

Use a checklist, such as the following, to evaluate materials for diversity and inclusivity.

Diversity Checklist for Educators

Cultural Representation
☐ Are different cultures and ethnic backgrounds represented?
☐ Do the materials highlight cultural achievements, not just struggles or stereotypes?
☐ Are cultural practices and perspectives accurately and respectfully portrayed?

Multiple Viewpoints
☐ Are historical events presented from multiple viewpoints?
☐ Is there an equal representation of genders?

Bias Indicators
☐ Does the curriculum present a single narrative about race or immigration, or does it offer multiple perspectives?
☐ Are MLEs' countries of origin represented accurately and respectfully?
☐ Does the curriculum include contributions from non-Western civilizations and cultures in a balanced way?
☐ Are stereotypical portrayals or unquestionable assumptions about social norms avoided?
☐ Does the curriculum acknowledge who the oppressors are in historical or contemporary contexts and present them from different viewpoints?
☐ Are the voices of oppressed groups amplified and given context within the broader historical narrative?

Historical Perspective
☐ Are historical events presented from multiple viewpoints, especially those of marginalized or underrepresented groups?
☐ Do the resources address both positive contributions and challenges faced by diverse communities?
☐ Are colonial, Indigenous, and global perspectives included where relevant?
☐ Are silenced or overlooked narratives from oppressed groups considered?
☐ Is there a clear distinction between oppressors and the oppressed, and is this distinction presented from multiple angles?

Gender Representation
☐ Is there equal representation of genders in the content, roles, and examples provided?
☐ Do the materials challenge traditional gender roles and avoid gender stereotypes?
☐ Are the achievements of women and gender-diverse individuals highlighted?

Socioeconomic Diversity
☐ Are characters or scenarios that reflect a range of socioeconomic backgrounds included?
☐ Do the resources avoid stereotypes related to socioeconomic status?

Ability and Neurodiversity
☐ Are people with different abilities and neurodiverse individuals represented?
☐ Are portrayals of disabilities positive and respectful, showing individuals' agency and capabilities?

Language and Communication
☐ Are there multilingual options or content that reflects linguistic diversity?
☐ Does the material consider MLEs in language use and accessibility?

Intersectionality
☐ Are characters or historical figures shown with intersecting identities (e.g., race, gender, and ability)?
☐ Do the resources address how multiple aspects of identity can affect experiences and perspectives?

Inclusivity in Imagery
☐ Are visuals inclusive of diverse skin tones, attire, physical abilities, and family structures?
☐ Do images reflect a balance of ages, ethnicities, and genders in various roles?

Stereotypes and Bias
☐ Do the materials avoid reinforcing stereotypes or biased perspectives?
☐ Is the language used neutral, respectful, and free from bias?

Authors and Contributors
☐ Are diverse voices and experts included in the development and authorship of the materials?
☐ Do the authors have lived experiences relevant to the topics covered?

Teachers should strive to present diverse perspectives and acknowledge the global impact of such conflicts to make all students feel included (Nieto, 2010). In another example from the Vietnam War, a teacher might downplay the contributions and suffering of Vietnamese civilians in favor of an American-centric perspective. This lack of perspective could alienate Vietnamese MLEs or other students from Southeast Asia, whose family histories may be directly tied to these events.

Language Use
Pay attention to language that might be biased or stereotypical. This includes not only explicit slurs but also more subtle forms of biased language. For example, a geography textbook might describe developing countries using terms like *Third World*, a biased and outdated term that reinforces negative stereotypes about those regions (McLaren, 1998). Instead, the teacher can talk to students about what terms are included in the text, what terms might be better, and why.

Creating an Inclusive and Equitable Curriculum

By including the different historical perspectives of cultural groups, especially with MLEs, we can create an inclusive and equitable curriculum. Teachers may do this by learning about their students' languages and cultural backgrounds, which enables them to create a curriculum that speaks to their experiences. Gay (2018) emphasizes that including MLEs' languages and histories enhances engagement and a sense of belonging. Teachers can use primary materials to balance covering different viewpoints while focusing on key events or persons that fit within the social study standards (Banks, 2019). This will allow them to present a more comprehensive yet efficient curriculum that reflects all students' identities.

Representing and incorporating marginalized narratives into the curriculum is essential to fostering a sense of belonging among MLEs, which enhances engagement and helps them personally connect with the material (Ladson-Billings, 1995; Nieto, 2010). For example, teachers can highlight the contributions of different groups, such as Asian American activists in the Civil Rights Movement (Paris & Alim, 2017) or share migration stories. The Zinn Education Project and Teaching for Change provide resources that support this approach, allowing teachers to integrate inclusive narratives while meeting academic requirements, validate MLEs' experiences, and promote a classroom culture of agency and belonging (Gay, 2018).

Actionable Strategies for a More Inclusive Curriculum

- Review Curricular Materials for Bias.
  - Use a checklist to evaluate textbooks and lesson plans for Eurocentrism, gender stereotypes, and omission of marginalized voices.
  - Teacher Checklist Example:
    - Are marginalized groups portrayed as agents of change or passive victims?
    - Whose perspectives are missing? (e.g., Filipino voices in WWII narratives)
- Engage in Critical Discussions.
  - Establish guidelines that encourage respect, challenge stereotypes, and promote critical thinking about identity and representation.
  - Activity Example: Stereotype Deconstruction
    - Students analyze a biased textbook passage (e.g., "Native Americans lacked civilization").
    - Students research and present counterevidence (e.g., Cahokia's urban planning).
    - Discuss how stereotypes like this in textbooks, if unchallenged, could affect people reading them today.
- Develop Media Literacy.
  - Train students to analyze bias in media and historical sources. Use current events to discuss how bias shapes public narratives.
  - Compare news coverage of global events (e.g., Western vs. Eastern news coverage on the genocide in Gaza) to identify framing biases.
- Model Reflective Teaching Practices.
  - Reflect on your biases through journaling, peer feedback, and professional learning communities.
  - Use student feedback and classroom observations to adjust your teaching strategies and better meet the needs of MLEs.

Conclusion: Every Teacher Is a Changemaker

To be culturally responsive, we educators must start with ourselves and explore our personal cultural iceberg. We must recognize how the hidden aspects of our cultural backgrounds have a lasting impact on how we have shaped our social studies teaching methods and how we interpret and interact with MLEs—not to reject our personal culture, but to become more aware of diverse backgrounds in order to better show respect for them.

Committing to daily self-reflection can improve our teaching and interactions with MLEs and help us make the necessary changes to promote social and linguistic justice. This approach can expose stereotypes, encourage critical thinking, and challenge the influence of media and government agendas on our curricula.

This task is not easy, but it is an honor. Education positions us as changemakers who inspire transformation. Educators nurture the minds, communities, and futures of those we teach to create a more just and compassionate world for all.

Reflection Questions

1. What misconceptions about MLEs in social studies are addressed in this chapter?
2. How can you create a more inclusive and culturally responsive social studies classroom?
3. How does the information in this chapter challenge or reinforce your current teaching practices?
4. After reading this chapter, how can you better support MLEs in understanding complex social studies concepts?
5. What role does diversity play in making social studies content more accessible for MLEs?

Classroom Connections

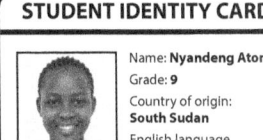

STUDENT IDENTITY CARD

Name: **Nyandeng Atong**
Grade: **9**
Country of origin: **South Sudan**
English language proficiency level: **Intermediate**

*An unconsidered comment by her teacher hurt **Nyandeng**, making her feel like her family's culture was not respected in her new home. The teacher did not mean to be intentionally harmful; she had simply never stopped to think that the way we talk about traditional cultures is often shaped by old ideas of one way of life being superior to another. As the teacher broadens her knowledge of cultural perspectives, increasing her awareness of the ways in which her students' experiences differ from her own, she finds it becomes easier to choose her words carefully to avoid unintended harm.*

STUDENT IDENTITY CARD

Name: **Reem Alshaibi**

Grade: **6**

Country of origin: **Syria**

English language
proficiency level: **Beginner**

*Not only is **Reem** deeply affected by the one-sided portrayal of Muslim people in her school's curriculum, but the way her classmates view her is also influenced. Aware of this, Reem's teacher works with his department leaders to revise the school's social studies curriculum to present a more balanced, accurate narrative of Islam. While working within state and local requirements, the department is able to enrich the curriculum by adding an emphasis on the contributions of Muslim scholars to mathematics, science, and medicine during the Golden Age of Islam, which coincides with the European Middle Ages, as well as situations in which Muslim people were the victims of violence instead of the aggressors, such as the displacement of Palestinian families during the Nakba. Both Reem and her classmates benefit from the deeper understanding of history and world cultures that this curriculum change provides.*

STUDENT IDENTITY CARD

Name:
Yadiel Ayala Gonzalez

Grade: **8**

Country of origin: **Cuba**

English language
proficiency: **Advanced**

*The changes that help **Yadiel** are so subtle that he is never aware that they are happening. He does not realize that his social studies teacher is learning about cultural differences in communication, but he starts getting in trouble less as his teacher comes to understand that when Yadiel avoids eye contact it is not defiance but the way he was raised to respond to correction from an adult. Yadiel does not really notice the shift in classroom activities toward more interaction among students, more opportunities to talk things out before writing, and different ways to demonstrate understanding; he just finds that it is getting easier to focus in class. Yadiel passes eighth-grade social studies without ever knowing how much work his teacher put into ensuring that her classroom was welcoming to people from all cultural backgrounds—but all those small changes made a big difference in Yadiel's success in her class.*

Chapter 5. Supporting Multilingual Learners of English at the School Level: Guidance and Resources for Administrators

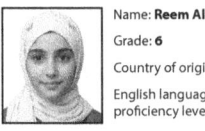

STUDENT IDENTITY CARD

Name: **Reem Alshaibi**
Grade: **6**
Country of origin: **Syria**
English language proficiency level: **Beginner**

*When teachers in **Reem**'s suburban school hear that several Syrian families will be resettled in their community, nobody really knows what to expect. They have heard about the civil war in Syria on the news, and they have lots of empathy for these kids who have been uprooted from everything they have ever known. They want to welcome them, but they are not sure how. Should they dig out ABC books, or are the kids likely already know some English from school? Can they seat the girls at table groups with boys? Do the kids need a place to pray during the day? Are the meatballs the cafeteria serves okay for Muslims to eat, or do they need to provide Halal and vegetarian meals? Are all Syrians even Muslim? As the teachers try to find reliable information about the students who will be arriving soon, rumors and conflicting information run wild.*

STUDENT IDENTITY CARD

Name: **Viktor Melnychuk**
Grade: **10**
Country of origin: **Ukraine**
English language proficiency level: **Beginner**

*In his preobservation meeting, the teacher of **Viktor**'s world history class shares that he would like to improve his differentiation to meet the needs of beginning multilingual learners of English (MLEs). For instance, Viktor takes notes in class and does his best to participate alongside his peers, but the teacher is not sure how much Viktor is actually taking in. The administrator promises to watch for opportunities for differentiation in the observation.*

As the class period unfolds, the administrator sees that the teacher is already doing a lot to meet the needs of a wide range of students—all the modifications and scaffolds she is used to looking for when she observes a Special Education classroom. But when it comes time for the exit ticket, Viktor stares blankly at the paper. The administrator wants to help the teacher grow but is not sure what she should be looking for to help the teacher support Viktor and other beginning MLEs.

STUDENT IDENTITY CARD

Name: **Minh Nguyen**
Grade: **11**
Country of origin:
Vietnam
English language
proficiency level:
Advanced

*When **Minh** gets into a conflict with a peer, her parents are called for a meeting. To the administrator's surprise, although Minh speaks English fluidly and is in advanced classes, her dad speaks only a few words of English. Without a common language, Minh's father and administrator end up relying on Minh to translate. The administrator feels terrible for putting that responsibility on a kid—and also wonders how accurately Minh translated everything to her father.*

In this chapter:
- Teachers' perspectives
- An administrator's guide
- Professional development
- Classroom observations

As schools become increasingly diverse, administrators play a vital role in ensuring that MLEs receive equitable, high-quality education in all subject areas, including social studies. This chapter is designed to guide administrators in recognizing and supporting effective teaching practices tailored to MLEs in the social studies classroom. By understanding the unique needs of MLEs and the strategies that promote their academic and linguistic success, administrators can foster environments where both teachers and students thrive. For teachers, it is important to know what role administrators can play in the social studies classroom and the support they can request to help make their teaching more inclusive and viable for all learners.

In social studies, MLEs face the dual challenge of mastering complex content while simultaneously developing their English language skills. Effective instruction requires intentional integration of language and content objectives, culturally responsive teaching, and the use of innovative technologies. Administrators must know what to look for during classroom observations and how to provide constructive feedback that empowers educators to refine their practices.

If you are an administrator, you are not alone. The great part of being in a school is that you have individuals to help and support you on this journey. For supporting teachers to meet the needs of MLEs, you have a partner in your English language teachers. This partnership is not about just giving them the opportunity to give a brief professional development (PD) session to your teachers, but it is about the process of working alongside them to create the best PD you can. The teachers know the students, and you know your staff. By collaborating with the English language teachers, you set the example for coteaching opportunities and show that you value the English language teachers, which promotes more discussion in your building. This collaboration can also lead to more coteaching opportunities and structures that allow English language teachers to be part of conversations during a common department planning time. Many buildings give these opportunities for coteaching and collaboration to Special Education teachers, but not English language teachers; this is a disservice to students. Through collaborative partnerships, administrators model valuing the expertise of English language teachers for other teachers in the building.

Administrators play a pivotal role in helping teachers meet the needs of MLEs by providing targeted PD, offering meaningful feedback through classroom walkthroughs, and ensuring teachers have access to resources and collaboration opportunities. Supporting teachers effectively not only enhances their ability to meet the needs of MLEs but also fosters a school culture of inclusion, innovation, and continuous learning. As you read through this chapter, think about teachers in your building that fit into these categories. Reflect on the activities and see which ones would support your teachers at the current stage in their teaching career.

Teachers' Perspectives

Overwhelm With Classroom Management and Curriculum Delivery

Being a first-year social studies teacher in a diverse urban school can be exciting, but such teachers can be overwhelmed by the demands of managing a classroom full of over 25 students, many of whom are multilingual and come from varying socioeconomic backgrounds. These teachers may have little to no prior experience with differentiating instruction for students at different levels of language proficiency. These students may include MLEs, students with varying levels of academic readiness, and students from refugee backgrounds, which create a unique challenge in making sure all students are engaged and can grasp the social studies content.

Thus, teachers should start by focusing on building classroom routines and establishing clear expectations. Utilizing cooperative learning strategies to foster peer support, especially pairing MLEs with students more proficient in English, can make lessons more accessible for students. Teachers can differentiate instruction by providing visual aids, using graphic organizers, and scaffolding content. Teachers can also take advantage of resources like online translation tools or collaborate with an experienced colleague or a bilingual aide to provide extra support. Using technology, such as educational apps that support language learning (e.g., Kahoot, Quizlet), can reinforce vocabulary and concepts, making the learning process more engaging and interactive. Additionally, mentoring or joining a teacher support network, such as TESOL International Association or other professional organizations, will help teachers navigate these challenges.

Burnout and Resistance to New Technology

Some seasoned teachers with 15 or more years of experience teaching social studies can also run into roadblocks. They may have deep content knowledge and strong classroom management, but they may still be struggling to adapt to the integration of new AI-driven tools in the classroom. These teachers fear that the overuse of technology affects student-teacher relationships and their ability to maintain a personal connection with students. They also fear the potential biases in AI systems and the effects on students, particularly those from historically marginalized groups. This reluctance stems from concerns that relying too heavily on technology could reduce the human element in education.

To handle this situation, teachers can attend PD workshops on integrating AI in a balanced and ethical way, such as learning to be selective in how and when to use AI, ensuring it complements rather than replaces meaningful interactions with students. AI tools can be leveraged to differentiate instruction, provide real-time feedback, and help track student progress, but these tools should always be used alongside traditional methods like group discussions and hands-on activities. Discussions with students about AI educates them on its limitations and biases, helps students engage critically with the technology, and also allows the teacher to guide them in using AI responsibly. When in doubt, teachers can seek advice from colleagues or mentors who have successfully navigated this transition, using their experiences to avoid potential pitfalls. (See Chapter 6 for an in-depth discussion on technology and AI.)

Balancing Differentiation With Time Constraints

As class sizes increase and student needs diversify, teachers struggle to balance differentiation with the limited time and resources available. With varying levels of language proficiency and districts implementing new standards for cultural responsiveness, many teachers get overwhelmed by the need to constantly adjust their teaching to ensure every student's success while managing their workload.

To succeed, teachers should start by setting clear, specific goals for differentiation. Prioritizing targeted support for MLEs using resources that streamline differentiation, such as digital platforms like Google Classroom, allows for differentiated assignments and real-time feedback that support teachers and students. By leveraging a blend of technology tools and hands-on approaches, such as collaborative group work and peer support, teachers can provide personalized support for students without becoming overburdened with graphic organizers, scaffolded reading materials, and video content to support diverse learners. Many of these strategies are discussed in Chapter 3.

In Chapter 2, we talked about student collaboration, but teachers should collaborate as well as students to balance differentiation with time constraints. Ideas for collaborating with colleagues include sharing lesson plans and strategies or even requesting the help of the English language teacher to provide support during class. To manage time, teachers can consider reducing the amount of time spent on direct lecturing and instead focus on student-centered activities, including collaborative projects, that allow for more personalized learning in small groups.

Finally, teachers should reflect on their practices by seeking feedback from students and adjusting based on their needs. By using professional learning communities and seeking guidance from experienced mentors, teachers can find efficient ways to manage the balance between high expectations and feasible strategies for differentiation.

Teaching MLEs in social studies classrooms presents unique opportunities and challenges that require tailored strategies and consistent support. These examples demonstrate the diversity of teacher experiences—ranging from new to seasoned professionals—and the barriers we face in fostering equitable learning environments for all students.

Empowering teachers to succeed in supporting MLEs requires intentional and ongoing efforts from school leadership. Administrators must recognize the unique needs of their teachers, offering tailored PD sessions that address specific barriers, such as classroom management, technology integration, and differentiation. Through structured walkthroughs, actionable feedback, and opportunities for coteaching and collaboration, administrators can help teachers build their confidence and refine their practices.

Ultimately, supporting educators in these ways benefits not only the teachers themselves but also their students, fostering a learning environment where MLEs can thrive academically and socially. By prioritizing equity, inclusion, and professional growth, administrators can ensure that all teachers are equipped to provide meaningful, culturally responsive education that prepares every student to succeed.

An Administrator's Guide

As student populations become increasingly diverse, school administrators need to lead the effort in adapting the social studies curriculum to address the varied language proficiency levels and cultural backgrounds of learners. Administrators play a pivotal role in overseeing the integration of culturally relevant materials and equitable language support into the curriculum. Although many administrators do not have a background as MLEs or as teachers of MLEs, they are still expected to support both educators and students in their learning journey. This section outlines strategic approaches for school leaders to ensure that social studies education is inclusive, culturally responsive, and accessible, allowing all students to engage meaningfully with the content. The guidance provided aligns with The 6 Principles for Exemplary Teaching of English Learners® as developed by TESOL International Association (2024).

Understanding the Diverse Classroom

Before implementing curriculum adaptations, school leaders must assess the linguistic and cultural diversity of their student body. Administrators should use schoolwide data to accomplish the following:

- **Assess Language Proficiency Levels:** Leverage formal language assessments and proficiency data to inform curriculum planning and resource allocation.
- **Engage With Cultural Backgrounds:** Facilitate surveys, parent–teacher meetings, and community engagement initiatives to gather insights into the cultural

backgrounds of students, which can then guide culturally relevant curriculum development.

Administrators should also promote collaboration between general education teachers and English language teachers to create a cohesive instructional approach.

As educational leaders, administrators play a vital role in creating systems and environments where all students, especially MLEs, can thrive. TESOL's (2024) 6 Principles provides a research-based framework that supports language development and academic success. From an administrator's lens, these principles are not just instructional guidelines, they serve as a foundation for school-wide practices, PD, and inclusive policies that ensure equity and access for every learner. By understanding and applying these principles at the leadership level, administrators can foster a culture of high expectations, collaboration, and continuous growth for both educators and students. Following are the principles:

1. **Know Your Learners**.

   Administrators should facilitate the collection and use of data on students' linguistic and cultural backgrounds to inform instruction. This collection can include conducting regular needs assessments and guiding the development of individualized learning plans based on the strengths and needs of each student.

2. **Create Conditions for Language Learning**.

   School leaders can foster a language-rich environment by ensuring that classrooms are equipped with language supports, such as bilingual resources, labeled diagrams, and culturally relevant materials. A schoolwide emphasis on inclusivity and respect for cultural diversity should be established through PD and administrative policies.

3. **Design High-Quality Lessons for Language Development**.

   Administrators should work with curriculum developers to ensure that lesson plans across all grade levels and classrooms incorporate both content and language objectives. Encourage the use of differentiated instruction and scaffolding techniques to help to ensure that students at various language proficiency levels can access social studies content.

4. **Adapt Lesson Delivery as Needed**.

   School leaders must provide teachers with the necessary tools and flexibility to adapt instruction for MLEs. This assistance includes promoting the use of visual supports, hands-on activities, and interactive teaching strategies to make lessons accessible to all learners. Administrators should monitor classroom implementation and provide targeted support where needed.

5. **Monitor and Assess Student Language Development**.

   Administrators should lead the design and implementation of formative assessment tools that measure both content knowledge and language proficiency. Regular data analysis will allow school leaders to make informed decisions about instructional adjustments and resource allocations. Additionally, constructive feedback systems should be embedded in classroom practice to support language development.

6. **Engage and Collaborate Within a Community of Practice**.

Administrators should foster a culture of collaboration by organizing professional learning communities in which teachers, staff, and community members can share best practices for supporting MLEs. School leaders must also engage families and local communities to build a strong support network for students, ensuring that all stakeholders are involved in the educational process. It is also beneficial for administrators to meet with other administrators in and around their districts to share ideas and challenges and to collaborate on area needs. For example, Colorado Springs has over nine different districts, and students transfer among them quite frequently. To alleviate confusion, district leaders meet monthly to discuss trends and needs and to collaborate on students' needs, PD, and support across the area.

Effective Communication in Action

Communication with families is crucial to building relationships and creating a successful learning environment for MLE students. This is not always easy when another language is involved. Many buildings use translation services like Language Link or apps like TalkingPoints that facilitate communication across language barriers. However, many buildings only provide accounts for English language teachers. *All teachers need access to these tools.* English language teachers are not the only ones who can and should be communicating with students and parents; administrators and content teachers should be reaching out as well. Parents want to know what is going on, and if you open the door of communication, they will participate in family nights, support discipline, and connect with the school community. Interpreters, Fluentalk, and Google are other great tools to help with communication, as you will see later in this chapter.

Administrators' Role in Supporting Social Studies

An administrator's role in the social studies classroom extends beyond observations and evaluation; it involves actively shaping the conditions that support high-quality, equitable instruction. Administrators are responsible for providing targeted PD that equips teachers with strategies to integrate culturally responsive content and effectively engage diverse learners, including MLEs. They ensure that resource allocation aligns with instructional goals by investing in digital tools that promote spatial thinking and enhance communication. By supporting teachers in selecting and implementing these resources, administrators help to foster critical thinking and historical analysis grounded in real-world connections. Not only are administrators supporting teachers, they also must uphold data privacy and address ethical use of AI, ensuring that emerging technologies are used responsibly and inclusively. Through strategic leadership, administrators empower educators to create dynamic, relevant social studies experiences that honor student identities and prepare learners for civic participation in a global society.

- **Professional Development**: Provide targeted PD on how teachers can use scaffolding techniques (e.g., visual timelines, simplified texts) to make social studies content more accessible to MLEs. For example, focus on how teachers can break down historical periods and leverage primary sources using simplified language. (Resources later in this chapter.)
- **Resource Allocation**: Ensure that your school has sufficient resources, such as bilingual historical texts, multimedia resources, and graphic organizers, to support visual learning and contextual understanding.
- **Support for Teachers:** Regularly review curriculum implementation to ensure teachers are able to support MLEs. For example, administrators might support teachers in the following ways:
  - Ensure teachers are provided with professional learning about designing lessons that use effective strategies, like those presented in Chapter 2 and Chapter 3.
  - Encourage collaboration between English language teachers and social studies departments to ensure that vocabulary development and content-level understanding are connected.
  - When observing social studies lessons, look for the effective use of visual supports, labeled maps, and digital tools in instruction.
  - Encourage schools to integrate simulations (e.g., mock elections or debates) into the social studies curriculum. Provide PD on how these activities can engage MLEs in civic learning while developing their academic language.
  - Provide curriculum materials that simplify social studies concepts (e.g., supply and demand) and include real-life applications that resonate with students' cultural and personal experiences.
  - Encourage the integration of financial literacy programs into the curriculum, offering students practical life skills alongside theoretical content. Ensure that differentiated materials are available for MLEs.

Integrating Culturally Responsive Content

Administrators must champion the development of a curriculum that reflects the diverse cultural backgrounds of students. This can be achieved by including stories, historical figures, and events from a variety of cultures and by promoting culturally responsive teaching practices. Additionally, school leaders can cultivate partnerships with local community organizations to bring culturally relevant resources into the curriculum.

- **Culturally Responsive Teaching:** Ensure that your social studies curriculum reflects the diverse cultures represented in your student body. Provide teachers with resources and training to integrate these perspectives meaningfully into their lessons.

- Organize schoolwide engagement activities, like multicultural fairs, language appreciation days, and heritage month celebrations.
- Encourage global pen pals, cultural clubs, a cultural appreciation bulletin board, and inclusive learning projects like cultural presentations that allow MLEs to celebrate their heritage while practicing academic language.

- **Community Engagement**: Build partnerships with local cultural organizations and community leaders who can provide guest lectures, field trip opportunities, or classroom visits to enrich the curriculum with lived experiences.
  - Build partnerships with local government and civic organizations to provide real-life engagement opportunities for students.
  - Connect with local cultural and nonprofit groups that support immigrant and refugee communities.

- **Data Privacy**: AI-driven educational tools often rely on vast amounts of personal data, which can raise serious concerns regarding privacy, data security, and compliance with legal regulations such as Family Educational Rights and Privacy Act (FERPA). Because of this, schools need to take care that whatever AI tools and other technology they use do not violate the regulations put in place by FERPA.

- **Ethical Considerations**: Ethical use of AI tools in education requires transparency about data collection practices. Schools should make it clear what data is being collected, how it will be used, and who will have access to it. This can help build trust with students and parents, ensuring that sensitive information is not exploited or mishandled. For example, AI systems should only collect data that is necessary for educational purposes and be transparent about how long this data will be retained. Moreover, data collection should not be used as a means of surveillance or control. Oversurveillance can lead to feelings of mistrust among students and parents, especially when AI systems monitor behaviors or provide insights into personal aspects of students' lives. Ethical use of AI in education must prioritize the dignity and autonomy of students, ensuring that data collection is strictly for enhancing educational outcomes rather than monitoring or manipulating students.

Leveraging Technology for Language and Content Learning

Administrators should ensure that technology, infrastructure supports MLEs by adopting educational tools that provide translation features, multimedia content, and platforms for collaborative learning. Schools can allocate budgetary resources for technology that enhances both language acquisition and content understanding, ensuring equity in access to digital tools.

Leveraging Technology for Spatial Thinking

Invest in interactive technology, such as digital maps and tools like Google Earth, that can engage

MLEs visually and contextually with geographic concepts.

- Ensure that teachers have access to interactive maps and technological resources and that they receive training on using these tools to promote language and content integration.
- Invest in classroom simulations, visual aids, and project-based activities that help teachers model processes in a way that is accessible for MLEs.

Leveraging Technology for Communication

Invest in technology tools that facilitate clear and inclusive communication with families, such as multilingual messaging apps, video conferencing platforms, and digital tools like Remind, ClassDojo, Language Link, Fluentalk, or TalkingPoints. These tools can bridge language barriers and ensure families stay informed and engaged in their children's education.

- Ensure teachers have access to user-friendly platforms that offer multilingual support and provide training on how to effectively use these tools to build strong home–school connections. Emphasize strategies for fostering trust, cultural understanding, and mutual collaboration through consistent and accessible communication.
- Invest in tools that allow families to engage in virtual conferences, access translated newsletters, or participate in interactive school events remotely. Offer guidance on using these resources to share updates, celebrate student achievements, and provide resources that support learning at home.
- Encourage the use of technology to create personalized communication strategies, such as video messages, interactive tutorials, or digital surveys, enabling teachers to connect meaningfully with families and build a supportive educational community.

Administrators have the unique opportunity to influence the entire learning ecosystem within their schools, ensuring that MLEs receive the support they need to succeed in social studies. By prioritizing PD, resource allocation, technology, and community involvement, administrators can create an inclusive, culturally responsive, and academically rigorous environment for all learners.

Professional Development Resources for Administrators

As administrators, you are tasked with leading your schools and managing the wide array of responsibilities that come with the role. While many of you may not have specialized in multilingual education, your dedication to supporting teachers and staff in unfamiliar areas is commendable. Throughout this book, we emphasize the power of small, incremental changes. You do not need to tackle everything at once to make a meaningful difference.

You invest significant time and effort in creating and presenting information that resonates with your staff and equips them with strategies to enhance their classrooms. Following are adaptable PD activities designed to support content and language teachers. These can be implemented individually or combined as part of a larger session, such as a beginning-of-the-year training.

Setting Up for Success

The two following activities are designed to help teachers understand the linguistic and cultural diversity within the school and develop empathy for MLEs. They are ideal for a training before the school year begins. Each activity should include the following materials:

- A note catcher, like a graphic organizer, with an action plan section
- Writing utensils
- Opportunities for discussion and reflection
- Visuals or props for engagement
- A calm and inclusive setting

Activity 1: Know Your MLEs

This activity uses stations to help teachers understand the diversity of home languages and cultures in your school.

1. Preparation:

- Collaborate with your English language teachers to create a list of the countries of origin and home languages represented in your building.
- Research each language and associated cultures, including a brief history of the home countries. This can include details like population, climate, beliefs, and holidays.
- Note that many countries with shared languages can vary significantly in culture and dialect. A Spanish speaker from Spain and one from Puerto Rico may have very different cultures; an Arabic speaker from Morocco and one from Syria may have difficulty understanding each other's regional dialects.

2. Station Set-Up:

- Prepare a station for each language, including one-pagers with cultural nuances (e.g., norms like removing shoes indoors or avoiding eye contact). Templates can be found on the companion website for this book (www.tesol.org/socialstudies-book).
- If additional information is needed, consider videos or articles on the language or culture.

3. Implementation:

- Rotate through stations, using note catchers to record insights and reflect on how this knowledge applies to current and past students.
- Discuss how understanding students' cultural and linguistic backgrounds fosters acceptance and enhances classroom connections.
- Use insights from this activity to guide future needs assessments for students, parents, and teachers.

Activity 2: What It Feels Like to Be an MLE

This activity builds empathy by simulating the experience of learning in a new language.

1. Watch and Reflect:

- Watch a portion of the video *What It Feels Like to Be an ELL* (Colorín Colorado, 2018, 3:45–9:08).
- Have teachers take notes (optional) and participate in a turn-and-talk discussion about what resonated with them.

2. Text Activity:

- Provide texts in different languages (e.g., Chinese, Arabic, French, Spanish, and English). Text examples can be found through websites like WorldStories (worldstories.org.uk).
- Begin with a text in a completely unfamiliar language, then progress to texts with some familiar elements (e.g., cognates).
- Discuss how students use their first language to bridge understanding of a second language, emphasizing the importance of scaffolding in supporting language acquisition.

3. Alternate Approach:

- Play a video of a lecture in an unfamiliar language for about 5 minutes. Observe when participants disengage and discuss strategies for providing comprehensible input and scaffolds in the classroom.

- Common terminology (refer to Appendix A)
- Questions tailored to your goals
- A device equipped with Google Translate (Even if not needed for every activity, it establishes the habit of including it for student support.)

Ongoing Professional Development Strategies

PD should be applicable, relevant, and adaptable across subjects. Consider the following universal strategies and use them as 5-minute PD activities at the beginning of staff meetings throughout the year.

Extend Students' First Language

Activity: *Translingual Collaboration*

    Materials: Sticky notes or index cards, chart paper, markers

Steps:

    1. Prompt: Write one way you could allow students to use their home language in class. Examples may include the following:

- "Provide bilingual glossaries."
    - "Pair students with the same home language for discussions."
2. Pair up with another participant and share your ideas.
3. Collaboratively, pick one practical idea to deepen content understanding and write it on the chart paper.
4. Briefly discuss: How can this strategy foster connection and understanding?
5. Display the chart for future reference.

Incorporate Cultural Contributions

Activity: *Cultural Contributions Carousel*

> **Materials:** Display the following premade prompts on chart paper:
> - "A tradition to highlight in the classroom"
> - "A way to incorporate cultural words"
> - "Unique perspectives we should invite students to share"

Steps:
1. Split participants into three small groups.
2. Each group rotates through the chart prompts, jotting ideas for 1 minute at each station.
3. Once all groups have visited all stations, a representative shares highlights from the group's chart.
4. Discuss how these contributions can enrich learning environments.

Use Layered Questions

Activity: *Question Ladder Simulation*

> **Materials:** Prepared question cards (one progressing question for each type of question: agree/disagree, multiple-choice, open-ended).

Steps:
1. Administrators model questioning progression using a sample topic (e.g., "Should students have homework?").
    - *Agree/Disagree*: "Homework is essential for learning. Agree or disagree?" (Thumbs up/down)
    - *Choices*: "Which is more helpful: daily homework or weekly projects?" (Choose corners or partners)
    - *Open-ended*: "How does homework help or hinder learning? Discuss in groups."
2. Participants simulate this progression with a new topic.
3. Debrief: How can layered questioning build confidence and understanding in students?

Build an Inclusive Environment

Representation in literature, family engagement, and visual representation all play a vital role in creating an inclusive and supportive learning environment. In the classroom and library, it is important to include books that reflect the diversity of the student population. Inclusive texts serve as both windows and mirrors—windows that offer students insight into others' cultures, identities, and experiences, and mirrors that reflect their own. This dual purpose fosters engagement, empathy, and self-affirmation. Children's books can also be powerful tools for introducing complex topics in an age-appropriate way, building a foundation for deeper learning. Connecting with families further strengthens this inclusive environment. Personalized comments about students, even when translated with technology, demonstrate care and effort, which families appreciate, even if the translations are imperfect. Finally, visual representation matters. Decorating bulletin boards with multiple languages and displaying flags from students' home countries helps create a welcoming space where all students feel seen and valued.

Activity: *Representation Brainstorm*

    Materials: Chart paper with categories: Books, Family Communication, Visuals

Steps:
1. Split participants into three groups, assigning each group one category.
2. Prompt: Write actionable ideas for your category.
   - *Books*: Title suggestions or strategies for finding inclusive texts.
   - *Family Communication*: Ideas for personalized or translated outreach.
   - *Visuals*: Ways to reflect student diversity through bulletin boards and decorations.
3. Share one actionable takeaway per group with the larger team.

Acknowledging multilingualism as an asset is crucial. Just as each staff member brings unique strengths to your building, each student enhances the learning environment with their experiences and perspectives.

Focus on key practices like scaffolding, academic conversations, culturally responsive teaching, and collaboration. These strategies not only support MLEs but also benefit all learners. Empower your staff by leveraging the expertise within your building and district, fostering a culture of continuous learning and improvement.

Classroom Observations

School administrators should ensure that these practices are observed and supported in classrooms through regular walkthroughs and teacher feedback. Social studies classrooms that integrate language learning with content create dynamic, inclusive environments where MLEs thrive. Administrators conducting walkthroughs in these classrooms should focus on several critical components to ensure effective teaching and meaningful learning. The following sections outline key elements administrators should observe, aligned with your

preexisting walkthrough forms (see examples on this book's companion webpage at www.
tesol.org/socialstudies-book), and provide practical examples of what excellence looks like as
your evidence of success, as provided in the following section.

Objectives: Clear Content and Language Goals

Administrators should look for the following:

Content/Language Objectives: Objectives should be clearly defined, visible, and aligned with social
studies standards. For example, a lesson on the American Civil War might have a combined content
and language objective such as, "Students will analyze the causes and consequences of the Civil War
by using academic vocabulary to describe key events."

Evidence of success:

- Objectives are posted visibly in student-friendly language.
- Objectives state not only the content but also the specific language students will be
  learning.
- Students can articulate what they are learning and why.

Preparation and Building Background

Administrators should look for the following:

- **Connections to Prior Knowledge**: The lesson should activate students' background
  knowledge, making connections to their cultural and personal experiences.
- **Cultural Relevance**: Instructional materials and examples reflect the diversity of
  students in the classroom.
- **Coplanning**: All the teachers in the room will have had the opportunity to
  communicate about the lesson well before the class in order to make sure that
  some strategies for MLEs are addressed in the lesson. This approach requires
  administrators to value the coteaching process by giving English language teachers
  the time to communicate and work alongside content teachers.

Evidence of success:

- Teachers use questioning techniques like, "How does this relate to what we learned
  about ___?" or "Does anyone recognize this from their own history or culture?"
- Materials include culturally relevant content, such as primary sources from diverse
  perspectives.
- Conversations from the teachers as they plan the lesson and implement the ideas in
  the lessons.

Comprehensible Input and Strategies

Administrators should look for the following:

- **Visual Aids**: Charts, timelines, maps, and graphic organizers help make complex content accessible.
- **Modeling**: When the teacher demonstrates both what the end product should look like *and* the thinking to get there, students have a better understanding of what they need to do to be successful.
- **Scaffolding and Effective Questioning**: Techniques such as sentence frames, think-alouds, and tiered questioning guide students toward deeper understanding.

Evidence of Success:

- Teachers use a variety of visual aids, such as charts and graphic organizers.
- Teachers model what they are asking students to do, such as analyze a primary source, write a paragraph, or create a graphic organizer.
- Teachers provide and help students use sentence stems or frames like, "This document shows __ because __."

Interaction and Practice or Application

Administrators should look for the following:

- **Group Work and Collaboration**: Students engage in structured group activities, such as analyzing a source together or debating historical perspectives.
- **Hands-On Activities**: Interactive tasks, such as creating timelines or role-playing historical events, encourage active learning.
- **Discussions and Debates**: Structured opportunities allow students to share ideas and defend positions.
- **Peer Learning**: Activities such as peer reviews or partner brainstorming promote interaction.

Evidence of Success:

- Students collaborate on tasks, using academic language and supporting each other's learning.
- Classroom buzz reflects engaged discussion and problem-solving.
- Students use academic language during discussions, supported by sentence frames.
- Teachers facilitate respectful dialogue and encourage diverse viewpoints.

Lesson Delivery

Administrators should look for the following:

- **Pacing**: Lessons are paced to maintain student engagement without overwhelming learners.

- **Engagement Strategies**: Teachers use storytelling, questioning, and multimedia to captivate attention.
- **Coteaching**: Building on successful collaboration on the lesson preparation by coplanning, coteaching should involve all teachers in the room working together to deliver content and support.

Evidence of success:
- The teacher frequently checks for understanding with techniques like quick polls or exit slips.
- Students stay on task and respond enthusiastically to prompts and activities.
- All teachers are actively teaching the class and working with all students. The teachers are creating a cohesive environment where students can ask either teacher a question and that teacher can answer it.

Culturally Responsive Teaching and Technology Integration

Administrators should look for the following:
- **Cultural Backgrounds and Resources**: Lessons incorporate students' cultural identities and community connections.
- **Technology Integration**: Digital tools, like interactive maps or collaborative platforms, enhance engagement and accessibility.

Evidence of success:
- Students see themselves represented in the curriculum and feel their experiences are valued.
- Technology is seamlessly integrated, with students actively using it for research, presentations, or collaborative projects.

These key elements are valuable additions to your classroom walkthrough forms. You can start small and add one or two at a time to help guide teachers toward what you are looking for. In addition, experienced teachers can use these to add to their goals for the year.

Conclusion: Leaders of Changemakers

A well-structured social studies classroom integrates content and language objectives to create a rich learning environment. Administrators should look for clear goals, effective scaffolding, collaborative learning opportunities, and culturally responsive teaching strategies supported by technology. When these elements are evident, the classroom becomes a space where MLEs can thrive academically, linguistically, and socially while building the skills and confidence needed for future success.

Classroom Connections

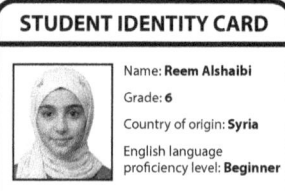

STUDENT IDENTITY CARD

Name: **Reem Alshaibi**
Grade: **6**
Country of origin: **Syria**
English language proficiency level: **Beginner**

*The administrator in **Reem**'s school, aware of the need for PD around the incoming students' background and culture, decides to devote the next staff meeting to building teachers' knowledge about Syria. He designs a jigsaw activity in which teachers read and share information from news articles about the civil war, the current situation in the country, and the experiences of Syrian refugees. In addition, he reaches out to the leaders of a local mosque, who put him in touch with a Syrian couple who come in to talk to the staff about their experiences and culture. The staff respond enthusiastically, and the administrator develops some optional professional learning for those who want to deepen their understanding: a book study of a memoir by a Syrian refugee, a mosque visit after school with the imam, and an online seminar about Syrian culture offered by a regional refugee resettlement organization. Because of the opportunities to build their cultural competency, the teachers are ready to provide a welcoming environment that meets the needs of Reem and the other Syrian children.*

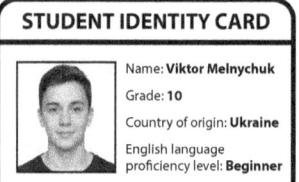

STUDENT IDENTITY CARD

Name: **Viktor Melnychuk**
Grade: **10**
Country of origin: **Ukraine**
English language proficiency level: **Beginner**

*After building her own knowledge on best practices for teaching MLEs, the administrator supporting **Viktor**'s history teacher comes to the next observation prepared with a walkthrough checklist that covers lesson design, comprehensible input, learning activities, and cultural responsiveness. Using this guide, she identifies that although Viktor's teacher is successfully connecting to Viktor's prior learning and experience, the lesson delivery and learning activities could be made more accessible for him. With the* *administrator's support, Viktor's teacher tries out some new strategies and discovers that sentence frames and vocabulary banks increase Viktor's ability to show what he does and does not understand.*

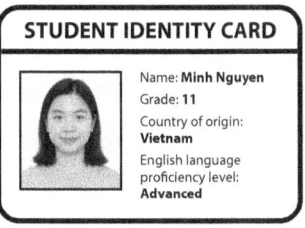

STUDENT IDENTITY CARD

Name: **Minh Nguyen**
Grade: **11**
Country of origin:
Vietnam
English language
proficiency level:
Advanced

*Upon leaving the disastrous parent meeting where **Minh** had to interpret, the administrator resolves to avoid something like this happening again. She works with her administrative staff to check that information on families' preferred languages is updated and made easily accessible in the student record management system. She also makes sure that all staff have access to the district's list of interpreting and translation services and that the instructions for using and billing these services are clear.*

Finally, she invests in a subscription for the entire school to a text messaging app that can translate messages to families automatically. Thanks to the administrator's efforts, communication with Minh's parents—and all the school's families who speak languages other than English—is greatly improved. Families feel more comfortable reaching out to the school when they need support, and teachers can more effectively communicate with families about their students' progress.

Chapter 6. Supporting Multilingual Learners of English Through Technology

STUDENT IDENTITY CARD

Name: **Nyandeng Atong**
Grade: **9**
Country of origin: **South Sudan**
English language proficiency level: **Intermediate**

Nyandeng had never touched a computer before moving to the United States. She now laughs as she recalls how confused she was the first time her newcomer class went to the computer lab and the teacher told them to look for the mouse—she pulled her feet up onto her chair so the animal wouldn't nibble her toes!

Now, she can use a computer just fine (although she still prefers her phone), but she does not see the point. Some of her classmates get excited when they have a WebQuest day or get to play a review game on the computers. For Nyandeng, using the computer requires so much reading that it does not seem worth the time and effort. She would much rather learn from another human being.

STUDENT IDENTITY CARD

Name: **Viktor Melnychuk**
Grade: **10**
Country of origin: **Ukraine**
English language proficiency level: **Beginner**

Viktor loves his Chromebook. It is where the soccer videos are.

Most of the time, Viktor feels lost in his classes, isolated from his peers by language and cultural barriers, anxious about everything. By far, the best part of his day is the 27 minutes between scarfing down his school lunch and the end-of-lunch bell: He pulls out his Chromebook, plugs in his headphones, and loads up ESPN FC on YouTube. And for just a few minutes, everything feels normal again.

STUDENT IDENTITY CARD

Name: **Yadiel Ayala Gonzalez**
Grade: **8**
Country of origin: **Cuba**
English language proficiency: **Advanced**

For *Yadiel*, technology is just one more way that school seems totally disconnected from his real life. In school, using technology means pulling out a clunky Chromebook and logging in to three or four different platforms before he can even find the thing he is supposed to be working on. Outside school, everything is right there on his phone at a single tap. Typing on a Chromebook is slow, and everything is covered in so many red squiggles that it is almost impossible to read anything.

But in his free time, Yadiel is an avid content creator, streaming on Twitch and creating gaming videos for his YouTube channel. Yadiel's teachers talk about the importance of evaluating online sources, using the URL extension and features of the website to determine a website's credibility; however, when Yadiel does online research, he just copies whatever quotation Google highlights in the first search result. Sometimes it *feels like the technology he uses at school and the technology that dominates his life at home are two completely different worlds.*

In this chapter:
- Technology and Artificial Intelligence (AI)
- Ethics of AI use
- Equity and access issues
- Digital literacy
- Strategies for integrating technology
- Digital resources

In Chapters 2 and 3, we shared a wide range of teaching strategies that can be implemented in various ways—high-tech and old-school. In this chapter, we focus specifically on how social studies teachers can make use of technology and AI tools to make these strategies more powerful and easier to implement. We also explore additional resources and technology tools that support language learning for multilingual learners of English (MLEs). This chapter starts with a brief introduction regarding the usefulness of technology and AI tools in language learning, followed by a collection of online resources and AI-powered language learning platforms. Finally, we present considerations for integrating technology into instruction using a case study.

Overview of Technology and AI for Teachers

We live in a digital era with the ever-evolving landscape of education technologies. The wide application of Zoom and other similar video conferencing platforms has made remote teaching possible during the COVID-19 pandemic, and the emerging development of generative AI technologies (e.g., ChatGPT) has brought new possibilities for teachers to plan, design, and deliver instruction. Besides the convenience these technologies bring, they have played an important role in language learning (e.g., Chapelle, 2024). For example, the Duolingo app allows users to learn foreign languages in their spare time, and machine translation tools (e.g., Google Translate) enable MLEs to translate texts and their own writing. More specifically, a brief review of existing literature (e.g., Chapelle, 2024; Gao, 2024; Godwin-Jones, 2024; Gonzalez-Lloret, 2024; Zhu & Wang, 2025) indicates that technology and AI tools can afford valuable opportunities for learning and using the language; increase students' motivation, interest, and engagement in language learning; and develop learner autonomy.

In social studies classrooms, instructors often teach a group of students with mixed-level English proficiency, a population which may increase with the growing enrollment of MLEs in public schools. Though it is not the primary job of social studies instructors to improve students' English proficiency, instructors often need to provide necessary language support to help students understand content-specific knowledge. Therefore, understanding and utilizing technology and AI tools in the social studies classroom can reduce instructors' workload and achieve better student learning outcomes (e.g., Taylor & Duran, 2006).

When districts support instructors in teaching MLEs through technology and AI tools, they also address other accessibility issues that districts face. AI can provide many benefits to learners and teachers in the classroom:

- **Personalized Learning**: AI can tailor content and resources to individual students' needs, enabling differentiated instruction that addresses diverse learning styles and abilities.
- **Increased Accessibility**: AI can provide accommodations for students with disabilities, such as text-to-speech for visually impaired learners or translation tools for MLEs.
- **Enhanced Engagement**: AI-powered tools, like interactive simulations, can make historical events and civic processes more engaging and immersive, fostering deeper understanding.
- **Support for Teachers**: AI can handle time-consuming tasks, such as grading and providing immediate feedback, freeing teachers to focus on more complex instructional strategies and relationship building.
- **Data-Driven Insights**: AI can analyze student performance to identify trends, misconceptions, or areas needing reinforcement, which enables informed decision-making.
- **Fostering Critical Thinking**: Using AI as a tool for research and analysis can help students critically evaluate sources, question biases, and learn about the ethics of technology in history and civic contexts.

Using AI to Reduce Teacher Workload

For the MLEs in her eighth-grade social studies class, Peggie needs differentiated resources. She can use Diffit and input a prompt such as "create a lesson on the Louisiana Purchase." She can indicate a second-grade reading level for her beginning and intermediate MLEs and then a sixth-grade reading level for her advanced proficiency students. In moments, the website will produce a lesson featuring adapted reading passages, a summary of key points, vocabulary words, and assessments with multiple-choice, short answer, and open-ended prompts. She can then insert visuals to accompany the vocabulary. Best of all, she can ask Diffit to translate the materials into Farsi, Arabic, and Ukrainian for her students to ensure comprehension after they use the English language resource.

The Ethics of Using AI in the Social Studies Classroom

AI integration in education holds immense potential but is accompanied by significant challenges, particularly the persistence of biases that can undermine equity and inclusivity. These biases often stem from data and algorithmic frameworks shaped by broader societal inequalities.

For example, Fatima noticed a pattern in the information she received when she asked ChatGPT about Palestine. Prior to October 7, 2023, ChatGPT referred to the Israeli presence in Gaza as an *occupation*, wording that implies support for Palestine. After October 7, ChatGPT's language shifted: It used *conflict*, a word that indicates a more neutral point of view. What happened with Fatima could happen with any student. When students use ChatGPT or any AI tools for research, they receive information shaped by those who controlled the data collection and human feedback process, both of which reflect inherent human biases (Schwartz et al., 2022). We see this discrepancy in education and technology. Technology is constantly evolving, but as educators, it is important to understand the *why* behind the programs and their bias. Each form of data collection has innate biases.

AI systems in the social studies classroom can unintentionally perpetuate systemic inequalities through various types of bias. Historical bias arises when algorithms trained on past data undervalue minority students' potential, leading to disparities in access to scholarships or advanced programs. Data-related bias occurs when diverse groups are excluded from or underrepresented in training datasets, resulting in poorer outcomes for these groups. For example, an AI system generating an image for *leader* may overlook diverse representations. Algorithmic bias can also emerge from model design, reinforcing stereotypes like steering male students toward STEM fields and female students toward the humanities. Interaction bias further perpetuates stereotypes as AI adapts to user behavior, particularly affecting marginalized groups. Additionally, oversurveillance by AI monitoring systems disproportionately targets certain groups, such as Black students, reinforcing stereotypes about behavioral issues and increasing punitive measures.

These biases risk reinforcing systemic discrimination, making the need for equity-centered AI development critical. Programs are starting to incorporate different forms of data collection (see sidebar), and these are decreasing the aforementioned biases.

The Greenlining Institute's *Algorithmic Bias Explained: How Automated Decision-Making Becomes Automated Discrimination* (Moya & Le, 2021) aimed to inform policy and decision-makers to use race-aware algorithms in place of ones that are not sensitive to diversity. This includes collecting race and ethnicity data within systems, which might be a concern, but "unlike humans, algorithms are not inherently biased. Instead, bias is introduced

- **Diverse Data:** Efforts to ensure training datasets are representative of all demographics reduce the likelihood of biased predictions. Diverse and inclusive data improve AI fairness.
- **Bias-Aware Algorithms:** Techniques like adversarial debiasing and re-weighting data samples during model training can reduce biases. Continuous monitoring and testing of AI models across different groups are essential for identifying disparities.
- **Transparency and Inclusion:** Engaging diverse stakeholders, including marginalized groups, in AI development helps identify potential biases early and ensures systems are designed with equity in mind.

to these systems by flawed assumptions in the algorithmic model" (Le, 2023, p. 3). The ultimate goal when choosing an AI-powered tool is finding an unbiased program that is collecting data.

The Teacher's Role in Addressing Bias

The integration of AI requires teachers to actively address biases in digital tools. Beyond student plagiarism concerns, educators should focus on the following actions:

- evaluating the fairness of AI resources
- diversifying multimedia and lesson content
- encouraging students to critically analyze AI outputs

Without proper oversight, these tools could trivialize or misrepresent the significance of sensitive topics. AI may oversimplify the human suffering associated with some historical events or present biased perspectives that reinforce harmful stereotypes, inadvertently perpetuating historical injustice. To mitigate this, the development of AI tools in educational settings should include diverse representation and historically accurate content. As emphasized by Le (2023) in his Race-Aware Algorithms blog, incorporating race-aware frameworks could ensure that AI systems present a more inclusive, accurate account of historical events and of the role racial injustice has played in shaping society. Ensuring that historical events not only are simulated with accuracy but also reflect diverse viewpoints would help students engage with these topics more critically and empathetically, fostering a deeper understanding of the complexities involved.

Educators should be proactive in teaching students how to question the outputs of AI systems, especially when it comes to portraying marginalized or historically oppressed groups. Encouraging students to examine multiple sources of information—diverse perspectives on a given topic, including from those underrepresented in mainstream narratives—will help foster a balanced and critical approach to historical learning and the use of AI.

Overreliance on AI in Education

One of the most pressing ethical concerns in the use of AI in education is the overreliance on technology both from the teacher and the student, which can undermine students' development of critical thinking and traditional research skills. AI tools, such as chatbots, recommendation systems, and automated essay graders, can provide students with quick answers or guide their learning in a personalized way, but this convenience comes at a cost. If students rely too heavily on AI for information, they may fail to engage in deeper cognitive processes, such as evaluating sources, making independent conclusions, or formulating questions. These skills are crucial for academic success and intellectual growth but may be sidelined in an AI-dominated classroom.

Critical thinking is an essential skill for students, one that AI cannot replace. AI is programmed to recognize patterns and generate responses based on data, but it lacks the ability to engage in higher order thinking, which is necessary for problem-solving, creativity, and decision-making. For example, while AI tools can assist students in research, they may not encourage students to question the validity of the sources or explore alternative viewpoints. Overreliance on technology could also reduce students' engagement in traditional research methods, such as manual data gathering, reading primary sources, or learning how to synthesize diverse perspectives—skills that are vital for their academic and professional futures.

Another critical ethical concern is teacher displacement. While AI has the potential to enhance instruction by offering personalized learning paths and administrative support, excessive reliance on AI tools might lead to reduced teacher autonomy. AI can certainly help teachers by automating tasks like grading or providing data-driven insights into student performance, but its overuse could lead to a devaluation of the teacher's role. Teachers are not only instructors but also mentors, facilitators, and emotional support for students, roles that AI cannot replicate.

The risk of devaluing teachers is especially prevalent in contexts where AI tools take over key aspects of instruction. If AI systems are used to deliver content without the necessary human oversight, students may miss out on the invaluable social and emotional learning experiences that teachers provide, such as fostering collaboration, managing classroom dynamics, and addressing students' emotional and social needs. Furthermore, excessive reliance on AI could reduce teachers' agency, limiting their ability to adapt teaching strategies based on their professional judgment and the specific needs of their students.

To maintain an ethical and balanced approach to education, AI tools should be seen as supplements to, not replacements for, the teacher's role. Teachers should be empowered to use AI in ways that enhance the learning experience—such as through personalized learning plans or administrative assistance—while retaining control over the learning environment. This balance ensures that AI enriches rather than diminishes the value of human expertise in education.

AI Ethical Use Guidelines for the Classroom

1. **Promoting Critical Thinking:** AI should be used to enhance, not replace, the development of critical thinking. Students should be encouraged to use AI tools to explore topics but also to question, debate, and critically assess the information they encounter (Kitson, 2025).

2. **Teacher Empowerment:** Teachers must be equipped to use AI tools in ways that complement their instructional strategies, not undermine their authority or creativity in the classroom.

3. **Human Connection:** AI should never replace the critical social and emotional role that teachers play in student development. Teachers should continue to serve as mentors, guiding students through both academic and personal challenges.

4. **Transparency and Autonomy:** Schools should provide teachers with the autonomy to make decisions about how AI is used in their classrooms and ensure that these tools are implemented transparently, with clear guidelines on privacy and data security.

In the context of AI integration in education, one of the most pressing ethical responsibilities is ensuring equity and access, particularly in underfunded districts. As AI tools become more prevalent in classrooms, they hold significant potential to enhance teaching and learning experiences. However, disparities in access to these technologies can exacerbate existing inequalities, particularly in schools that already face financial challenges.

Equity and Access Issues

Schools in underfunded districts often struggle to afford the latest technologies, including AI tools, which can create a significant digital divide. AI-powered educational tools, such as personalized learning platforms, automated tutoring systems, or data-driven instructional aids, have the potential to transform learning outcomes, particularly for students in underserved communities. However, if these tools are not accessible due to financial constraints, students in wealthier districts will likely benefit disproportionately from their advanced capabilities. This disparity could further entrench educational inequalities, as students in underfunded schools may lack the resources that their peers have access to, reducing their chances of academic success.

Equity in Action: Integrating AI With Purpose

Addressing these equity challenges requires a thoughtful approach to integrating AI tools into education systems. To ensure that AI benefits are distributed equitably across all schools, especially those in underfunded areas, several strategies must be implemented:

1. **Targeted Funding:** Governments and educational bodies should allocate targeted funding to ensure that underfunded districts have the resources needed to invest in AI tools. This could include grants or partnerships with technology companies to provide affordable AI solutions or even free access to certain platforms designed for educational use. Schools could also work with nonprofits and technology companies to secure donations of hardware and software that help bridge the digital divide.

2. **Accessible AI Tools:** When integrating AI into education, it is essential to choose tools that are cost-effective and accessible to all schools. Some AI systems are expensive to implement and maintain, but there are also affordable, open-source platforms that provide many of the same benefits. These tools could be especially beneficial in districts with limited resources. The key is to prioritize AI systems that enhance learning while being mindful of the financial constraints of these schools.

3. **Teacher Training and Support:** To fully realize the benefits of AI, teachers need adequate training. In many underfunded districts, professional development opportunities are scarce. AI tools can be used to provide continuous, accessible training for teachers, particularly in schools that may not have the budget for in-person workshops or coaching. AI-based teacher development programs can help

educators in these districts stay up to date with best practices and instructional strategies.

4. **Fostering Collaboration:** Districts can collaborate to share resources and knowledge. For example, school districts could partner to pool resources, allowing smaller, underfunded districts to access expensive AI tools by sharing costs. Collaboration also provides an opportunity for educators to exchange ideas on the best practices for integrating AI into classrooms, ensuring that all students benefit from these technologies, regardless of their school's funding level.

5. **Monitoring and Evaluation:** Once AI tools are introduced, it is crucial to monitor their impact on students' outcomes across all districts. Regular assessments can help determine whether AI tools are meeting their objectives and whether there are disparities in outcomes that need to be addressed. This process can guide future investment decisions and ensure that AI systems are truly improving educational equity.

In the long run, addressing equity and access in education requires systemic changes beyond AI tools. Educational policies must focus on creating more equitable funding structures, so that all students—regardless of their socioeconomic status—have access to the same high-quality resources. This includes not only AI but also other forms of technology, infrastructure, and educational support.

By strategically integrating AI in a way that is mindful of financial constraints and actively working to close the gap, educators, policymakers, and communities can ensure that AI serves as a tool for equitable education. AI integration in education holds immense potential to enhance learning experiences, improve personalized instruction, and streamline administrative processes. However, this integration comes with significant challenges, particularly the persistence of biases that can undermine equity and inclusivity. These biases often originate from the data and algorithmic frameworks that AI systems rely on, which are frequently shaped by broader societal inequalities. Whether through historical biases in student performance predictions, data-related biases in underrepresented groups, or algorithmic biases reinforcing stereotypes, AI has the potential to perpetuate existing disparities in education.

As we move forward with AI in education, it is essential to address these issues by implementing strategies that promote fairness and equity. This includes diversifying training data, developing bias-aware algorithms, and ensuring continuous monitoring to identify disparities. Additionally, educators must be equipped with the tools and knowledge to use AI responsibly, ensuring that technology supports, rather than replaces, critical human interactions in the classroom. Thoughtful and ethical integration of AI, combined with careful attention to the challenges of equity, can help ensure that the benefits of AI are accessible to all students, regardless of background or socioeconomic status (Kitson, 2025).

Digital Literacy

Digital literacy encompasses more than just basic computer skills; it includes "the skills associated with using technology to enable users to find, evaluate, organize, create, and communicate information; and developing digital citizenship and the responsible use of technology" (Museum and Library Services Act, 2018). Especially in the social studies classroom, digital literacy is becoming increasingly important and closely linked to citizenship skills, emphasizing critical awareness of media and its influence on thinking and behavior (Berson & Berson, 2003).

Challenges

MLEs who have never seen or used a computer are missing critical digital literacy skills necessary to navigate today's technology-driven world. Even those MLEs who are part of the "digital generation" have huge gaps in their understanding because all their digital experience has been on smartphones and apps. They have little or no foundational skills, such as sending emails, navigating internet browsers, searching websites, reading digital maps, and using digital calendars.

Understanding the interaction of technology requires some proficiency in language and literacy (Harris, 2015). Limited English language proficiency makes it especially challenging for MLEs. For instance, many MLEs find it difficult to interpret buttons, menus, instructions, and feedback presented only in English. Without explicit instruction and visual supports, they could miss important dates, like deadlines for homework assignments and projects.

Many MLEs come from different socioeconomic backgrounds, so some may not have access to a computer or the internet in their home, do not know about or struggle to find technology support, or may be unable to get to the library on a regular basis to use the internet or computers.

Strategies

Despite these challenges, we present different instructional strategies in the next section to help educators teach digital literacy skills to MLEs.

Integrating Basic Digital Skills Into Instruction

Teach foundational skills by first teaching basic computer skills and then high-level digital literacy skills once students are ready. Use direct instructions as needed and put the skills into practice in relevant activities that focus on digital technology.

- **Example:** Have MLEs spend time practicing turning the computer on and off, keyboarding, using a mouse, right- and left-clicking, etc.
- **Tool:** laptop, Chromebook, or desktop computer

Teach Relevant Vocabulary for Using Computer Skills

MLEs must understand and use the language of the computer skills in settings where the primary language of technology instruction is in English. Put MLEs in small groups, pass out word lists, and ask students to circle the words they know. This activity helps you determine how many computer-related words they know. Take some time explaining the new words and demonstrate how to use them. Then, have students practice using the new vocabulary.

- **Example:** Students may know that the word *mouse* refers to an animal, but they may not know it is the tool that moves the computer cursor.
- **Tools:** word list, computer mouse

Reading Information Online

For MLEs, finding and reading information on the internet can be difficult. It involves specific reading skills such as scanning for what is important and accurate, skimming irrelevant content, and close reading. In addition, it requires a strong ability to distinguish between main content and advertisements and to know when to follow hyperlinks and engage with multimedia.

- **Example:** Teach students to search for historical events using specific keywords on platforms like Google or academic databases. Instead of simply typing "World War I," guide students to use more specific keywords like "causes of World War I" or "alliances before 1914." Encourage students to break research questions into smaller parts, use quotation marks for exact phrases such as "Treaty of Versailles," and include dates or locations to narrow their results, like "immigration laws 1920s USA."
- **Tools:** Google SafeSearch, school-subscribed databases (e.g., JSTOR)

Evaluating Credibility

To interpret online information, MLEs need to learn how to ask critical questions to address bias, credibility, accuracy, and reliability. Some of the key critical questions to evaluate information online come from *wh*–questions:

- Who wrote this?
- What is the message behind it?
- When did they write it?
- Where did they get the data?
- Why did they write it?
- How might the reader understand the message differently?
  a. **Example Activity**: Compare two articles about a historical event—one from a reputable source and one from an unreliable blog. Discuss the differences in language and sources.
     Tool: Fact-checking websites like Snopes.com
  b. **Example Activity**: Analyze a social media post or YouTube video about a current event. Discuss how visuals, music, and editing influence opinions.
     Tool: Canva for creating simple infographics that showcase findings

Extending Learning Beyond the Classroom

MLEs can use technology beyond the classroom walls in independent online learning opportunities to improve speaking, listening, reading, and writing in English. Independent learning also allows teachers to differentiate instruction and better meet students' needs, interests, and abilities (Kitson, 2025). Students can be highly motivated to practice the grammar and vocabulary needed to interact with the community outside the classroom.

Independent Learning Activities
- **Writing**: Have students create a blog or digital poster about a historical figure, including multimedia elements like images, videos, and hyperlinks.
  - ◆ **Tool**: platforms like Google Sites or Padlet
- **Speaking:** Have students create a digital story that is recorded by students reading it out loud and that uses visual supports.
  - ◆ **Tool:** platforms like CapCut or Adobe Express
- **Reading:** After reading a text, provide access to a digital copy and have students practice reading on their own and receive immediate feedback.
  - ◆ **Tool:** Microsoft Reading Coach
- **Listening:** Have students listen to videos or recorded interviews or talks.
  - ◆ **Tool**: TED talks, YouTube videos, or podcasts

Developing Digital Literacy in Social Studies for Multilingual Learners of English

Although cultural stereotypes and misrepresentations can spread online, the internet can also effectively be used to debunk these stereotypes. The following activity shows MLEs how to use technology through critical thinking, digital literacy, and collaborative problem-solving to add their voice and speak the truth to raise awareness of cultural stereotypes in the broader community on the web.

Teachers begin the activity by preteaching vocabulary, introducing the concept of stereotypes, and watching a video on the definition of stereotypes and their harmful effects. Support MLEs by providing multilingual dictionaries and visual aids.

After teachers lead discussions to identify examples of stereotypes, students use multimedia tools (e.g., Flip, Padlet, or Canva) to record video reflections, create digital posters, or design slideshows to reflect on their experiences with stereotypes and share their thoughts. Once they finish, students analyze a common stereotype through graded readings and visuals, and students evaluate online articles for bias and reliability to build critical media literacy. Teachers can find these resources on platforms like Newsela, Rewordify, or the British Council website; or they can create their own by simplifying texts, adding glossaries, and pairing content with images or infographics that support comprehension. Later, students examine cultural misrepresentations in the media, compare perspectives, and brainstorm strategies to address bias while promoting ethical digital citizenship.

Lastly, students use readings and visuals they previously analyzed to explore the misleading nature of stereotypes to create blogs, videos, or podcasts that address stereotypes and contribute to positive cultural representations on learning platforms, focusing on diversity and inclusion.

In the end, students take action to respond to misrepresentations, present their work, and receive feedback based on critical thinking, creativity, collaboration, and digital literacy skills.

Strategies for Integrating Technology and AI Into Social Studies Instruction

The use of technology tools in the classroom can distract learners if teachers do not follow certain practices. Following are some necessary considerations to help social studies instructors thrive in using technology to create engaging and interactive learning environments.

- **Know Yourself and Your Learners.** Before using technology tools in the classroom, teachers should first reflect on their comfort level and familiarity with certain technologies. Teachers should also develop a general understanding of students' digital literacy and proficiency in using technology because MLEs do not always have experience. Getting to know them and their previous schooling experience will help set your expectations and starting points for students.
- **Set Clear Goals.** Teachers should clearly understand the purpose of using certain technologies in the classroom and should allocate time for teaching and using these technologies in advance.
- **Select Appropriate Tools.** Teachers should select appropriate tools according to teaching purposes, students' digital literacy, and students' English proficiency. Also, teachers should select tools that are accessible to students and protect their privacy.

One technology tool that supports MLEs is real-time language assistance through AI. Tools like translation apps and speech-to-text programs help bridge language gaps, enabling students to access content and participate in discussions. AI is also used in adaptive language learning platforms that tailor vocabulary, grammar, and comprehension exercises to individual proficiency levels, allowing students to progress at their own pace.

To make abstract concepts more accessible, AI-powered content creation tools can generate customized instructional materials, such as visual aids, simplified texts, and multimedia resources. Virtual tutors and chatbots offer instant feedback, explanations, and practice opportunities, helping MLEs reinforce their understanding outside the classroom.

Moreover, AI can facilitate culturally responsive teaching by enabling educators to incorporate diverse perspectives and materials into the curriculum. Many AI tools use machine learning algorithms that can analyze students' cultural backgrounds and learning styles, helping teachers design lessons that resonate with their experiences.

For assessments, AI provides innovative tools like voice recognition software for oral presentations, automated scoring for written work, and interactive simulations that allow MLEs to demonstrate their knowledge in meaningful ways. These tools ensure that evaluations are fair and reflective of students' abilities, regardless of their language proficiency. For example, Write & Improve by Cambridge focuses on content and structure rather than grammar alone, supporting MLEs without penalizing emerging language skills.

AI can also automate administrative tasks, freeing up teachers' time to focus on building relationships and providing individualized support. These programs also offer valuable insights through data analytics, helping educators track progress and identify areas where additional support may be needed.

When used thoughtfully, AI can be a powerful ally in fostering an inclusive, dynamic, and effective learning environment for MLEs, empowering them to achieve both academic and linguistic success.

Digital Resources for Supporting Language and Social Studies Content

This section highlights a variety of digital and nondigital tools designed to support both language development and social studies instruction. Resources are organized by type and purpose: for example, those that enhance vocabulary, build background knowledge, support primary source analysis, or promote collaboration. It is important to note that digital tools frequently update their features, pricing, or availability. Some programs may no longer exist or may evolve after publication, and newer resources may emerge. While every effort has been made to include a representative selection, this is not an exhaustive list. Additionally, pricing structures vary—some platforms are free, others require a fee or are available through subscription-based models. Educators are encouraged to explore each tool to determine the best fit for their students and context.

Know Your Learner:
- Interest Inventories and Learning Surveys (Google Forms): Gather student preferences, tech comfort levels, and learning styles.
- One-on-One Conferences: Schedule short check-ins at the beginning of the semester to build relationships and better understand student goals.
- Digital Portfolio (Google Sites or Slides): Let students showcase their work and reflect on strengths and growth areas.

Set Clear Goals:
- SMART Goal Sheet (Google Forms): Guide students in setting Specific, Measurable, Achievable, Relevant, and Time-bound goals.
- Canva for Education: Guide students with visual templates to cocreate class expectations and tech use agreements.

Select Appropriate Tools:

- EdTech Evaluation Rubrics (EdTech equity evaluation toolkit, ISTE AI tool checklist, or your district expectations): Assess AI tools for bias, accessibility, and pedagogical values.
- Common Sense Education Reviews: Check tool ratings and read educator feedback on classroom tech and AI platforms.

Interactive and Collaborative Tools

- Padlet [padlet.com]: An interactive, collaborative digital bulletin board where teachers can assess students' familiarity with technology through surveys or discussions.
- Google Forms [www.google.com/forms/about]: A web-based software used to create surveys or quizzes for formative feedback.
- Kahoot! [kahoot.com]: A game-based learning platform that provides an engaging way to review learning by incorporating vocabulary and visuals.
- Blooket [www.blooket.com]: A game-based learning platform that provides an engaging way to incorporate review questions for students using teacher-created or pre-existing question sets.
- Knowt [knowt.com]: An AI study tool that provides flashcards and notes and is FERPA, COPPA, and SOPPA compliant.

Tools for Content Design and Video Learning

- Canva for Education [www.canva.com/]: Allows teachers to design visuals for students.
- Edpuzzle [edpuzzle.com]: Enables teachers to analyze student interaction with videos and revise content based on analytics. Provides videos and scaffolds questions for students at their level.
- Screencastify [www.screencastify.com]: An easy-to-use screen recording tool for teachers to create how-to guides for students.

Language Support and Translation Tools

AI-powered tools like Google Translate or Grammarly can support comprehension by translating social studies content into students' home languages or providing simplified versions. The following are a few AI tools that can translate primary source documents or articles into students' home languages while retaining historical context:

- Google Translate [translate.google.com]: Translates text and documents into one of over 240 languages, enabling students to access primary source materials in their home languages.
- Microsoft Translator [translator.microsoft.com]: Offers real-time translation for conversations and documents, useful for multilingual classrooms.
- Microsoft Reading Coach [coach.microsoft.com]: Generates stories and provides reading feedback for MLEs to practice.

Reading and Leveled Text Tools

Educators can use a variety of AI and technology resources to level texts for MLEs, making academic content more accessible. Here are some tools to adjust reading levels, simplify language, and provide support for MLEs in the social studies classroom:

- NewsELA [newsela.com]: This website offers a large selection of news articles and social studies content that can be adjusted to different reading levels. Each text is available at a range of reading levels, with many going as low as a second-grade level. Many articles are also available at multiple levels in Spanish. In addition to current events and historical topics, NewsELA has begun adding significant primary sources to their collection, also available at various reading levels. This tool is highly beneficial for providing leveled texts that cover grade-level topics at a more accessible reading level.
- Diffit [app.diffit.me]: This AI-powered tool is designed to help educators differentiate instruction and make content more accessible for MLEs and students with diverse needs. The platform allows teachers to adapt reading materials and assignments, adjusting the complexity of texts to match the proficiency levels of individual students. By simplifying vocabulary, sentence structure, and overall text complexity, Diffit ensures that all students, regardless of their language background, can engage with content meaningfully.

Conclusion: Purposeful Integration of Technology

Integrating technology and AI into social studies instruction offers educators powerful tools to enhance engagement, accessibility, and inclusivity in the classroom. By following general principles—such as understanding their own and their students' proficiency with technology, setting clear objectives, and thoughtfully selecting appropriate tools—teachers can create interactive and meaningful learning experiences. Leveraging AI for language support, cultural responsiveness, and scaffolding academic vocabulary ensures that MLEs and diverse student populations feel empowered and represented. Furthermore, employing technology for speaking and listening practice, immediate feedback, and multimodal learning enriches students' understanding of complex social studies content. As educators reflect on and revise their strategies, they can continue to adapt technology effectively, fostering an environment where all learners thrive academically and develop critical thinking skills for the 21st century.

Reflection Questions

1. How can technology be used to enhance your social studies instruction for MLEs?
2. How can technology empower MLEs to express their unique identities and perspectives?
3. How can technology support the simultaneous development of content knowledge and language proficiency?
4. Based on what you have read, what is one new technology strategy you would like to implement with your MLEs?
5. How will you evaluate the effectiveness of this strategy in supporting both language development and academic success?

Classroom Connections

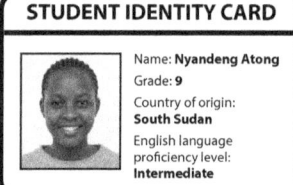

STUDENT IDENTITY CARD

Name: **Nyandeng Atong**
Grade: **9**
Country of origin: **South Sudan**
English language proficiency level: **Intermediate**

Nyandeng has already developed basic computer literacy (although she may need some extra support developing skills like touch typing in order to become a fluent computer user). However, she does not have a lot of interest in using technology because she does not see any benefits to it; doing her work on paper is easier and learning through talking to others is more interesting. However, many of the technological supports available to Nyandeng can totally transform her learning by helping her get past the barrier of low print literacy. By using the built-in text-to-speech features on many websites and programs, Nyandeng can learn from sources that were previously inaccessible to her because the reading level was too challenging. This technology allows her to access grade-level content while still building her reading ability. Nyandeng can also use speech-to-text tools to more fluidly express her ideas in writing without having to struggle with the English spelling system. These tools allow Nyandeng to learn and express her learning at a level that matches her high speaking and listening proficiency in English.

Better yet, Nyandeng's teachers can use technology to tap into one of her key motivating factors—connecting with others. After all, the internet is just a way of connecting to people around the world. Using blogs, podcasts, video sharing websites, and other types of social media, Nyandeng can share her ideas with a real audience and participate in conversations about what matters to her.

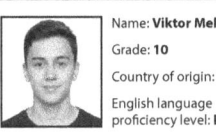

STUDENT IDENTITY CARD

Name: **Viktor Melnychuk**
Grade: **10**
Country of origin: **Ukraine**
English language
proficiency level: **Beginner**

*Technology allows **Viktor** to feel a precious few minutes of normalcy. But that does not have to end when the end-of-lunch bell rings! By seeking out resources in Ukrainian, which Viktor reads fluently, Viktor's teachers can help him feel like a normal high schooler again in the classroom: reading a text that is both at a comfortable reading level and about actual high school–level content, understanding the passage perfectly instead of grasping at meaning from a few familiar words. Translation tools also help Viktor express himself. Instead of fumbling around in English, all too aware that his writing sounds like that of a 5-year-old kid, Viktor can produce sophisticated, thoughtful pieces in his own language and then translate them to English to share his thinking with his teachers.*

As well as allowing Viktor to access grade-level content and fully express himself in writing, technology can support Viktor's English language development. Even a beginner like Viktor can meaningfully participate in the social studies classroom in English—but this requires a lot of work on the teacher's part to prepare vocabulary lists, leveled texts, and other modifications and support. AI tools designed for education lessen the workload for Viktor's teachers, making it actually possible to provide these supports on a daily basis for him and other students at a range of proficiency levels.

STUDENT IDENTITY CARD

Name:
Yadiel Ayala Gonzalez
Grade: **8**
Country of origin: **Cuba**
English language
proficiency: **Advanced**

***Yadiel** is an avid user of technology outside of school, but the ways his teachers use technology in school have never seemed to have anything to do with the real world. This changes when his social studies teacher introduces a unit on evaluating the reliability of sources with a discussion about a scam Yadiel saw on TikTok a week ago. For the first time, Yadiel can see how questions about sources and reliability actually matter in the real world. Confident in his prior knowledge about how to identify fake social media accounts, he participates eagerly in the lessons, and as the teacher moves from online safety to identifying propaganda and other misleading media the students might encounter in U.S. History, Yadiel knows he has the skills to be successful.*

Yadiel's teachers also use technology to support his growth in English. Using powerful data tools, his teachers can analyze his past results on standardized tests and pinpoint the types of questions where Yadiel is not successful. This analysis reveals that, although Yadiel has a good grasp of the content, he struggles with Tier 2 vocabulary, especially words related to causes and effects. Based on this data, Yadiel's English language teacher starts including extra practice with cause-and-effect vocabulary into instruction—something that the teachers find benefits all their students.

Chapter 7. Lesson Plans for Supporting Multilingual Learners of English

In this chapter:
- Integration of strategies from previous chapters within the content
- Lesson plans for middle school classrooms
- Lesson plans for high school classrooms

The work you see in this book reflects an ongoing journey—a process of growth, experimentation, and purposeful change. Supporting multilingual learners of English (MLEs) does not require a complete curriculum rewrite. It starts with small, thoughtful shifts: modifying one lesson at a time, adjusting strategies bit by bit, and staying open to learning along the way.

One of the most effective ways to grow in this work is by seeing how other educators have adapted their instruction to meet the needs of MLEs. That is why we have included a collection of model social studies lessons to give you a starting point. These lessons are ready to use, but they are also meant to inspire. You can adapt them, remix them, or simply use them as a springboard to try something new in your own classroom.

Each lesson reflects a commitment to inclusive, engaging, and rigorous learning. They showcase how history, geography, civics, and economics can come alive for MLEs through culturally responsive, linguistically accessible instruction. Grounded in the C3 Framework and enhanced with research-based strategies and purposeful technology, these lessons are designed to build content knowledge, deepen critical thinking, and promote language development—all at the same time.

Key Features of the Lessons

1. **Student-Centered Learning**: Lessons are scaffolded to meet diverse language needs, incorporating visuals, sentence frames, and collaborative activities to promote active participation.

2. **Culturally Responsive Content**: Topics are presented through a global lens, valuing students' cultural backgrounds while exploring connections to broader historical and social themes.

3. **Technology Integration**: Digital tools, such as interactive timelines, multimedia resources, and AI-supported language apps, support both teaching and learning by enhancing engagement and accessibility.

4. **Teacher Support**: Each lesson includes explanations of the differentiation strategies used, highlighting how the principles in this book can be applied to specific content.

These lessons are not just about teaching social studies; they are about fostering curiosity, critical inquiry, and meaningful language development in a supportive, technology-enhanced environment. Together, we will help MLEs navigate the past and present while preparing for the future.

Teaching History, Building Language: Instruction for Multilingual Learners of English in the Middle School Classroom

Lesson 1: The American Civil War
Lesson by Mary Brennan

Table 7.1.1 *Middle School Lesson Overview: The American Civil War*

	The American Civil War
Duration	110 minutes
Differentiation Strategies	• chunking • sentence frames
C3 Framework Standards	**D1.2.6–8.** Explain points of agreement experts have about interpretations and applications of disciplinary concepts and ideas associated with a compelling question. **D1.5.6–8.** Determine the kinds of sources that will be helpful in answering compelling and supporting questions, taking into consideration multiple points of views represented in the sources. **D2.His.9.6–8.** Classify the kinds of historical sources used in a secondary interpretation. **D2.His.10.6–8.** Detect possible limitations in the historical record based on evidence collected from different kinds of historical sources. **D2.His.11.6–8.** Use other historical sources to infer a plausible maker, date, place of origin, and intended audience for historical sources where this information is not easily identified. **D2.His.12.6–8.** Use questions generated about multiple historical sources to identify further areas of inquiry and additional sources. **D2.His.13.6–8.** Evaluate the relevancy and utility of a historical source based on information such as maker, date, place of origin, intended audience, and purpose. **D3.1.6–8.** Gather relevant information from multiple sources while using the origin, authority, structure, context, and corroborative value of the sources to guide the selection. **D3.3.6–8.** Identify evidence that draws information from multiple sources to support claims, noting evidentiary limitations. **D3.4.6–8.** Develop claims and counterclaims while pointing out the strengths and limitations of both. **D4.2.6–8.** Construct explanations using reasoning, correct sequence, examples, and details with relevant information and data, while acknowledging the strengths and weaknesses of the explanations.
Content/Language Objectives	1. Students will understand the causes and consequences of the American Civil War by using academic vocabulary related to the war in their discussions and writing. 2. Students will analyze key events, figures, and battles of the American Civil War by articulating their thoughts in discussions and written work. 3. Students will evaluate the impact of the Civil War on American society, including issues of slavery and states' rights by analyzing primary and secondary sources including timelines.
Materials and Technology	• textbook chapters on the Civil War • primary source documents (letters, speeches, photographs) • multimedia resources (videos, documentaries) • whiteboard and markers • chart paper and markers for group work • handouts with questions for group discussions • Civil War vocabulary guide (Table 7.1.3) • overview of the Civil War, if needed (Table 7.1.4)

Teacher Background	The teacher should have a thorough understanding of the American Civil War, including its key causes (e.g., slavery, economic differences, states' rights), major battles (e.g., Gettysburg, Antietam), influential figures (e.g., Abraham Lincoln, Frederick Douglass), and its lasting impact on the United States. Familiarity with different teaching strategies, including collaborative learning and critical thinking exercises, will aid the lesson's success.
Assessment	For beginning MLEs, monitor group discussions, pair shares, and individual sentence constructions to assess understanding and language use. Then allow students to share ideas before they write.

Table 7.1.2 *Middle School Lesson Procedures and Differentiation: The American Civil War*

Lesson Procedures	Differentiation Strategies

Introduction (15 minutes)
1. Chunk:
  a. Begin with the KWL chart (5 minutes): Have students discuss their prior knowledge in small groups before sharing with the class.
  b. Introduce vocabulary (10 minutes): Provide a Civil War vocabulary sheet with visuals and definitions. Use a mix of direct instruction and matching activities to ensure understanding.
2. Activity:
  a. Pair students to highlight or underline key terms in their vocabulary sheets related to the day's focus (e.g., slavery, states' rights).
	Sometimes when we talk about chunking, it is not just what students are reading but how they are learning. Many teachers have a lot of content to fit into lectures and tend to run everything together. This lesson chunks things out for students to understand in pieces. Sometimes just having purposeful chunks of activities and information can help students. An example of chunking text is included in Figure 7.1.4 (Overview of the Civil War).

Main Activity (30 minutes)
1. Chunk:
  a. **Part A (10 minutes):** Divide students into small groups. Assign each group a specific cause of the Civil War and give them simplified primary sources alongside translations (if available). Use sentence frames to support analysis:
    i. "This source shows that ___ because ___ ."
    ii. "A key event described is ___, which impacted ___ by ___ ."
  b. **Part B (20 minutes):** Students collaboratively analyze their source and create a mini-presentation (use a graphic organizer for notes).
2. Activity:
  a. As part of the presentation, have each group place their cause or event on a **large class timeline** on chart paper or a digital platform. Groups will discuss where their assigned topic fits and why.
	Because the Civil War is a large topic and has many causes, it is less overwhelming if each group digests one cause. Then, the groups share and pull out similarities.
	
	Sentence frames are structured sentence starters that provide students with a scaffold to support their speaking or writing. They help learners, especially multilingual students, express their ideas using academic language and complete thoughts. By offering a consistent structure, sentence frames build confidence, model correct grammar and syntax, and promote language development while students focus on content understanding

Small Group Discussion (20 minutes)
• **Chunk:**
  ○ Groups present their findings (12–15 minutes): Keep presentations concise, focusing on 2–3 main points.
  ○ Question time (5–8 minutes): Students ask clarifying questions, using sentence stems for support:
    ▪ "Can you explain why ___ happened?"
    ▪ "How did ___ lead to ___?"
• **Activity:**
  ○ Add student-generated events to the timeline during presentations to build a visual representation of the Civil War's progression.
	Chunking materials for MLEs involves breaking down content into smaller, manageable parts to support understanding and reduce cognitive overload. This strategy allows students to focus on key concepts one step at a time, making complex information more accessible. Chunking can include dividing texts into sections, using visuals to support meaning, and providing clear headings or guiding questions to help students process and retain new information. In small groups, chunking can be much more targeted and responsive to students' language proficiency levels and individual needs. Teachers can adjust the size and complexity of the chunks, offer more frequent checks for understanding, and use tailored supports such as sentence frames, bilingual glossaries, or additional modeling. Small groups also allow for more interaction and immediate feedback, helping MLEs process information more deeply and confidently.

Whole Class Discussion (15 minutes)
• **Chunk:**
  ○ Use visuals (e.g., the developing timeline) as discussion anchors.
  ○ Scaffold questions to foster deeper connections between causes and events:
    ▪ "What patterns do you see on the timeline?"
    ▪ "Why do you think ___ led to ___?"
	In a whole-class setting, chunking tends to be more general and designed to support a wide range of learners. Teachers might break a lesson into clear sections with visual aids, pauses for processing, and structured note-taking strategies. They may use guiding questions or brief turn-and-talk opportunities to help all students stay engaged and make sense of the content at a collective pace.

Timeline Creation Activity (20 minutes)
• **Activity:**
  ○ Have students work individually or in pairs to create their own **personal timeline of the Civil War**, incorporating events from the class timeline.
  ○ Provide a structured template:
    ▪ Columns for **Date, Event, Cause/Effect, and Importance**.
    ▪ Prefill 1–2 entries to model expectations.
  ○ Students illustrate 1 event and write 1–2 sentences using academic vocabulary (sentence frames: "In ___, ___ happened, which caused ___ because ___").
	Offer a scaffolded version with dates already filled in or some events placed in order. Students can focus on filling in missing information or labeling events using sentence frames.
	
	Pair MLEs with supportive peers in mixed-ability groups or create language-level groups with tailored instruction. In small groups, students can discuss the sequence and meaning of events before writing.
	
	Let students present their timelines orally, digitally, or with drawings instead of full written explanations, depending on their language development level.

Reflective Writing and Assessment (10 minutes) • Students respond to the essential question in writing, referencing their timeline and using evidence discussed during the lesson. • Provide a word bank and sentence frames for additional support: "One main cause of the Civil War was ___ . This led to ___ because ___ . Another important event was ___, which impacted ___ . "	

Table 7.1.3 *Vocabulary Guide: The American Civil War*

Word	Tier	Definition	Example	Translation
abolitionist	3	person who worked to abolish, or end, slavery		
civil war	3	a war between different groups or regions in the same country		
Confederacy	3	the government formed by the states in the South after they withdrew from the United States		
economy	3	the system by which people produce and trade goods		
Emancipation Proclamation	3	the official document, or announcement, that all slaves would be set free		
expand	2	to spread out; to become greater in size		

issue	2	a problem or topic that people are talking about and may disagree about		
plantations	3	large farms where crops are raised		
rebels	3	the nickname given to the Confederate soldiers		
secede	3	to leave a group		
slavery	3	the practice of forcing people to work without pay as enslaved people and denying them the freedom to decide how to live their lives		
Union	3	the northern states that did not secede from the United States		

Yankees	3	Union soldiers during the Civil War; people from the northern states		

Note. Image for "abolitionist" from portrait of Harriet Tubman [Photograph], by B. F. Powelson, 1868–1869, Library of Congress (www.loc.gov/item/2018645050). In the public domain. Image for "civil war" from *Battle of Kenesaw Mountain* [Lithograph], by Kurz & Allison, 1891, Library of Congress (www.loc.gov/item/91482215). In the public domain. Image for "Confederacy" from *The Civil War in America* [Engraving], by F. Vizetelly, 1862, The New York Public Library (https://digitalcollections.nypl.org/items/510d47e0-f9ca-a3d9-e040-e00a18064a99). In the public domain. Image for "Emancipation Proclamation" from *Abraham Lincoln and his Emancipation Proclamation* [Illustration], by Strobridge & Co., 1888, Library of Congress (www.loc.gov/item/97507511). In the public domain. Image for "plantation" from *Plantation Residence, Louisiana* [Photograph] by Detroit Publishing Co., 1890, Library of Congress (www.loc.gov/item/2016818856). In the public domain. Image for "rebels" from *Unidentified Soldier in Confederate Uniform* [Photograph], 1861–1865, Library of Congress (www.loc.gov/item/2022633084). In the public domain. Image for "slavery" from *People with baskets and sacks pick cotton on a plantation* [Lithograph], by J. R. Barfoot, 1840, Wellcome Collection (https://wellcomecollection.org/works/mf7r354u/images?id=dctev2ms). In the public domain. Image for "Union" from *Union Generals* [Lithograph], by Mayer & Stetfield, 1861, Library of Congress (www.loc.gov/item/90714113). In the public domain. Image for "Yankees" from *Unidentified soldier in Union Uniform* [Photograph], 1861–1865, Library of Congress (www.loc.gov/item/2022642437). In the public domain.

Table 7.1.4 *Overview of the Civil War*

The Civil War: An Overview

Paragraph Number	Content	Notes (e.g., keywords, ideas, dates)
1	The **Civil War** started in 1861. Tensions between the North and the South grew, leading to a conflict that almost split the United States in two. The reasons for this tension were different and so were the opinions of people living in the young country.	
2	As the United States grew, it faced the **issue** of **slavery**. Many people in the North opposed slavery and became **abolitionists**, while many in the South supported slavery, believing it was important for their **economy**. These differences created a divide in the country. The Missouri Compromise of 1820 and the Compromise of 1850 temporarily brought both sides together, but the disagreements continued to lead the country toward war.	
3	In 1852, Harriet Beecher Stowe published a novel called *Uncle Tom's Cabin*. The book tells the fictional story of an enslaved man named Tom, who dies after being severely beaten. This book became very popular, and abolitionists used it to show the horrors of slavery. Many people started to see slavery as a moral issue. However, Southerners argued that since the book was a work of fiction, it did not accurately represent the life of enslaved people.	
4	In March 1857, the United States Supreme Court made a significant ruling against anti-slavery supporters. Dred Scott, a formerly enslaved man, sued for his freedom with the help of lawyers. The Supreme Court decided that Scott was not free for two main reasons: First, he had no right to sue because he was not considered a citizen; second, the court said that slaves were property. They also ruled that Congress could not prohibit slavery in any territory. Supporters of slavery were happy with this decision, while abolitionists were shocked.	
5	In the 1860 election, Abraham Lincoln ran against Stephen Douglas, John Bell, and John Breckinridge. Each candidate had a different view on slavery. Lincoln won the election even though he received only 40% of the popular vote because he got enough electoral votes. Lincoln's election upset many in the South. They felt that the government was now very much against slavery, and South Carolina decided to **secede** from the United States. Soon, several other states followed. The nation was on the edge of war.	
6	When Lincoln took office, he faced a divided country. Despite many attempts to find compromises and assurances, bringing the country back together peacefully was not possible. It would take several years and a terrible war to achieve that goal.	

Note. This summary can be put into a technology tool to be translated or simplified by grade level for students. You can also chunk this into readable pieces for students. The chunking of text makes reading manageable for students because it helps them slow down and understand what they read. You can have them put a blank paper over the rest of the text and just focus on one paragraph at a time.

Lesson 2: Ancient Egypt

Lesson by Peggie Cypher

Table 7.2.1 *Middle School Lesson Overview: Ancient Egypt*

Ancient Egypt Brochure	
Duration	Two 40-minute class periods
Differentiation Strategies	guided notes alternative assessment
C3 Framework Standards	**D1.4.6–8.** Explain how the relationship between supporting questions and compelling questions is mutually reinforcing. **D2.His.2.6–8.** Classify a series of historical events and developments as examples of change and/or continuity. **D3.1.6–8.** Gather relevant information from multiple sources while using the origin, authority, structure, context, and corroborative value of the sources to guide the selection. **D3.2.6–8.** Evaluate the credibility of a source by determining its relevance and intended use. **D4.2.6–8.** Construct explanations using reasoning, correct sequence, examples, and details with relevant information and data, while acknowledging the strengths and weaknesses of the explanations.
Content/Language Objectives	Students will use information from their textbooks and guided notes to compile the most relevant information about ancient Egypt.
Materials and Technology	• textbook, websites, or class notes • brochure template (Figure 7.2.3) • sample brochure (can be found via internet search) • grading rubric (Figure 7.2.4)
Teacher Background	At the end of a unit on ancient Egypt, this activity can be used as an alternative assessment for MLEs and general education students alike. A review of the main points may be necessary.
Assessment	For beginning MLEs, assess on the main content points only, such as the following: • Do they include the main achievements of ancient Egypt? • Does the map include the Nile? If students struggle with writing, modify the assignment to include one achievement, one fact about social structure, etc. Intermediate and advanced MLEs can be required to write using correct sentence structure, but assessment can be more lenient concerning correct grammar, spelling, and punctuation. Grade assessment on rubric.

Table 7.2.2 *Middle School Lesson Procedures and Differentiation: Ancient Egypt*

Lesson Procedures	Differentiation Strategies
Introduction (15 minutes) Explain to students that they will be creating a travel brochure of ancient Egypt instead of a traditional assessment. 1. Review key information together as a class, or direct students to the textbook or other resources to find the relevant information. 2. Pass out the travel brochure template and rubric. If possible, project these materials. 3. Show students an example of a complete project. (Sample brochures can be found on Google Images.) 4. Explain the instructions while reviewing the rubric. 5. Ensure MLEs understand each category on the brochure and rubric. 6. Translate the rubric if needed.	Alternative Assessment: a hands-on way to review key information and have students present it in a way that does not challenge their language proficiency. Ensure students understand the categories of the brochure. Allow them to translate if needed.
Main Activity Students work independently to find information and fill out the brochure. Circulate the room to see if help is needed.	You may have to guide newcomers on how to search for and upload images. All MLEs may need assistance locating information in the textbook or their notes.

Table 7.2.3 *Ancient Egypt Brochure Template*

Achievements (include 3)	Map	Cover
	Fun Facts	**Name**_____

Table 7.2.3 *Ancient Egypt Brochure Template (back)*

Social Structure (include 2)	Religious Beliefs (include 2)	Early Geography

Table 7.2.4 *Ancient Egypt Brochure Rubric*

You need:	Points Total = 20 points
Drawings or images for	
• Cover	/1
• Achievements section (things done successfully)	/1
• Early Geography section (features of the land and water such as mountains, rivers, seas)	/1 /1
• Religious Beliefs section	/1
• Social Structure section (rank, groups, roles, jobs)	/5
Details and explanations *in your own words*	
• Achievements section	/2
• Early Geography section	/2
• Religious Beliefs section	/2
• Social Structure section	/2
	/8
Map of ancient Egypt including	
• The Nile	
• The Mediterranean Sea	
• The Red Sea	
• Upper Egypt	
• Lower Egypt	
• Cairo	
	/6
Two Fun Facts	/1
Total	/20

Lesson 3: Understanding Supply and Demand

Lesson by Mary Brennan

Table 7.3.1 *Middle School Lesson Overview: Understanding Supply and Demand*

Understanding Supply and Demand	
Duration	70 minutes
Differentiation Strategies	• graphic organizer • technology support (videos) • visuals
C3 Framework Standards	**D1.1.6–8.** Explain how a question represents key ideas in the field. **D1.5.6–8.** Determine the kinds of sources that will be helpful in answering compelling and supporting questions, taking into consideration multiple points of views represented in the sources. **D2.Eco.3.6–8.** Explain the roles of buyers and sellers in product, labor, and financial markets. **D2.Eco.6.6–8.** Explain how changes in supply and demand cause changes in prices and quantities of goods and services, labor, credit, and foreign currencies. **D3.2.6–8.** Evaluate the credibility of a source by determining its relevance and intended use. **D3.4.6–8.** Develop claims and counterclaims while pointing out the strengths and limitations of both. **D4.6.6–8.** Draw on multiple disciplinary lenses to analyze how a specific problem can manifest itself at local, regional, and global levels over time, identifying its characteristics and causes, and the challenges and opportunities faced by those trying to address the problem.
Content/Language Objectives	1. Students will understand the concepts of supply and demand by using economic vocabulary such as *supply, demand, price,* and *market.* 2. Students will analyze how supply and demand affect prices in a market by constructing sentences to explain the relationship among supply, demand, and price.
Materials and Technology	• whiteboard and markers • interactive digital market simulation (e.g., online supply-and-demand simulator such as Simbound) • vocabulary guide (Table 7.3.3) • graphic organizers (e.g., supply-and-demand graphs, Table 7.3.4) • visual aids (pictures of goods and services) • sentence starters (Table 7.3.5) • computers or tablets • handouts with simplified texts about supply and demand • projector and screen
Teacher Background	This lesson will focus on the basic economic concepts of supply and demand, and their effects on prices in a market. The lesson will integrate both content and language objectives with differentiated strategies to support MLEs and struggling students.
Assessment	1. **Formative Assessment**: Use group discussions, pair shares, and individual sentence constructions to assess understanding and language use. 2. **Summative Assessment**: Evaluate group presentations based on content accuracy, use of economic vocabulary, and explanations of supply-and-demand scenarios.

Table 7.3.2 *Middle School Lesson Procedures and Differentiation: Understanding Supply and Demand*

Lesson Procedures	Differentiation Strategies
Introduction (10 minutes) 1. **Hook**: Show a short video clip explaining the basic concepts of supply and demand with real-life examples. 2. **Discussion**: Ask students to share their thoughts on the video and give examples of goods and services they use daily. 3. **Objective Overview**: Explain the content and language objectives of the lesson.	Here is an opportunity to modify the content through a video. After completing an anticipation guide, pick a video that fits your students' knowledge, background, and age. During the video, have students create a two-column graphic organizer to write notes about goods and services based on the video. When modifying, you are selecting the most important "need to know" content for your MLEs and emphasizing its importance. Be sure to still include the more in-depth connections but know that, due to background knowledge, students may struggle with some concepts.
Main Activity: *Exploring Supply and Demand* (15 minutes) 1. **Interactive Market Simulation**: Use the digital market simulation to demonstrate how changes in supply and demand affect prices. Let students interact with the simulation. 2. **Group Work**: Divide students into small groups and assign each group a scenario (e.g., increase in demand, decrease in supply) to explore using the simulation. 3. **Graphic Organizer**: Provide groups with a supply-and-demand graphic organizer (Table 7.3.4) to record their observations and outcomes from the simulation.	Technology simulations help students see the process of the market and make it easier for them to connect the process to something they already know.
Small Group: *Vocabulary and Sentence Construction* (15 minutes) 1. **Vocabulary Introduction**: Introduce key economic vocabulary using visual aids and vocabulary guide (Table 7.3.3). 2. **Sentence Construction**: Provide sentence starters (Table 7.3.5) to help students explain supply-and-demand scenarios. 3. **Pair Share**: Have students work in pairs to practice constructing sentences using the provided vocabulary and sentence structures.	For example, "When the demand for a product increases, the price usually ___ " "If the supply of a product decreases, the price will ___ ." (More sentence starters are included in Figure 7.3.5.)

Whole Group: *Real-Life Application* (10 minutes) 1. **Explanation**: Discuss real-life examples of supply and demand, such as seasonal products or popular trends. 2. **Modeling**: Model a few examples on the board, such as "During the holiday season, the demand for toys increases; therefore, the prices go up." 3. **Practice**: Ask students to think of their own real-life examples and explain them using the sentence starters and word banks. **Activity: Presentation and Sharing** (10 minutes) 1. **Group Presentations**: Each group presents their supply-and-demand scenario from the simulation, describing the changes and outcomes using descriptive and academic language. 2. **Class Discussion**: Facilitate a discussion on the different scenarios and their effects on prices.	There are many scenarios that can help students understand these ideas. You can use videos, role-playing, or just stories: 1. Search YouTube for videos about supply and demand. 2. Use the "Supply and Demand Game" from Council for Economic Education (preview2.econedlink.org/resources/supply-and-demand-game). 3. Use the lesson and/or resources from the "Supply and Demand of Toy Fads" lesson from EconEdLink (econedlink.org/resources/a-lesson-on-the-supply-and-demand-of-toy-fads). 4. Consult the "Market Equilibrium" resource from the Federal Reserve Education website (www.federalreserveeducation.org/teaching-resources/economics/markets/market-equilibrium). Have Google Translate available for students so that they can communicate their thoughts during the class discussion.
Conclusion (10 minutes) 1. **Review**: Recap the key points of the lesson, highlighting the concepts of supply and demand and their effects on prices. 2. **Exit Ticket**: Ask students to write one thing they learned about supply and demand and one example of how it affects prices in real life. 3. **Homework**: Assign a short research task in which students find an example of a recent price change in a product they are interested in and write a paragraph explaining the supply-and-demand factors involved.	If students are newcomers, have them answer the question for the exit ticket verbally to either you or another teacher in the room.

Table 7.3.3 *Vocabulary Guide: Understanding Supply and Demand*

Word	Tier	Definition	Example	Translation
demand	2	amount of goods that are wanted		
supply	2	amount of goods available		

Table 7.3.4 *Graphic Organizer: Understanding Supply and Demand*

supply	market equality	demand
What is *supply*?	What is *market equality*?	What is *demand*?
[insert picture]	[insert picture]	[insert picture]
[define in your own words]	[define in your own words]	[define in your own words]
[write a sentence using a sentence starter]	[write a sentence using a sentence starter]	[write a sentence using a sentence starter]

Table 7.3.5 *Sentence Starters: Understanding Supply and Demand*

Category	Sentence Starter
General Supply-and-Demand Concepts	• When the demand for ___ increases, ___ tends to happen because ___. • As the supply of ___ decreases, ___ occurs due to ___. • The relationship between supply and demand is evident when ___. • An increase in ___ results in ___, demonstrating the law of supply/demand.
Explaining Shifts in Supply or Demand	• A shift in demand occurs when ___, causing ___. • The supply of ___ changes when ___, which leads to ___. • As consumers' preferences for ___ change, the demand ___. • An external factor, such as ___, influenced the supply/demand of ___ by ___.
Market Equilibrium	• Market equilibrium is reached when ___. • If supply exceeds demand, ___ occurs, leading to ___. • When demand surpasses supply, the result is ___.
Specific Scenarios	• For example, when ___ is in high demand, ___ happens in the market because ___. • A real-world example of supply and demand is ___, where ___ caused ___. • In the case of ___, a surplus/shortage occurred because ___.
Predicting Outcomes	• If ___ happens, it is likely that ___ because of the principles of supply and demand. • Based on current trends, we can expect ___ to impact ___ due to ___.

Lesson 4: Exploring Landforms and Physical Features

Lesson by Mary Brennan

Table 7.4.1 *Middle School Lesson Overview: Exploring Landforms and Physical Features*

Exploring Landforms and Physical Features	
Duration	75 minutes
Differentiation Strategies	• visuals • digital maps • sentence frames • graphic organizers • verbal responses
C3 Framework Standards	**D1.4.6–8.** Explain how the relationship between supporting questions and compelling questions is mutually reinforcing. **D1.5.6–8.** Determine the kinds of sources that will be helpful in answering compelling and supporting questions, taking into consideration multiple points of views represented in the sources. **D2.Geo.1.6–8.** Construct maps to represent and explain the spatial patterns of cultural and environmental characteristics. **D2.Geo.2.6–8.** Use maps, satellite images, photographs, and other representations to explain relationships between the locations of places and regions, and changes in their environmental characteristics. **D2.Geo.3.6–8.** Use paper based and electronic mapping and graphing techniques to represent and analyze spatial patterns of different environmental and cultural characteristics. **D3.3.6–8.** Identify evidence that draws information from multiple sources to support claims, noting evidentiary limitations. **D4.2.6–8.** Construct explanations using reasoning, correct sequence, examples, and details with relevant information and data, while acknowledging the strengths and weaknesses of the explanations. **D4.3.6–8.** Present adaptations of arguments and explanations on topics of interest to others to reach audiences and venues outside the classroom using print and oral technologies (e.g., posters, essays, letters, debates, speeches, reports, and maps) and digital technologies (e.g., Internet, social media, and digital documentary).

Content/Language Objectives	1. Students will identify, describe, and explain different types of landforms and physical features using descriptive language. 2. Students will understand the formation of these landforms, their features, and their significance by using academic vocabulary in both oral and written forms. This lesson combines the content and language objectives. By combining the language objective with the content objective, teachers give students a clear understanding of what is expected and how they can demonstrate their knowledge. Language Objectives 1. Students will use descriptive language to explain the characteristics of various landforms. 2. Students will use academic vocabulary related to geography in both oral and written forms. Content Objectives 1. Students will identify and describe different types of landforms and physical features. 2. Students will understand the formation of these landforms, their features, and their significance.
Materials and Technology	• world map and physical feature maps • interactive digital map (e.g., Google Earth) • graphic organizers (e.g., chart for listing features and descriptions) • visual aids (pictures of different landforms) • vocabulary guide (Table 7.4.3) • sentence starters (Table 7.4.4) • computers or tablets • handouts with simplified texts about landforms • projector and screen
Teacher Background	This lesson will focus on understanding various landforms and physical features of the Earth, such as mountains, rivers, valleys, and plateaus. The lesson will integrate both content and language objectives with differentiated strategies to support MLEs and struggling students.
Assessment	1. **Formative Assessment**: Use group discussions, pair shares, and individual sentence constructions to assess understanding and language use. 2. **Summative Assessment**: Evaluate group presentations and written descriptions based on content accuracy, use of descriptive language, and explanations of formation. This lesson is designed to support students' success in the summative assessment.

Table 7.4.2 *Middle School Lesson Procedures and Differentiation: Exploring Landforms and Physical Features*

Lesson Procedures	Differentiation Strategies
Introduction (10 minutes) 1. **Hook**: Show a short video clip connected to your textbook featuring diverse landforms and physical features from around the world. 2. **Discussion**: Ask students to share their thoughts on the video and list different landforms they recognized. 3. **Objectives Overview**: Explain the content and language objectives of the lesson.	Videos are excellent materials for MLEs because they combine visual, auditory, and contextual clues to support language development and content understanding. They help make abstract ideas more concrete, provide models of academic language in use, and can be paused or replayed for clarity. Videos also engage learners with diverse learning styles and offer opportunities for discussion, vocabulary development, and comprehension practice
Main Activity: *Exploring Landforms (15 minutes)* 1. **Interactive Map Exploration**: Using the digital map, guide students through various landforms around the world. 2. **Group Work**: Divide students into small groups and assign each group a specific landform to explore (e.g., mountains, rivers, valleys, plateaus). 3. **Graphic Organizer**: Provide groups with a chart to list characteristics of their assigned landform and examples of where they are found.	Use interactive digital maps that include multilingual support. Many of these will translate on the computer for students to make better connections.
Small Group Discussion: *Descriptive Language Practice (15 minutes)* 1. **Vocabulary Introduction**: Introduce key vocabulary related to landforms using visual aids and a vocabulary guide (Table 7.4.3). 2. **Sentence Construction**: Provide sentence starters (Figure 7.4.4) to help students describe their landforms. For example, "Mountains are characterized by __" "Rivers flow through __ because __." 3. **Pair Share**: Have students work in pairs to practice describing their landforms using the provided vocabulary and sentence structures.	See the simplified description of terms in Table 7.4.3. You can put these on the board, create a graphic organizer, or have students draw a picture of and label each term. See the sentence starters in Figure 7.4.4 to support students.

Whole Class Discussion:

Form and Function (10 minutes)

1. **Explanation**: Discuss how different landforms are formed (e.g., tectonic activity for mountains, erosion for valleys).
2. **Modeling**: Model a few examples on the board, such as "Mountains are formed by tectonic activity; therefore, they are often found at plate boundaries."
3. **Practice**: Ask students to create their own explanations about how their assigned landforms are formed using the sentence starters and word banks.

Activity:

Presentation and Sharing (15 minutes)

1. **Group Presentations**: Each group presents their landform, describing its characteristics, formation, and examples using descriptive and academic language.
2. **Class Discussion**: Facilitate a discussion on the similarities and differences among the landforms.
3. **Assessment**: As groups present, the teacher assesses their content accuracy, use of descriptive language, and explanations of formation.

Modeling and allowing discussion are powerful strategies for supporting MLEs. Modeling provides clear examples of language use, academic tasks, or problem-solving processes, helping students understand expectations and reduce confusion. When teachers think aloud or demonstrate step-by-step actions, MLEs can connect language with meaning. Allowing structured discussions gives MLEs the chance to practice using new vocabulary and language structures in a low-pressure setting. Peer interaction builds confidence, reinforces understanding, and encourages the use of academic language in meaningful ways.

Conclusion (10 minutes)

1. **Review**: Recap the key points of the lesson, highlighting the characteristics of different landforms and their formation.
2. **Exit Ticket**: Ask students to write one thing they learned about landforms and one example of a landform they find interesting.
3. **Homework**: Assign a short research task where students find an example of a landform in their local area or a famous landform worldwide and write a paragraph describing it.

If students are newcomers, have them answer the question for the exit ticket verbally to either you or another teacher in the room.

Table 7.4.3 *Vocabulary Guide: Exploring Landforms and Physical Features*

Word	Tier	Definition	Example	Translation
desert	1	dry land with very little rain		
hill	1	smaller and round mountain		
island	1	land surrounded by water		
lake	1	still water surrounded by land		
mountain	1	tall and rocky area that rises high above the land		
plain	1	flat and wide area of land		
river	1	flowing water that moves across the land		
valley	1	low area between mountains or hills		

Table 7.4.4 *Sentence Starters: Exploring Landforms and Physical Features*

Category	Sentence Starters
Describing Landforms	• A [landform] is a natural feature on Earth, such as ____. • The [landform] is found in ____. • This landform is usually ____ (tall, flat, dry, etc.) and is made by ____.
Comparing and Contrasting	• A [landform] is similar to a [landform] because ____. • A [landform] is different from a [landform] because ____. • Unlike [landform], a [landform] is ____.
Sharing Facts	• One interesting fact about [landform] is ____. • [Landform] is formed by ____. • People use [landform] for ____.
Asking Questions	• What makes a [landform] special? • How is a [landform] formed? • Where can we find a [landform]?

Lesson 5: Thanksgiving

Lesson by Mary Brennan

Table 7.5.1 *Middle School Lesson Overview: Thanksgiving*

Understanding Bias in the Thanksgiving Story	
Duration	60 minutes
Differentiation Strategies	• sentence starters • graphic organizers • vocabulary
C3 Framework Standards	**D1.2.6–8.** Explain points of agreement experts have about interpretations and applications of disciplinary concepts and ideas associated with a compelling question. **D1.5.6–8.** Determine the kinds of sources that will be helpful in answering compelling and supporting questions, taking into consideration multiple points of views represented in the sources. **D2.His.4.6–8.** Analyze multiple factors that influenced the perspectives of people during different historical eras. **D3.1.6–8.** Gather relevant information from multiple sources while using the origin, authority, structure, context, and corroborative value of the sources to guide the selection. **D3.2.6–8.** Evaluate the credibility of a source by determining its relevance and intended use. **D4.2.6–8.** Construct explanations using reasoning, correct sequence, examples, and details with relevant information and data, while acknowledging the strengths and weaknesses of the explanations. **D4.1.6–8.** Construct arguments using claims and evidence from multiple sources, while acknowledging the strengths and limitations of the arguments.
Content/Language Objectives	1. Students will explore multiple perspectives of the Thanksgiving story, including the perspectives of the Pilgrims, Native Americans, and modern interpretations using vocabulary such as *bias, perspective, narrative,* and *primary/secondary sources.* 2. Students will identify how bias influences historical narratives and popular traditions by comparing two or more perspectives. 3. Students will reflect on how understanding multiple perspectives deepens historical understanding by sharing their findings and opinions through structured discussions and writing.

Materials and Technology	• graphic organizer, such as a Venn diagram or comparison chart (Table 7.5.3)
	• texts (Figure 7.5.1):
	  ◦ The Traditional Story of Thanksgiving (False)
	  ◦ How the Holiday Was Established
	  ◦ Historical Narrative
	• multimedia: Short video clips or infographics on Thanksgiving history from both perspectives
	• vocabulary guide (e.g., *bias, perspective, harvest*)
	• sentence frames: Structured prompts for analysis and discussion
	• art supplies: For creative reflection activities, if time permits

Teacher Background	Almost everything we know and celebrate about Thanksgiving is a lie. We teach many of the victors' stories, but how many of them are not true or half-truths? We teach about Columbus who "sailed the ocean blue in 1492," but this is only one perspective. Teaching about Thanksgiving for MLEs and Indigenous students requires a thoughtful approach because they may not be familiar with the historical context or may have a different cultural perspective. It is important to provide accurate, inclusive, and respectful information that helps all students understand the complex history behind the holiday, rather than relying on simplified or traditional narratives. As you research various historical perspectives, keep in mind the stories students have been taught. Empathy will be a key piece. Teachers should understand • The traditional Thanksgiving story, its origins, and its cultural significance; and • Indigenous perspectives on Thanksgiving, including critiques of the holiday. For this lesson, it is crucial to consider perspective. How many of you were taught things about Thanksgiving that you later found out were not true? Did you know that Thanksgiving was not even a federal holiday until the Civil War? Check out some archival information from the National Archives (2021). The Oklahoma City Public Schools Native American Student Services (n.d.) created a resource that gives great background information for both teachers and students.
Assessment	1. **Creative Reflection:** Have students create a poster or infographic showing both perspectives of Thanksgiving. 2. **Writing Assignment:** Students write a short essay answering, "What does Thanksgiving mean to you after learning about different perspectives?"

Table 7.5.2 *Middle School Lesson Procedures: Thanksgiving*

Lesson Procedures	Differentiation Strategies
Introduction (10 minutes) 1. **Hook**: Show contrasting images of a traditional Thanksgiving feast and a National Day of Mourning protest. 2. **Discussion Questions**: • What do you see in these images? • Why might people have different feelings about Thanksgiving? 3. **Vocabulary Introduction**: Define *bias and perspective*, linking the definitions to how stories about the past are told.	Teaching Thanksgiving to MLEs without a frame of reference requires providing background knowledge about U.S. history, cultural traditions, and the significance of the holiday. Instruction needs to start with building context: explaining who the Pilgrims and Native Americans were, why people left Europe, and how early settlers interacted with Indigenous communities. Visuals, timelines, maps, and simplified texts are especially helpful. It is also important to clarify common myths and present multiple perspectives, especially Indigenous voices, to provide a fuller picture. Teachers should connect the concept of giving thanks to students' own cultural traditions to make the content more relatable and meaningful. For a story of the Day of Mourning for Native Americans, see Mayflower 400 (n.d.).

Main Activity (20 minutes) 1. **Mini-Lecture**: Explain the traditional Thanksgiving story (e.g., Pilgrims and Wampanoag sharing a meal after a successful harvest). Highlight the positive aspects of cooperation and survival. 2. **Discussion**: Introduce Indigenous perspectives, focusing on how Thanksgiving is seen by some as a time of mourning and a reminder of colonization and loss. Use examples of oral histories or modern reflections. 3. **Model analysis**: Read short excerpts from the traditional narrative and an Indigenous perspective. Think aloud to identify bias (e.g., word choice, missing voices).	Use sentence starters like "The Pilgrims' story says _____, but the Native American (Indigenous) perspective says _____." Refer to how you were taught about Thanksgiving and give historical reasons for making this a holiday. Read about the Wampanoag perspective in a resource from the National Museum of the American Indian (McVay, 2017). **Simplified Texts**: Provide shorter or adapted versions of the texts for analysis (see Figure 7.5.1).

Guided Practice (20 minutes)
• Group Work:
  ○ Divide students into small groups and give each group excerpts from two perspectives:
    ◆ Example 1: Traditional Thanksgiving story
    ◆ Example 2: An Indigenous reflection on the same event .
  ○ Use a graphic organizer to compare:
    ◆ Who is telling the story?
    ◆ What details are included or left out?
    ◆ What feelings or opinions are expressed?
  ○ Provide sentence frames to support discussion:
    ◆ In this story, the Pilgrims are described as ____.
    ◆ In the other story, the Wampanoag are described as ____.
	Collaborative Work: Pair MLEs with peers who can support language development.
	
	Students need the opportunity to hear other students' interpretation of the reading and discussions.
	
	The graphic organizer (Table 7.5.3) can be modified to fit your resources.

Collaborative Sharing and Reflection (10 minutes)
• Class Discussion: Groups share their findings using structured prompts.
  ○ Reflection Questions:
    ◆ Why do people tell different stories about the same event?
    ◆ How can understanding different perspectives help us think critically about history?
  ○ Encourage students to share personal reflections or connections to their own cultural traditions.
	Sentence Frames: Offer structured templates for discussing and writing.
	
	PBS Kids gives practical advice for guiding a discussion about Thanksgiving as a celebration of gratitude (Turner, 2019).

Table 7.5.3 *Thanksgiving Graphic Organizer*

Topic	Perspective 1	Perspective 2	Similarities (What is the same?)
Historical Context: What happened in the story?			
Key Characters or Group: Who is in the story?			
Major Events: What do they believe?			
Values and Beliefs: What do they celebrate?			
Impact on Modern Views: How do they feel?			

Figure 7.5.1 *Thanksgiving Readings*

The Traditional Story of Thanksgiving (False)

The holiday commemorates when the pilgrims, who arrived in Plymouth, Massachusetts, on the Mayflower, celebrated a successful harvest. They are said to have shared a meal with their Native American neighbors in a spirit of cooperation and friendship.

In modern-day elementary schools, younger students often make turkey crafts or dress up as pilgrims and Native Americans for Thanksgiving plays. As students get older, they learn more about the reasons the pilgrims left Europe, their journey across the Atlantic, and the connection between their hard work and survival and the founding ideas of the United States.

Modified version

A long time ago, the pilgrims came to a place called Plymouth, Massachusetts, on a ship called the Mayflower. After working hard to grow food, they had a big harvest (picking food). To celebrate, they shared a meal with their Native American neighbors.

In some classrooms today, young children draw turkeys shaped like their hands or dress up as pilgrims and Native Americans for plays about Thanksgiving. Older students learn why the pilgrims came to America and how they worked hard to start a new life. This is often connected to the important ideas that shaped the United States.

How the Holiday Was Established[1]

Thanksgiving today is very different from the Plymouth harvest festival 400 years ago, but it has an interesting history. In colonial New England, Thanksgiving started as a serious and quiet day. Instead of feasting, people fasted and spent time reflecting.

Over time, different states and the federal government announced days of Thanksgiving, but they did not happen regularly. In the mid-1800s, after years of work by magazine editor Sarah Josepha Hale, Thanksgiving became a national holiday. As the holiday grew, people wanted an American story to go with it, so the Plymouth harvest festival was reimagined as the "First Thanksgiving."

Today, Thanksgiving continues to change as each generation adds its own traditions. However, coming together to share a meal and give thanks remains an important part of the holiday.

Modified version

Thanksgiving today is very different from the first celebration 400 years ago. In colonial early America, it was a serious day. People did not eat big meals; they fasted and thought about life quietly.

Later, states and the U.S. government created days of Thanksgiving, but they were not regular. In the 1800s, a magazine editor named Sarah Josepha Hale worked hard to make it a national holiday. She was successful. Over time, people wanted a special American story, so they made the Plymouth harvest into the "First Thanksgiving."

Thanksgiving changes with every generation, but families still come together to share food and say thank you for what they have.

Historical Narrative[2]

In 1621, with help from their new Wampanoag allies, the Europeans were able to survive their first year in America and have a successful harvest. They planted crops using seeds from Europe and corn provided by Massasoit, a Wampanoag leader. Although the European seeds did not grow well, the corn saved them.

To celebrate, the Europeans held a festival called the Harvest Home, a tradition many had experienced as children in Europe. This festival included feasting, drinking, sports, and parading while firing muskets. Edward Winslow, a leader of the group, wrote a letter on December 11, 1621, describing the celebration.[3] This letter is the main written account of what we now call the "First Thanksgiving."

The celebration did not focus on giving thanks, but it is remembered as the beginning of the modern Thanksgiving holiday. The feast was based on European traditions but also included contributions from the Wampanoag. Native foods like wild duck, goose, turkey, and five deer provided by the Wampanoag were served alongside ale made from barley grown by the Europeans.

This three-day event is seen as a symbol of peaceful coexistence between Native Americans and Europeans, something that was rare in the 1600s.

Modified version

In 1621, the Europeans survived their first year in America with help from their Wampanoag allies (friends). They planted seeds from Europe and corn given to them by Massasoit, a Wampanoag leader. The European seeds did not grow well, but the corn saved them.

To celebrate, the Europeans held a festival called the Harvest Home. This was a European tradition with feasting (eating), drinking, sports, and firing muskets (guns). Edward Winslow, a leader of the group, wrote a letter on December 11, 1621, describing this celebration.[3] This letter is the main record of what we call the "First Thanksgiving."

The festival was not about giving thanks, but it became the start of today's Thanksgiving holiday. The Wampanoag contributed to the feast with wild duck, goose, turkey, and five deer. The Europeans added ale (beer) made from barley.

This three-day festival is remembered as a rare time when Native Americans and Europeans lived peacefully together.

Notes

1. Adapted from Sherman (2019).
2. Adapted from National Museum of the American Indian (n.d.).
3. Following is Edward Winslow's account. You can incorporate it into the texts or read it aloud to students.

> Our harvest being gotten in, our governor sent four men on fowling, that so we might after a special manner rejoice together after we had gathered the fruit of our labors. They four in one day killed as much fowl as, with a little help beside, served the company almost a week. At which time, amongst other recreations, we exercised our arms, many of the Indians coming amongst us, and among the rest their greatest king Massasoit, with some ninety men, whom for three days we entertained and feasted, and they went out and killed five deer, which they brought to the plantation and bestowed on our governor, and upon the captain and other. (as cited in Heath, 1963, p. 82)

Access and Engagement: Designing Instruction for Multilingual Learners of English in the High School Classroom

Lesson 6: Articles of Confederation
Lesson by Peggie Cypher and Mary Brennan

Table 7.6.1 *High School Lesson Overview: Articles of Confederation*

Articles of Confederation	
Duration	40 minutes
Differentiation Strategies	• vocabulary guide • simplified passages with audio or videos from BrainPOP or Simple History on YouTube • sentence starters
C3 Framework Standards	**D2.His.13.9-12.** Critique the appropriateness of the historical sources used in a secondary interpretation. **D3.3.9-12.** Identify evidence that draws information directly and substantively from multiple sources to detect inconsistencies in evidence in order to revise or strengthen claims.
Content/Language Objectives	Students will engage in collaborative discussions to comprehend key concepts, strengths, and vocabulary related to the Articles of Confederation.
Materials and Technology	• vocabulary guide (Table 7.6.3) • whiteboard and markers • Chromebook or other devices, if available • easy-to-comprehend passage with audio or a video with translation • copies of simplified Articles of Confederation text (translated if necessary) • a graphic organizer of the strengths and weaknesses of the Articles (Table 7.6.4) • sentence starter frames
Teacher Background	Use this lesson in its entirety or use parts to modify your regular lesson for MLEs. Talk to your MLEs to find out how much they already know about the topic and what background knowledge they have about it in their culture. This will help you connect the new information to what they already understand. For example, ask them about the type of government, constitution, or laws that exist in their home countries.
Assessment	1. Observe students' participation in group discussions and their ability to articulate key concepts. 2. Review students' graphic organizers to assess their understanding of the strengths and weaknesses of the Articles of Confederation. 3. Evaluate students' written paragraphs for accuracy and clarity.

Table 7.6.2 *High School Lesson Procedures: Articles of Confederation*

Lesson Procedures	Differentiation Strategies
Introduction (5 minutes) 1. Provide MLEs with a vocabulary guide including Tier 2 (general academic vocabulary used across contexts) and Tier 3 (content-specific words) with images and space for translation, drawings, or notes (Table 7.6.3). 2. With the whole class, brainstorm what a government does and write ideas on the whiteboard. 3. Remind students that the colonies needed to unify and plan a government after declaring American independence from Britain. 4. Introduce the Articles of Confederation as the first constitution (plan of government) of the United States.	Giving MLEs a vocabulary guide ahead of time or at the beginning of class allows them to use it as a reference during the lesson and after as a study guide. *Note.* Use websites like Diffit to generate lists such as this with images and to translate it into various languages.
Main Activity (25 minutes) Assign a short independent reading for background and comprehension. ***For Intermediate and High-Level MLEs*** Use a simplified passage with audio from Ducksters or websites such as Britannica Kids. ***For Beginning-Level MLEs*** Use a video from BrainPOP or Edpuzzle (if subscribed) or a video on YouTube (Pursuit of History; History Heroes), translating the subtitles into MLEs' home language as needed.	While MLEs can participate in most of the same activities as their grade-level peers, assigning alternative, simplified readings on complex or unfamiliar topics, such as historical documents, can ensure comprehension and grow MLEs' reading skills.
Talk (15 minutes) 1. Divide the class into groups of 4, mixing MLEs and non-MLEs. 2. Pass out the graphic organizer on strengths and weaknesses of the Articles of Confederation, and have students work together to fill it in (Table 7.6.4). 3. Bring the class back together and have groups share their responses. 4. Write them on the board in simple English. 5. Emphasize the challenges faced by the new nation under the Articles of Confederation, such as the lack of a strong central government.	MLEs learn by engaging with non-MLEs. Rather than grouping all MLEs together, create groups that mix MLEs and non-MLEs. Use a graphic organizer to guide the discussion.
Write (10 minutes) Ask students to write a 1-paragraph summary of the strengths and weaknesses of the Articles of Confederation.	Distribute sentence starters or write sentences such as the following on a board: The Articles of Confederation had both strengths and weaknesses. The strengths are _____. The weaknesses are _____.

Table 7.6.3 *Vocabulary Guide: Articles of Confederation*

Key Vocabulary				
Word	**Tier**	**Definition**	**Example**	**Translation**
amendment	3	change to a law		
constitution	3	the laws of government		
federal system	3	the structure of a government that divides power between a large national government and smaller state or local government		
government	2	the people who rule a country or area, including a president		
law	2	rule made by the government		
tax	2	money paid to the government by the people to build roads and schools		
unite	2	to bring together		

Table 7.6.4 *Graphic Organizer: Articles of Confederation*

Strengths	Weaknesses
Example: Congress could declare war.	Example: Congress could not collect taxes.

Lesson 7: The Bill of Rights
Lesson by Peggie Cypher

Table 7.7.1 *High School Lesson Overview: Bill of Rights*

Bill of Rights Scenarios	
Duration	40–50 minutes
Differentiation Strategies	This is a modified lesson on the amendments. It includes an easy-to-understand handout from the free iCivics Amendment Mini-Lesson and an amendments scenarios worksheet written in simple English.
C3 Framework Standards	**D2.His.11.9–12.** Critique the usefulness of historical sources for a specific historical inquiry based on their maker, date, place of origin, intended audience, and purpose. **D4.1.9–12.** Construct arguments using precise and knowledgeable claims, with evidence from multiple sources, while acknowledging counterclaims and evidentiary weaknesses.
Content/Language Objectives	Students will understand the essential vocabulary and meanings of the first 10 amendments and work in small groups to apply the amendments to a variety of scenarios.
Materials and Technology	• Big Ideas Sheet (Figure 7.7.1) • Amendment Guide from the iCivics Amendment Mini-Lesson with graphics of each amendment (optional) • essential Tier 2 and Tier 3 vocabulary guide (can be made on Diffit; Table 7.7.3) • modified Bill of Rights scenarios in simple English and with relevant examples (Figure 7.7.2)
Teacher Background	This lesson can serve as an introductory, review, or extension lesson on the Bill of Rights.
Assessment	1. Observe students' participation in group discussions and pair work. 2. Evaluate students' scenario worksheets for understanding of the main concepts.

Table 7.7.2 *High School Lesson Procedures: Bill of Rights*

Lesson Procedures	Differentiation Strategies
Introduction (5 minutes) 1. Provide MLEs with the vocabulary guide (Table 7.7.3) and the Big Ideas Sheet (Figure 7.7.1). 2. Tell students your new class rule is that when the bell rings, they must stand and say the Pledge of Allegiance (Hindu prayer, Muslim prayer, etc.) or they will automatically fail the class. Elicit responses to the new rule and ask students if they think the rule is fair. Why or why not?	A study sheet or summary of the essential ideas in simple English can provide background for those who are unfamiliar with the Bill of Rights.
Activity 1 *Talk (15 minutes)* 1. Explain that the Bill of Rights is the first 10 amendments that were added to the Constitution of the United States. It lists many of our basic rights. 2. Pass out and project the Amendment Advantage Guide from iCivics or something similar that includes an image and brief description of each amendment. 3. Ask students to look at the pictures while a volunteer reads each amendment. 4. Stop after each amendment to discuss.	Often, you will not have time to modify instructions for your MLEs. Take advantage of sites such iCivics that include social studies lessons complete with graphics, videos, and engaging games.
Activity 2 *Read & Write (15 minutes)* 1. Divide the class into pairs, placing an MLE with a friendly non-MLE student. 2. Distribute the scenarios worksheets (Figure 7.7.2). 3. Have the student pairs work together to read the scenarios and figure out which amendment each scenario violates. 4. Have students write the amendment number and paraphrase it in their own words.	These scenarios are written in simple sentence structures to enable MLEs to comprehend them. They are inclusive of students from various cultural backgrounds. The non-MLE student may need to do the writing, but if able, encourage the MLE to write some of it, telling them not to worry about spelling and grammar.
Conclusion *Talk (10 minutes)* 1. Bring the class together and discuss how the United States might be different without some of our fundamental rights. 2. If time allows, have students rate three rights that are most important to them.	

Table 7.7.3 *Vocabulary Guide: Bill of Rights*

Word	Tier	Definition	Example	Translation
assembly	2	a group of people who are gathered together		
double jeopardy	3	being tried in court twice for the same crime	**2X**	
due process	3	the government and courts must follow the law in a fair way		
expression	2	a way to show how you feel, such as talking, writing, or protesting		
police search	2	when the police look for something in a house or a car		
trial	2	a court hearing where a judge or jury decides if someone did something wrong (is guilty or innocent)		
warrant	2	a paper that gives the police permission (the okay) to search someone's house		
weapon	2	a thing used to fight, such as a gun or a sword		

Note. Image for *assembly* from "an assembly at school" prompt, Canva Dream Lab, 13 January 2025, www.canva.com/dream-lab. Image for *due process* by Sora Shimazaki, Pexels, www.pexels.com/photo/judges-desk-with-gavel-and-scales-5669619. Image for *police search* from "police search" prompt, Canva Dream Lab, 13 January 2025, www.canva.com/dream-lab. Image for *warrant* from "police warrant" prompt, Canva Dream Lab, 13 January 2025, www.canva.com/dream-lab.

Figure 7.7.1 *Big Ideas for Bill of Rights*

The Big Ideas

- The Bill of Rights is the first 10 rights (freedoms) in the U.S. Constitution.
- They guarantee (promise) that each person will have rights such as the freedom to speak freely and practice any religion.
- The rights also put restrictions (limits) on what the government can do.
- They were added to the Constitution so that the federal government would not have too much power.

Figure 7.7.2 *Bill of Rights Worksheet*

Bill of Rights Scenarios Worksheet

Instructions: Read the scenarios and write which Amendment was violated (goes against; fails to respect) in each story and why.

1. EXAMPLE: Ivan was driving down Sylvania Avenue. A police officer stopped him and searched his car. The police officer also took his phone and searched Ivan's text messages. Ivan was arrested for texting while driving. Which amendment was violated?

ANSWER: The 4th Amendment was violated because searches are not allowed without the consent of a judge.

2. Sixteen-year-old Juman wore her hijab to school. The principal told her to take it off or she would be sent home.

_____

3. Home robberies keep happening near Northstar High School. To keep everyone safe, the mayor ordered soldiers to sleep in the houses of the people in that neighborhood.

_____

4. Juan was at a high school soccer game. He bought some candy. He threw the wrappers in the garbage but missed. Ten minutes later, a police officer arrested him for littering. Juan was sent to jail for 25 years.

_____

5. Ming was talking to a friend about how she did not like the president of the United States. She was arrested and put in jail.

_____

6. An older woman bought a gun to protect herself. Her neighbor told the police. The woman was arrested and sent to jail.

_____

7. A young man named Helal was arrested for computer hacking. He had to wait in jail for 10 years before he was put on trial.

_____

8. Maria wanted to visit her family in California. When she got there, she was arrested for traveling out of her state.

_____

9. Seventeen-year-old Hamz was arrested for a robbery near downtown Chicago. He was in New York at the time. Later, he was taken to the courthouse, and the judge quickly decided he was guilty.

_____

10. The police were looking for a lost dog. They entered each house in the neighborhood, turning over furniture and searching for it.

Lesson 8: Jim Crow Laws

Lesson by Peggie Cypher

Table 7.8.1 *High School Lesson Overview: Jim Crow Laws*

Jim Crow Laws & Segregation	
Duration	40–50 minutes
Differentiation Strategies	• vocabulary guide • sentence starters
C3 Framework Standards	**D2.His.4.9–12.** Analyze complex and interacting factors that influenced the perspectives of people during different historical eras. **D3.1.9–12.** Gather relevant information from multiple sources representing a wide range of views while using the origin, authority, structure, context, and corroborative value of the sources to guide the selection.
Content/Language Objectives	Students will collaborate in groups to read and summarize Jim Crow laws.
Materials and Technology	• projector • key vocabulary (Table 7.8.3) • Big Ideas sheet (Figure 7.8.1) • historical photographs (Figure 7.8.2) • Jim Crow WebQuest worksheet (Figure 7.8.3)
Teacher Background	This lesson uses collaborative learning to complete a WebQuest on the Jim Crow laws some states enacted after the Civil War. It can be part of a Reconstruction unit or a starting point on the Civil Rights Movement. It gives multileveled MLEs an opportunity to work with their general education peers.
Assessment	Evaluate worksheets for accuracy and simple paraphrasing.

Table 7.8.2 *High School Lesson Procedures: Jim Crow Laws*

Lesson Procedures	Differentiation Strategies
Introduction (10 minutes) 1. Project two Library of Congress photographs of distinct classrooms during the Jim Crow era (Figure 7.8.2). Leave out the title, date, and other information. 2. Ask the students to name some details they see in the photographs. Lead a discussion on the differences between the photographs and what that might mean. 3. Explain that both photographs were taken by Jack Delano in Green County, Georgia, in 1941. 4. Tell students that the photographs represent an example of the Jim Crow laws enacted in many states after the Civil War until 1965. 5. Project a photograph of Jim Crow (Thomas Rice) and explain who he was.	Introducing or reviewing a lesson with photographs allows MLEs an additional comprehension component in addition to listening and reading.

Main Activity (20 minutes)	Provide sheets of the Big Ideas and essential Tier 2 vocabulary to aid in growing background knowledge and general comprehension.
1. Provide MLEs with the Big Ideas summary (Figure 7.8.1) and Tier 2 and 3 vocabulary guide (Table 7.8.3). 2. Divide students into groups of 4, mixing MLEs and non-MLEs. 3. Tell students they are going on a WebQuest to learn about Jim Crow laws and the unwritten rules that were expected. 4. Project the following sites: • Black Past webpage about Jim Crow Laws in Tennessee [www.blackpast.org/african-american-history/jim-crow-laws-tennessee-1866–1955] • The Jim Crow Museum webpage *What Was Jim Crow?* [jimcrowmuseum.ferris.edu/what.htm] • Getty Images collection of images of the Jim Crow era [www.gettyimages.com/photos/jim-crow-laws] 5. Distribute the Jim Crow WebQuest Worksheet (Figure 7.8.3) and ask students to work together to complete it. 6. After the allotted time, have students share the information from their worksheets with the class. This may need to wait until the next class period.	Mixing groups with MLEs and non-MLEs allows MLEs to interact in informal ways and to model students' speaking and writing structures.
Conclusion (10 minutes) As an exit ticket, have each student write a short reflection on how groups of people today, immigrants, the unhoused, Native Americans, LGBTQ+, or people of certain religions or ethnicities may still face challenges to acceptance and full rights.	Check in with MLEs to elicit connections they can make in their lives about being treated unfairly. Provide sentence starters for their reflections, such as the following: • One group that is still treated unfairly is ___. • An example of this is ___.

Figure 7.8.1 *Big Ideas for Jim Crow*

The Big Ideas
Segregation is keeping specific groups of people apart. After the Civil War between the northern and the southern states, enslaved people gained their freedom. However, people in the South made laws called Jim Crow to keep Black and white people separate. These laws were not fair to Black people.

Table 7.8.3 *Vocabulary Guide: Jim Crow Laws*

Word	Tier	Definition	Example	Translation
14th Amendment	3	the law that guaranteed (promised) equal protection under law for all people born in the United States (all citizens)		
equal treatment	2	all people have the same rights under the law		

interracial marriage	2	the marriage of two people from different races or ethnic backgrounds (such as Black and white people)		
Jim Crow Laws	3	unfair laws that Southern states created to keep Black people and white people separate		
Plessy v. Ferguson	3	an important decision the made by the Supreme Court, saying it was legal for Black and white people to use separate facilities such as restrooms, drinking fountains, and trains		
racism	2	the belief that one race or group of people is better than another		
segregation	2	separating people (Black people at this time were required to live in separate neighborhoods, go to separate schools, and play on separate sports teams)		
separate	2	to keep apart		

Note. Image for "14th Amendment" from "The 14th Amendment" prompt, Canva Dream Lab, 13 January 2025 (www.canva.com/dream-lab). Image for "Jim Crow Laws" from *Drinking fountain on the county courthouse lawn, Halifax, North Carolina* [Photograph], by J. Vachon, 1938, Library of Congress (www.loc.gov/resource/fsa.8a03228). In the public domain. Image for "Plessy v. Ferguson" from *Negro Expulsion From Railway Car, Philadelphia* [Illustration], 1856, The Illustrated London News, Library of Congress (www.loc.gov/item/2007678048). In the public domain. Image for "segregation" from *Negro Drinking at "Colored" Water Cooler in Streetcar Terminal, Oklahoma City, Oklahoma* [Photograph], by R. Lee, 1939, Library of Congress (www.loc.gov/item/2017740552). In the public domain. Image for "separate" from "white ball separate from blue balls" prompt, Canva Dream Lab, 12 April 2025 (www.canva.com/dream-lab).

Figure 7.8.2 *Historical Photographs by Jack Delano*

Note. From *White Plains, Greene County, Georgia. The three-teacher Negro school* [Photograph], by J. Delano, October 1941, Library of Congress (www.loc.gov/item/2017796644). In the public domain.

Note. From *White Plains, Greene County, Georgia. Studying insects in a classroom at the school* [Photograph], by J. Delano, October 1941, Library of Congress (www.loc.gov/item/2017796546). In the public domain.

Figure 7.8.3 *Jim Crow WebQuest Worksheet*

<h3 style="text-align:center">Jim Crow Webquest</h3>

Names _____ Class _____

Part I

Look over the Black Past webpage about Jim Crow laws in Tennessee [www.blackpast.org/african-american-history/jim-crow-laws-tennessee-1866–1955]. Use your own words to summarize two statutes (laws) in Tennessee that apply to each category.

Marriage
1.
2.

Education
1.
2.

Public Accommodations (parks, theaters, etc.)
1.
2.

Transportation
1.
2.

Part II

A. Go to the Jim Crow Museum's webpage *What Was Jim Crow?* (jimcrowmuseum.ferris.edu/what.htm). Look at the first bulleted list. Paraphrase (use your own words) three unwritten rules of etiquette norms (polite behavior) that were expected of Black people.
1.
2.
3.

Lesson 9: The Industrial Revolution
Lesson by Kaedmon Fulton

Table 7.9.1 *High School Lesson Overview: The Industrial Revolution*

The Industrial Revolution	
Duration	50 minutes
Differentiation Strategies	• visuals • primary source documents at progressive levels • alternative document activity for beginning MLEs • sentence frames
C3 Framework Standards	**D2.His.2.9–12.** Analyze change and continuity in historical eras. **D2.His.16.9–12.** Integrate evidence from multiple relevant historical sources and interpretations into a reasoned argument about the past. **D3.3.9–12.** Identify evidence that draws information directly and substantively from multiple sources to detect inconsistencies in evidence in order to revise or strengthen claims. **D4.2.9–12.** Construct explanations using sound reasoning, correct sequence (linear or non-linear), examples, and details with significant and pertinent information and data, while acknowledging the strengths and weaknesses of the explanation given its purpose (e.g., cause and effect, chronological, procedural, technical).
Content/Language Objectives	Students will describe how the industrial revolution changed the way people worked and lived by using time phrases in speaking and writing.
Materials and Technology	• interactive whiteboard or other display system • vocabulary guide (Table 7.9.3) • student packet (includes do-now image and graphic organizer, gallery walk organizer, documents and questions, exit ticket) • image sets (posted around the room before class starts) • for beginning MLEs: set of sentence frames and word bank
Teacher Background	This lesson introduces students to the industrial revolution as an economic and social turning point in Britain. It builds on previous lessons about the causes of the industrial revolution and the innovations that came into use during this time.
Assessment	**Formative:** Circulate through the room as students work, monitoring progress and checking for understanding. **Summative:** Students answer the question "Why was the industrial revolution a turning point?" by writing a paragraph about how people's ways of living and working changed. To be successful, students need to be able to • identify and describe specific ways life changed because of the industrial revolution, • use evidence from documents (images or text) to support their claims, and • use time phrases (e.g., *before the industrial revolution, after the industrial revolution*) to put their observations in context.

Table 7.9.2 *High School Lesson Procedures: The Industrial Revolution*

Lesson Procedures	Differentiation Strategies
Introduction (10 minutes) 1. Students study a photograph of children working in a factory and make observations, using a See, Think, Wonder organizer. 2. Students turn and talk with an elbow partner, sharing their observations and ideas about the image. 3. Whole-class discussion: The teacher invites students to share out what they observed.	This activity allows every student to participate at their own level—whether they are responding in full sentences or single words, and whether they have lots of background knowledge to recall or are simply making observations about the images. Additionally, having students share with an elbow partner before full-group discussion can give MLEs a chance to prepare their ideas before sharing in front of the whole class.
Gallery Walk (15 minutes): *Setup: Before class, post the image sets around the room. (Each image set shows an aspect of life or work before and after the industrial revolution.)* 1. The teacher reviews the expectations for the gallery walk protocol (e.g., move at your own pace, discuss with the people around you before writing down your observations, write your ideas in whatever language is most comfortable). 2. The teacher models using the first image set, making and recording specific observations about how people worked before and after the industrial revolution. 3. Students move around the room at their own pace, discussing the image sets and writing down their observations.	Strategy: Using visuals Gallery walks are a great activity for classrooms with diverse language proficiency because everyone can participate at their own level. The information in the photographs is equally accessible to all students, regardless of language.
Document Work (15 minutes): 1. Students work individually or in pairs to analyze documents about living and working conditions during the industrial revolution. Scaffolding questions move from basic comprehension to analysis of the source. 2. The first provided document is at a lower reading level than the second one; MLEs and other students with lower reading proficiency can work with the first document only while other students can work with both documents or only with the second, as time allows. *Alternate activity for beginning MLEs:* 1. Instead of document work, beginning MLEs work in a small group to use sentence frames ("Before the industrial revolution, people worked ___." "After the industrial revolution, people worked ___.") and a word bank to make observations about the image sets in full sentences. Depending on what kind of practice the students need, they can copy the sentences they create or practice saying them out loud (or both).	A convenient way to differentiate the main document work activity is to have the practice period of the lesson move from easier to more challenging reading levels. Students who need a challenge will make it to the more difficult texts; those who need a lower reading level can just work with the first document.

Summary/Assessment (10 minutes):	Strategy: Sentence frames
1. The teacher reminds the class that, in history, a *turning point* is a major change; the industrial revolution is one example of a turning point. The students now need to explain why that is, using what they have learned from the photographs and documents. The teacher displays the sentence frames on the board and reminds students that they need to clearly explain how things were before and after when they are writing about a change. 2. Students complete the exit ticket (Why was the industrial Rrevolution a turning point?). The teacher circulates and reminds students to use their resources (sentence frames, observations from the gallery walk and source work, etc.).	In this assessment, sentence frames are provided for all students; those who need them will use them, and those who do not can just ignore them. For beginning MLEs, more practice may be needed. For this reason, a practice activity is provided for this group of students to complete instead of the document work.

Table 7.9.3 *Vocabulary Guide: The Industrial Revolution*

Word	Tier	Definition	Example	Translation
agriculture	3	farming		
factory	2	a place where people use machines to make things		
industry / industrial	2	making products using machines		
labor	2	work		
turning point	3	an important change		

Figure 7.9.1

See 👁	Think ☁	Wonder 🤔
I observe ...	I think ...	I want to know ...

Gallery Walk Notes

Image Set	Observe (1): Before the industrial revolution ...	Observe (2): After the industrial revolution ...	Evaluate: This change is positive/negative because ...
A			
B			
C			
D			
E			

Document 1

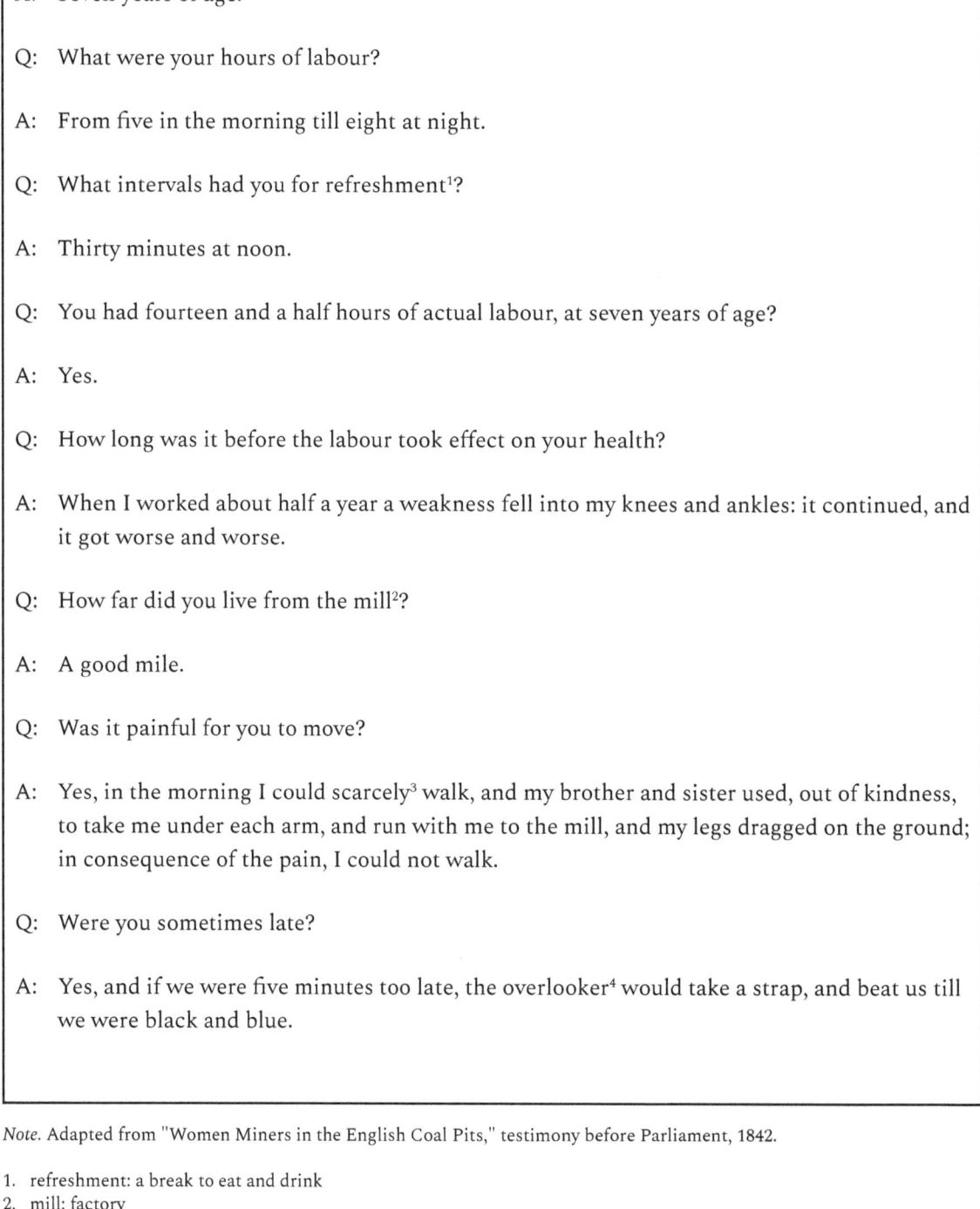

Q: At what age did you start work?

A: Seven years of age.

Q: What were your hours of labour?

A: From five in the morning till eight at night.

Q: What intervals had you for refreshment[1]?

A: Thirty minutes at noon.

Q: You had fourteen and a half hours of actual labour, at seven years of age?

A: Yes.

Q: How long was it before the labour took effect on your health?

A: When I worked about half a year a weakness fell into my knees and ankles: it continued, and it got worse and worse.

Q: How far did you live from the mill[2]?

A: A good mile.

Q: Was it painful for you to move?

A: Yes, in the morning I could scarcely[3] walk, and my brother and sister used, out of kindness, to take me under each arm, and run with me to the mill, and my legs dragged on the ground; in consequence of the pain, I could not walk.

Q: Were you sometimes late?

A: Yes, and if we were five minutes too late, the overlooker[4] would take a strap, and beat us till we were black and blue.

Note. Adapted from "Women Miners in the English Coal Pits," testimony before Parliament, 1842.

1. refreshment: a break to eat and drink
2. mill: factory
3. scarcely: hardly, almost not
4. overlooker: supervisor, boss

Document 1 Questions

In-the-text questions (do these first!):	Analysis questions:
1. How old was Joseph (the person giving the answers) when he started working in the factory?	6. Who is Joseph talking to in this interview[1]? (Look at the source.)
2. How many hours a day did he work?	7. What do you think was the purpose of this interview?
3. *Inference:* Was Joseph able to go to school? Why?	8. What is Joseph's point of view[2] about factory work?
4. How did factory work affect Joseph's health?	9. How might Joseph's health problems affect him later in life?
5. What happened when Joseph was late to work?	10. How will Joseph's lack[3] of education affect him later in life?

1. interview: an official conversation
2. point of view: opinion
3. lack: missing

Document 2

Every great city has one or more slums[1], where the working-class is crowded together. True, poverty often dwells in hidden alleys close to the palaces of the rich; but, in general, a separate territory has been assigned to it, where, removed from the sight of the happier classes, it may struggle along as it can.

These slums are pretty equally arranged in all the great towns of England, the worst houses in the worst quarters of the towns; usually one- or two-storied cottages in long rows, perhaps with cellars[2] used as dwellings,[3] almost always irregularly built. These houses of three or four rooms and a kitchens form, throughout England, some parts of London excepted, the general dwellings of the working-class.

The streets are generally unpaved, rough, dirty, filled with vegetable and animal refuse,[4] without sewers or gutters, but supplied with foul,[5] stagnant pools instead. Moreover, ventilation is impeded[6] by the bad, confused method of building of the whole quarter, and since many human beings here live crowded into a small space, the atmosphere[7] that prevails in these working-men's quarters may readily be imagined. Further, the streets serve as drying grounds in fine weather; lines are stretched across from house to house and hung with wet clothing.

Note. Adapted from *The Condition of the Working Class in England in 1844*, by Friedrich Engels.

1. slums: areas of bad housing
2. cellars: basements
3. dwellings: places to live
4. refuse: garbage
5. foul: nasty
6. impeded: blocked
7. atmosphere: air

Document 2 Questions

In-the-text questions (do these first!):	Analysis questions:
1. What does Engels emphasize about the location of the slums (in the first paragraph)?	5. What is Engels's point of view regarding working-class living conditions in England?
2. Describe the conditions of the houses in English cities, according to this source.	6. What does the title of this source tell us about the author's purpose for writing this book?
3. Describe the sanitation (process of keeping something clean) in the slums, according to this source.	7. Look up the author. What is he known for? How does this connect to his purpose in writing this book?
4. According to Engels, why is the air quality so bad in the slums?	

Exit Ticket

Remember! A turning point is an important change.

Write a paragraph in which you answer the question below. Use specific details from what you learned today (photographs and documents) to support your answer. Remember to clearly describe what life was like both before and after the Industrial Revolution.

Why is the Industrial Revolution considered a turning point in world history?

_____

_____

_____

_____

_____

_____

_____

_____

_____

_____

_____

_____

_____

_____

_____

_____

_____

_____

_____

_____

_____

_____

Sentence Frames and Word Bank for Beginner Activity

Before the Industrial Revolution, people ☆_____ → _____

_____.

After the Industrial Revolution, people ☆_____ → _____

_____.

☆ (main idea)	→ (how?)	
worked	in dirty places	in clean places
traveled	by machine	by hand
lived	in agriculture	in factories
made things	with one family	with many families
	by train	by horse

Figure 7.9.2

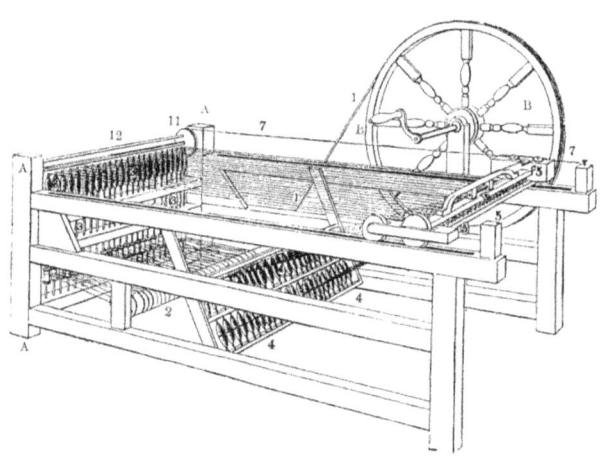

Figure 7.9.3

Teacher Resource: Image Set B

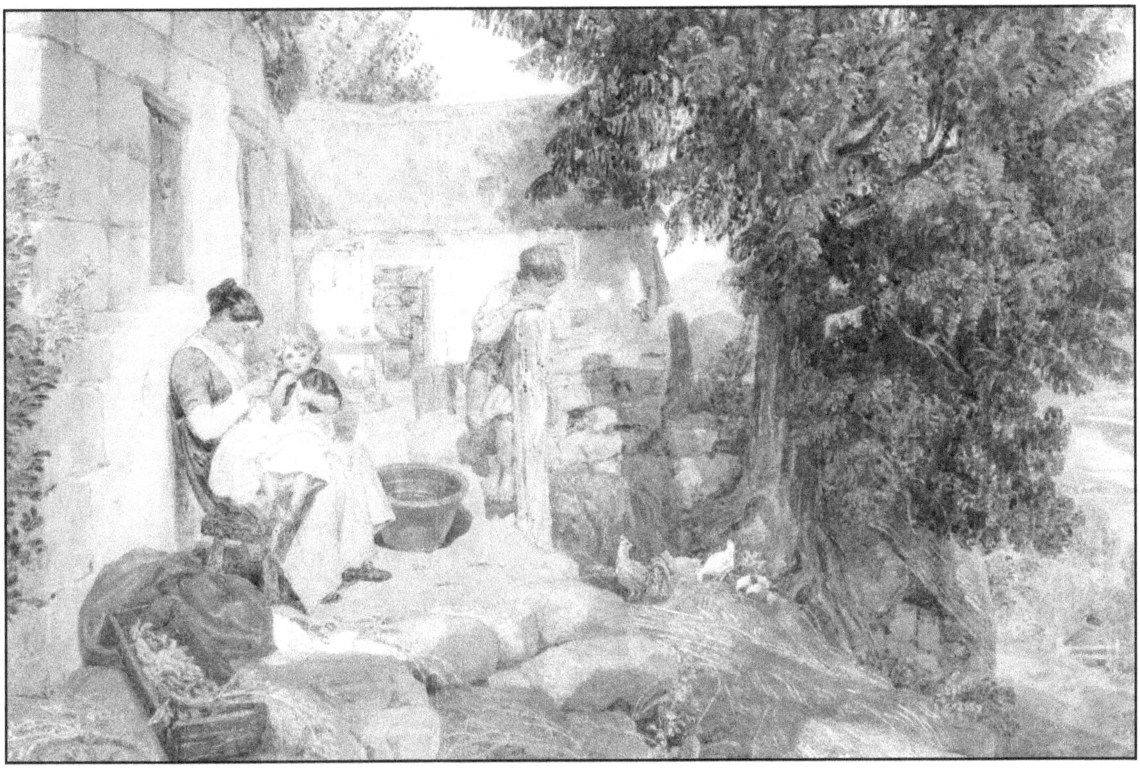

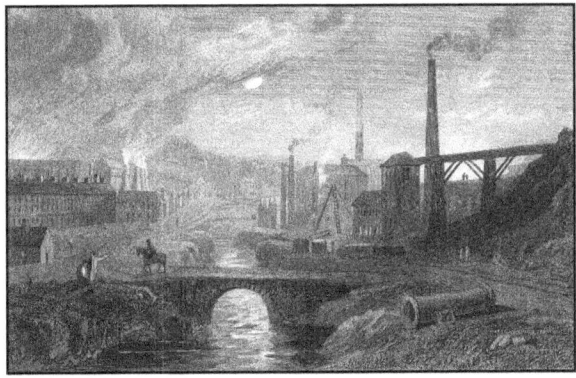

Figure 7.9.4

Figure 7.9.5

Figure 7.9.6

Figure 7.9.7

Figure 7.9.8

Figure 7.9.9

Figure 7.9.10

Figure 7.9.11

Image Credits for Student Packet and Image Sets

Document 1. Adapted from "Women Miners in the English Coal Pits," in *Parliamentary Papers: Vol. XVI*, 1842, Internet Modern History Sourcebook, Fordham University. (https://origin.web.fordham.edu/Halsall/mod/1842womenminers.asp).

Document 2. Adapted from *The Condition of the Working-Class in England in 1844*, by F. Engels, translated by F. Kelley, 1845, Project Gutenberg (https://www.gutenberg.org/ebooks/17306). In the public domain.

Figure 7.9.1. Cropped from *Child labour Vivian Cotton Mills* [Photograph], by L. Hine, 1908, Leiden University Libraries (https://digitalcollections.universiteitleiden.nl/view/item/1659529). In the public domain.

Figure 7.9.2. From *Häusliche Szene mit Musikanten und Spinnerin* [Painting], by G. Cipper, 1725, Städel Museum (https://sammlung.staedelmuseum.de/en/work/domestic-scene-with-musicians-and-woman-spinning). In the public domain.

Figure 7.9.3. Diagram of Hargreaves' Spinning Jenny [Engraving], from *The Cotton Manufacture of Great Britain: Investigated and Illustrated*, Volume 1, by A. Ure and P. L. Simmonds, 1861, Internet Archive, p. 231 (https://archive.org/details/dli.ministry.01503). In the public domain.

Figure 7.9.4. From *A Cottage on the Side of Symond's Rock Near Goodrich, Herefordshire* [Painting], by J. Cristall, 1825, Wikimedia (https://commons.wikimedia.org/wiki/File:Joshua_Cristall_A_Cottage_on_the_side_of_Symond%27s_Rock.jpg). In the public domain.

Figure 7.9.5. From *Nant y Glo, Monmouthshire* [Engraving], by H. G. Gastineau & S. Lacey, ca. 1830, Llyfrgell Genedlaethol Cymru—National Library of Wales (http://hdl.handle.net/10107/1131349). In the public domain.

Figure 7.9.6. From *A Study From Nature (Horse-Drawn Cart With Two Men)* [Illustration], by W. Brockedon, 1787–1854, Yale Center for British Art, Paul Mellon Collection, B1977.14.1490(47) (https://collections.britishart.yale.edu/catalog/tms:13255). In the public domain.

Figure 7.9.7. From *Virginia & Truckee Railroad 11, Reno, With the Lightning Express at Virginia City* [Photograph], photographer unknown, ca. 1880, Wikimedia (https://commons.wikimedia.org/wiki/File:Virginia_%26_Truckee_Railroad_11,_Reno,_with_the_Lightning_Express_at_Virginia_City_(early_1880s%3F).jpg). In the public domain.

Figure 7.9.8. From *Cottage at Adel*, [Illustration] by W. Braithwaite, 1878, Leeds Libraries (https://commons.wikimedia.org/wiki/File:1878_Cottage_at_Adel.jpg). In the public domain.

Figure 7.9.9. From *Crowded Tenement Used by Cranberry Pickers* [Photograph], by L. Hine, September 1911, Library of Congress (www.loc.gov/item/2018676025/).

Figure 7.9.10. From a photograph of farm workers in the 1800s, National Archives and Records Administration, ca. 1800, Flickr (www.flickr.com/photos/usdagov/6510688255/). In the public domain.

Figure 7.9.11. From an illustration of machine works of Richard Hartmann in Chemnitz, Germany, by unknown artist, 1868, Wikimedia (https://commons.wikimedia.org/wiki/File:Hartmann_Maschinenhalle_1868_(01).jpg). In the public domain.

Lesson 10: Women's Suffrage
Lesson by Peggie Cypher

Table 7.10.1 *High School Lesson Overview: Women's Suffrage*

Women's Suffrage	
Duration	40–60 minutes
Differentiation Strategies	Modified reading passages for two levels of MLEs with audio support from the Ducksters and TED-Ed websites.
C3 Framework Standards	**D2.Civ.2.9–12.** Analyze the role of citizens in the U.S. political system, with attention to various theories of democracy, changes in Americans' participation over time, and alternative models from other countries, past and present. **D2.His.4.9–12.** Analyze complex and interacting factors that influenced the perspectives of people during different historical eras. **D3.4.9–12.** Refine claims and counterclaims attending to precision, significance, and knowledge conveyed through the claim while pointing out the strengths and limitations of both.
Content/Language Objectives	Students will learn about women's suffrage and its opposition by looking at historical cartoons and pamphlets and by reading or listening to a passage that summarizes the movement.
Materials and Technology	• candy (optional) • timeline of the suffrage movement from Jewish Women's Archive (http://jwa.org/media/chronology-of-womens-suffrage-in-america) • online historical cartoons and pamphlets from "12 Cruel Anti-Suffragette Cartoons," by T. O'Neill, January 2015, The Week (theweek.com/articles/461455/12-cruel-antisuffragette-cartoons). • Pamphet on the National Association Opposed to Women Suffrage from Anti-Woman Suffrage Circular: Household Hints, State Archives of North Carolina (digital.ncdcr.gov/Documents/Detail/anti-woman-suffrage-circular-household-hints/764614). • vocabulary guide (Table 7.10.3) • Ducksters article and quiz about women's suffrage (www.ducksters.com/history/civil_rights/womens_suffrage.php) • TedEd video and quiz about 1913 women's suffrage march (https://ed.ted.com/lessons/the-historic-women-s-suffrage-march-on-washington-michelle-mehrtens)
Teacher Background	The teacher should know about women's suffrage and its opposition. This lesson introduces women's suffrage using primary source materials and leveled reading texts. It is an example of integrating leveled passages and comprehension questions from established websites. Ensure your MLEs understand the words *vote*, *suffrage*, and other essential vocabulary.
Assessment	Evaluate worksheets for accuracy.

Table 7.10.2 *High School Lesson Procedures: Women's Suffrage*

Lesson Procedures	Differentiation Strategies
Introduction (10 minutes) 1. Ask students to vote for their choice of two different treats to be shared in class, such as Jolly Ranchers or Skittles. Ask them to raise their hands and then tell them that only the boys' votes will count. When students object, introduce the meaning of women's suffrage. Elicit responses about how the girls felt or how others might feel if they were excluded from voting based on their height, weight, hair color, religion, or whether their parents own a boat. Pass out the candy to the class (optional). 2. Introduce the suffrage movement with a timeline. 3. Remind students how an amendment to the Constitution gets ratified. 4. Project a series of antisuffrage cartoons. 5. Ask students to describe what they see and what they think the main message is. 6. Elicit responses as to why women's right to vote was seen as a threat to society and culture.	Simulations or role-playing can deepen MLEs' understanding of being excluded from voting. Timelines can be essential visual tools for comprehension of the context of political change. Call on beginning MLEs and ask simple yes/no or agree/disagree questions, such as: *Do you think this cartoon favors women's right to vote?*
Main Activity READ & WRITE (15 minutes) 1. Divide the class into groups of 4, mixing MLEs and non-MLEs. 2. Project the pamphlet on the National Association Opposed to Woman Suffrage. 3. For pamphlet part 1 (p. 2), have students write down 4 chores that do not require a ballot. 4. For pamphlet part 2 (p. 3), have groups write 4 reasons why some people thought women did not need the right to vote. 5. Lastly, have students write down what the two parts of the pamphlet imply about women, society, and U.S. culture at the time.	Without much time to modify the lesson, teachers can take advantage of the myriad of websites that feature leveled reading passages with audio and comprehension questions.
Activity 3 LISTEN (15 minutes) 1. Listen to a recorded reading of the Women's Suffrage webpage on Ducksters, and have students take the 10-question quiz. 2. Watch the TED-Ed video *The Historic Women's Suffrage March on Washington*, by Michelle Mehrtens, and have students take the accompanying quiz (ed.ted.com/lessons/the-historic-women-s-suffrage-march-on-washington-michelle-mehrtens/think).	Listening practice is often a neglected activity for MLEs and, when accompanied by a simplified reading passage, can greatly improve comprehension of content. Ducksters and TED-Ed have a wealth of resources on social studies. Teachers can have students do the quizzes online or print the quizzes. For beginning MLEs, teachers can reduce the choices in the multiple-choice quizzes. This approach is also useful for students with disabilities and students with lower reading levels.

Table 7.10.3 *Vocabulary Guide: Women's Suffrage*

Word	Tier	Definition	Example	Translation
march	2	protest; people gathering to express ideas or disagree with things they want to change		
the 19th Amendment	3	a law added to the U.S. Constitution that gave women the right to vote		
vote	2	choosing between two or more people or ideas		
women's suffrage	3	the right of women to vote		

Note. Image for "The 19th Amendment" from *Woman Suffrage Button* [Photograph], National Museum of American History (https://www.si.edu/object/nmah_1437164). In the public domain. Image for "women's suffrage" from *Mary Winsor (Penn.) '17* [Photograph], by Harris & Ewing, 1917, Library of Congress (https://www.loc.gov/item/mnwp000225/). In the public domain.

Lesson 11: Causes of World War I
Lesson by Kaedmon Fulton

Table 7.11.1 *High School Lesson Overview: World War I*

The MAIN Causes of World War I	
Duration	50 minutes
Differentiation Strategies	• simplified guided notes • scaffolding questions for political cartoons
C3 Framework Standards	**D2.His.14.9–12.** Analyze multiple and complex causes and effects of events in the past. **D4.2.9–12.** Construct explanations using sound reasoning, correct sequence (linear or nonlinear), examples, and details with significant and pertinent information and data, while acknowledging the strengths and weaknesses of the explanation given its purpose (e.g., cause and effect, chronological, procedural, technical).
Content/Language Objectives	1. Students will be able to explain how militarism, alliances, imperialism, and nationalism contributed to World War I by using cause–effect transitions to connect their ideas in writing. 2. Students will be able to interpret political cartoons by identifying and explaining symbolic images.
Materials and Technology	• interactive whiteboard or other display system • lesson slides on MAIN causes • vocabulary guide (Table 7.11.3) • student packet (guided notes sheets, political cartoons with scaffolding questions, exit tickets)
Teacher Background	This lesson will focus on the MAIN (militarism, alliances, imperialism, and nationalism) causes of World War I, with a focus on not just identifying the causal factors but explaining each factor's contribution to a regional conflict that turned into a world war.
Assessment	**Formative:** Checks for understanding after each cause is presented. **Summative:** At the end of class, students write a paragraph making a claim about the most important of the MAIN causes. Whichever cause they choose, students should be able to • explain the meaning of the cause, • explain how this cause made a small conflict larger, and • use cause–effect transitions in their writing.

Table 7.11.2 *High School Lesson Procedures: World War I*

Lesson Procedures	Differentiation Strategies
Introduction (5 minutes) 1. Show the clip "The Inciting Event" from the Netflix show *Beef*. (In this clip, a minor parking lot incident becomes a major road rage event.) Lead a discussion on what a huge problem this was (e.g., How did this affect the drivers? What might happen next?). 2. Then ask what caused this huge problem. If students are stuck on the main character's poor driving, replay the first 10 seconds of the video, when the main character is already clearly upset about something before he even gets into the car. Ask if the students can relate, if they have ever been so frustrated or upset that a little thing made them really angry. Explain that this is similar to what happened in Europe in the early 1900s. *Note.* On the official Netflix YouTube channel, the language in the clip from *Beef* is censored but includes an obscene hand gesture. This introductory activity—showing how a small problem can become a big problem—can also be taught using the opening scene from *Ice Age*, in which the squirrel tries to bury an acorn and ultimately causes a series of avalanches.	Videos are a good resource for MLEs because they can present information in an easily comprehended format; however, not all videos are a good fit for language learners. The video used here is a good example of a clip where a viewer does not actually need to know the meaning of the words to understand what is happening.

Notes Reflection (20 minutes)
 	
1. The teacher presents the MAIN causes of World War I, while the students take notes using the guided notes sheet. Slides and notes use clear, simple language and support understanding with images.
2. Check for understanding: After each cause, students pause to process the information and answer the question, "How did this factor make a small conflict bigger?" Remind students to write their answer using cause–effect transitions, and circulate as students work, helping out with the language as needed.
    a. Students first think about the question on their own and write down their ideas.
    b. Then students share their ideas with an elbow partner.
3. After discussing with a partner, students can add on to what they originally wrote.
	Strategy: Simplified notes
	
	In order to focus students' cognitive effort on understanding rather than searching for and copying long answers, the guided notes in this lesson are very minimal. Most information is already included, and students are only writing a few key words in order to focus attention on the important points and to stay engaged.

Source Work (15 minutes) 1. Explain that each cartoon helps to show how one of the MAIN factors contributed to World War I becoming a major conflict. 2. With the help of scaffolding questions that move from literal observations to inferences about symbolism to interpretation, students identify the factor portrayed in each cartoon and explain how it contributed to the war.	Strategy: Supporting work with political cartoons Here, the students' understanding of political cartoons is scaffolded by guiding questions. The questions prompt the students to start with observations and help them focus on the important details in the cartoon. With continued practice, the students will eventually be able to approach political cartoons on their own without guiding questions.
Summary/Assessment (10 minutes) 1. Review the MAIN causes and then tell students that they are going to make a claim answering the question, "Which cause contributed the most to World War I becoming a world war?" Outline the criteria for success (defining the cause you chose, using cause–effect transitions, giving specific reasons, etc.). 2. As students write, circulate through the room, prompting students to draw on the ideas and language generated in the checks for understanding if they are stuck and reminding them to use cause–effect transitions to connect their ideas.	Differentiation: Keep everyone busy for the full time without overloading the lower proficiency students by adding on a challenge for advanced students and fast writers: Ask students to make their argument stronger by explaining how the cause they chose ties in with all other causes. (For example, a student could argue that nations built up their militaries because they felt pride in their nation and wanted to defend it from others, so it all comes back to nationalism in the end.)

Table 7.11.3 *Vocabulary Guide: World War I*

		Key Vocabulary		
Word	**Tier**	**Definition**	**Example**	**Translation**
alliance	3	an agreement between two countries, promising to help each other in war		
compete	2	to try to get the same thing		
conflict	2	a fight or problem between two people or countries		
contribute	2	to help to cause something		
imperialism	3	taking control of a weaker country		
militarism	3	increasing a country's military to be ready to fight		

| nationalism | 3 | believing your country is the best | | |
| represent | 2 | to use a picture to show an idea | | |

Note. Image for "imperialism" from *English Imperialism Octopus* [Illustration], 1888, Wikimedia Commons (https://commons.wikimedia.org/wiki/File:English_imperialism_octopus.jpg). In the public domain.

The MAIN Causes: How Did a Small Conflict Become a World War?

---

1. Militarism
- Militarism means increasing a country's _____.
- At first, European countries needed stronger armies in order to take and maintain[1] control of more _____.
- Later on, European countries continued to build up their armies and military _____ because they were afraid of their neighbors.

Stop and think: How did *militarism* contribute[2] to a small conflict becoming a world war?

---

2. Alliances
- An alliance is an _____ between two countries: The countries promise that if one is in trouble, the other one will help.
- There were _____ important alliances in Europe in the early 1900s.
- The Triple Alliance was an agreement among Austria–Hungary, _____, and Italy.
- The Triple Entente was an alliance among _____, France, and Russia.

Stop and think: How did *alliances* contribute to a small conflict becoming a world war?

---

3. Imperialism
- Imperialism is when a strong country _____ another country, taking advantage of it economically and culturally.
- European countries took control of many regions of Africa and Asia because they wanted _____ to use in factories.
- European countries began to _____ for colonies; nobody wanted to have fewer colonies than their neighbors.

Stop and think: How did *imperialism* contribute to a small conflict becoming a world war?

---

4. Nationalism
- Nationalism is believing that your nation (country) is _____.
- Nationalism can be good: It can help v people to work together.
- It can also be negative if you love your country so much that you _____ all other countries.

Stop and think: How did *nationalism* contribute to a small conflict becoming a world war?

---

1. maintain: keep
2. contribute: help to cause

Document 1

A NEW LEGEND IN AN OLD DRESS.

The men's swords are labeled "Germany" (left) and "France" (right). The women in the tower are labeled "Alsace" and "Lorraine."

Document 1 Questions

Observe 👀	Connect 🔗	Infer 🤔
How many people do you see?	What do the men represent?	What were Germany and France probably doing at this time?
What are they doing?	What do the women represent?	
		Which cause of WWI does this show? Why?
Is there any text in the picture?	What do the chains represent?	

Document 2

"Japan—I see your Cruisers and raise you a Dreadnought!" (a cruiser is a military ship; a dreadnought is a bigger military ship).

Document 2 Questions

Observe 👀	Connect 🔗	Infer 🤔
How many people do you see?	What countries do the people at the table represent?	What's the artist's point of view* on this competition? How do you know?
What are they doing?	How are they competing?	Which cause of WWI does this show? Why?
What else is in the picture?		

*point of view: opinion (Does the artist think this is good or bad for the countries?)

Document 3

By Joseph Simpson, R.B.A.

" YOUR MOTHERLAND WILL NEVER FORGET "

Document 3 Questions

Observe 👀	Connect 🔗	Infer 🤔
How many people do you see?	What is the man in the image doing?	How did the artist want the audience* to feel about the war? How do you know?
What are they doing?	What does the woman in the image represent?	Which cause of WWI does this show? Why?
What else is in the picture?		

*audience: people who see the picture

Exit Ticket

Write a paragraph in which you make a claim in response to the question below. Use specific details from what you learned today to support your answer.

Which cause contributed most to World War I becoming a world war?

In your answer, remember to do the following: ☐ Define the cause you chose. ☐ Use at least two cause–effect transitions to connect your ideas. ☐ Give specific reasons to support your claim.	Cause–Effect Transitions *Use at least 2!* ☐ As a result, ☐ Because of this, ☐ Consequently, ☐ Due to this,

_____

_____

_____

_____

_____

_____

_____

_____

_____

_____

_____

_____

_____

_____

_____

_____

_____

_____

_____

_____

_____

_____

_____

Guided Notes Key: The MAIN Causes—How Did a Small Conflict Become a World War?

---

1. Militarism
- Militarism means increasing a country's **military** (**army and weapons**).
- At first, European countries needed stronger armies in order to take and maintain control of more colonies.
- Later on, European countries continued to build up their armies and military technology (tanks, airplanes, guns) because they were afraid of their neighbors.

---

2. Alliances
- An alliance is an **agreement** between two countries: The countries promise that if one is in trouble, the other one will help.
- There were **two** important alliances in Europe in the early 1900s.
- The Triple Alliance was an agreement among Austria-Hungary, **Germany**, and Italy.
- The Triple Entente was an alliance among **Britain**, France, and Russia.

---

3. Imperialism
- Imperialism is when a strong country **controls** another country, taking advantage of it economically and culturally.
- European countries took control of many regions of Africa and Asia because they wanted **raw materials** to use in factories.
- European countries began to **compete** for colonies; nobody wanted to have fewer colonies than their neighbors.

---

4. Nationalism
- Nationalism is believing that your nation (country) is **the best**.
- Nationalism can be good: It can help **unite** people to work together.
- It can also be negative, if you love your country so much that you **hate** all other countries.

Image Credits

Document 1. From *A New Legend in an Old Dress* [Illustration], by U. J. Keppler, February 16, 1898, *Puck*, 43(1093), centerfold, Library of Congress (www.loc.gov/item/2012647516/). In the public domain.

Document 2. From *No Limit* [Illustration], by L. M. Glackens, September 22, 1909, *Puck*, 66(1699), cover, Library of Congress (https://www.loc.gov/resource/ppmsca.26411/). In the public domain.

Document 3. From *Your Motherland Will Never Forget* [Illustration], by J. Simpson, c. 1917–1919, *Canada in Khaki*, British Library, Wikimedia (https://commons.wikimedia.org/wiki/File:Your_motherland_will_never_forget.jpg). In the public domain.

Conclusion

And at the end of the day, hello and welcome is the key word. We just want to make
sure that everyone, no matter where they're from, no matter what tribe they're from,
is welcome.

—2022 World Cup Opening Ceremony

If you take one thing away from this book, we hope it is this: Everything starts with knowing your students. Although they are identified by districts simply as language learners, multilingual learners of English (MLEs) are in fact a diverse group of students, comprising a wide range of language proficiencies, backgrounds, cultures, and experiences. Incorporating the appropriate strategies and activities to make social studies content and skills accessible to MLEs starts with getting to know each student's individual background, abilities, and challenges. And once you really know your students, you will understand that they bring a great number of assets and inner strengths that will help them surmount the daunting range of obstacles set up against them.

In an increasingly interconnected world, the need for inclusive and culturally responsive education has never been greater, particularly for MLEs. While numerous resources exist for teaching history and language arts, there is a gap when it comes to integrating social studies with language development. This book fills that gap by offering practical strategies for educators working with MLEs, helping to bridge the divide between students' linguistic and cultural assets and the instructional practices that can empower them.

Through this work, we have shared our observations of how MLEs, when given the right support, can excel in social studies. We have seen students like Viktor, Reem, Nyandeng, Minh, and Yadiel not just survive but thrive when their linguistic and cultural backgrounds are recognized and respected. Whether writing complex essays, engaging with primary sources in their home language and English, or sharing powerful personal histories with their peers, MLEs can bring history to life in ways that benefit all students in the classroom.

The diverse linguistic landscape of U.S. classrooms is changing, with MLEs now comprising a significant portion of the student body. To meet their needs, we must rethink traditional teaching methods and adopt strategies that foster both academic growth and cultural competence. Social studies, with its focus on history, civics, and cultural studies, offers a rich opportunity for language development, critical thinking, and civic engagement. These subjects do not just teach students about the world; they prepare them to actively participate in it, equipped with the tools needed for success in college, career, and civic life.

Our aim in this book is not only to provide educators with effective instructional practices but also to inspire them to see MLEs as invaluable contributors to the learning community. MLEs bring a wealth of diverse experiences and cultural perspectives that can enrich all students' understanding of the world. By integrating their backgrounds and cultures into social studies instruction, we can create a learning environment where social studies comes alive.

The strategies and examples presented here are meant to serve as both inspiration and a practical guide for teachers, administrators, and school leaders. By working together, we can build a future where MLEs are not on the sidelines but are actively shaping their educational experience—and ultimately, the world around them.

Appendix A
Common Terminology

Students who are learning English are referred to in many different ways: Some common terms that are used by legislation and individual states are *English learners* (EL), *English language learners* (ELL), *multilingual learners* (ML/MLL), *emergent bilinguals* (EB), *English as an additional language* (EAL) learners, *English for speakers of other languages* (ESOL) students, and *English as a second language* (ESL) students. Throughout this book, we have used the term *multilingual learners of English* (MLEs), focusing on the assets of the learner.

The following terminologies are commonly used in this book:

- **asset-based pedagogy**: A practice that focuses on the diversity that students bring to the classroom, including culture and language that add value and strength to classrooms and communities.
- **bilingual:** A student who speaks and understands, to varying degrees, two languages.
- **biliteracy:** The ability to speak, read, and write in two languages.
- **coteaching:** A teaching strategy where two or more teachers work together to plan, teach, and assess students in the same class.
- **culturally and linguistically responsive teaching:** An instructional approach that leverages the cultural and linguistic experiences of students to make learning relevant and meaningful.
- **dual language learner:** A child aged birth to 5 who is learning two or more languages at the same time or is starting to learn a second language while developing their first language.
- **first language**: Also *native language, heritage language*, or *home language*. A language spoken in a student's family or home as reported on the Home Language Survey.
- **home language survey:** Also *home language questionnaire*. A set of questions asked about a student's language background when they enroll in a school district. This is given to all students from Pre-K to Grade 12.
- **long-term English learner:** A student who has been enrolled in schools in the United States for 6 years or more and is still classified as an English learner.
- **multilingual student:** A student who speaks or understands, to varying degrees, one or more languages.
- **translanguaging:** (1) A practice of using multiple languages to communicate (books, verbal). (2) An educational approach that encourages students to use their full linguistic repertoire to learn.

Appendix B
Digital Resources for Language Support

(1) Flashcard Programs

The following programs allow instructors and students to create their own flashcards for vocabulary and important concepts. Alternatively, they can use available decks shared by others.

- *Anki* [apps.ankiweb.net/]
- *Quizlet* [quizlet.com/gb]

(2) Grammar Instruction and Tools

- *Grammar Bytes* [www.chompchomp.com/] introduces definitions of common grammar terms, provides learning quizzes and handouts, and even offers ready-to-use slides.
- *Grammarly* [app.grammarly.com/] and *Hemingway Editor* [hemingwayapp.com/] are powerful tools to provide automated feedback on writing, especially grammatical and mechanical issues.

(3) Listening Practice

- Randall's ESL Cyber Listening Lab [www.esl-lab.com/] provides opportunities for students to practice listening and speaking skills through everyday conversations.
- DailyDictation [dailydictation.com/] offers multi-level dictation exercises for students to practice their listening skills.

(4) Writing Practice

- Write & Improve [writeandimprove.com/free] allows students to practice writing and receive instant feedback.
- Quill [www.quill.org] offers interactive grammar and writing activities tailored to student skill levels, with real-time feedback and teacher monitoring tools.

(5) Online Learning

- British Council's LearnEnglish [learnenglish.britishcouncil.org/] offers free courses and materials for students to improve their English skills.
- BBC Learning English [www.bbc.co.uk/learningenglish/] offers free multimodal materials for worldwide learners to improve their English proficiencies.

(6) Online Collections of Digital Resources

- Amaya Garcia and Elise Franchino provide an extensive list of digital resources for MLE students: [www.newamerica.org/education-policy/edcentral/digital-resources-el-students/].
- Language Teachers' Association of the Northern Territory shares a list of digital learning resources: [www.ltant.org/digital-learning-resources].
- TESOL Blog [www.tesol.org/blog/] actively shares teaching tips and activities related to multilingual learners of English and English language teaching.

(7) AI-Powered Language Learning Platforms

- Duolingo [www.duolingo.com/] engages users to learn English or other languages in a free, fun, and effective way.
- Online collections of AI-powered language learning apps
  - 20 Best AI Language Learning Apps in 2024 [makesyoufluent.com/ai-language-learning-apps/].
  - Which is the best AI conversation practice app for language learners? [oh-yeah-sarah. medium.com/which-is-the-best-ai-conversation-practice-app-for-language-learners-68fccc6942ad].

Appendix C

Recommended Reading Resources

Multilingual Education and Language Acquisition

Castro, D. C., Garcia, E. E., & Markos, A. M. (2013). *Dual language learners: Research informing policy*. The University of North Carolina, Frank Porter Graham Child Development Institute, Center for Early Care and Education—Dual Language Learners. https://fpg.unc.edu/sites/fpg.unc.edu/files/resource-files/FPG_CECER-DLL_ResearchInformingPolicyPaper.pdf

de Oliveira, L. C., & Jones, L. (2023). *Teaching young multilingual learners: Key issues and new insights*. Cambridge University Press. https://doi.org/10.1017/9781108934138

Turkan, S., Bicknell, J., & Croft, A. (2014). Effective practices for developing the literacy skills of English language learners in the English language arts classroom. *ETS Research Report Series, 2012*(1), i–31. https://doi.org/10.1002/j.2333–8504.2012.tb02285.x

Culturally Responsive Teaching

Gay, G. (2018). *Culturally responsive teaching: Theory, research, and practice* (3rd ed.). Teachers College Press.

Hammond, Z. (2014). *Culturally responsive teaching and the brain: Promoting authentic engagement and rigor among culturally and linguistically diverse students*. Corwin.

Hollie, S. (2017). *Culturally and linguistically responsive teaching and learning: Classroom practices for student success* (2nd ed.). Shell Education.

Martell, C. C., & Stevens, K. M. (2020). *Teaching history for justice: Centering activism in students' study of the past*. Teachers College Press.

Technology

Chapelle, C. A. (2008). Technology and second language acquisition. *Annual Review of Applied Linguistics, 27*, 98–114. https://doi.org/10.1017/S0267190508070050

Warschauer, M., & Healey, D. (1998). Computers and language learning: An overview. *Language Teaching, 31*(2), 57–71. https://doi.org/10.1017/S0261444800012970

Zhu, M., & Wang, C. (2025). A systematic review of research on AI in language education: Current status and future implications. *Language Learning & Technology, 29*(1), 1–29. https://hdl.handle.net/10125/73606

Authentic Assessments

Gulikers, J. T. M., Bastiaens, T. J., & Kirschner, P. A. (2004). A five-dimensional framework for authentic assessment. *Educational Technology Research and Development, 52*, 67–86. https://doi.org/10.1007/BF02504676

Sherrin, D. (2020). *Authentic assessments in social studies: A guide to keeping it real*. Routledge. https://doi.org/10.4324/9780429261114

Educational Research Journals

- *Journal of Multilingual and Multicultural Development* [https://www.tandfonline.com/journals/rmmm20] focuses on multilingualism and multicultural education, with articles relevant to language acquisition and educational policy.
- *Journal of Social Studies Research* [https://journals.sagepub.com/home/ssra] publishes research on effective social studies teaching practices, including articles on culturally responsive teaching and inclusive curriculum.
- *TESOL Quarterly* [https://onlinelibrary.wiley.com/journal/15457249] publishes research articles on language learning and teaching, including studies on multilingual learners of English.

Reports and Resources From Educational Organizations

- **Center for Applied Linguistics** (CAL; https://www.cal.org/) publishes reports and resources on language education policy and effective practices for multilingual learners of English.
- **National Council for the Social Studies** (NCSS; https://www.socialstudies.org/) offers resources and publications on social studies education, including articles on teaching diverse perspectives and inclusive curriculum.
- *Teaching History for Social Justice: Centering Activism in Students' Study of the Past* (Teachers College Press; www.tcpress.com/teaching-history-for-justice-9780807764749) discusses strategies for incorporating diverse perspectives and critical thinking in teaching history, which aligns with culturally responsive social studies education.
- **TESOL International Association** (TESOL; https://www.tesol.org/) provides resources and reports on language education policies and practices.

Legislative Initiatives and Policy Reports

- **Advancing Equity for K–12 English Learners** (Office of English Language Acquisition) provides an overview of policy recommendations to support educational equity for MLEs, including legislative initiatives (https://ncela.ed.gov/sites/default/files/2024-09/oelaequityinfographic-20240906-508.pdf).
- **"Ensuring English Learner Students Can Participate Meaningfully and Equally in Educational Programs"** (U.S. Department of Justice; U.S. Department of Education) discusses the protections and implications of Title VI for English learners in education (www.ed.gov/media/document/dcl-factsheet-el-students-201501pdf-21469.pdf).
- **"Policy Discourses and U.S. Language in Education Policies"** compares state policies on language education and their impact on MLEs. By E. J. de Jong, *Peabody Journal of Education*, 88, 98–111, 2013 (https://doi.org/10.1080/0161956X.2013.752310)

Appendix D
Types of Programs

This is just a handful of examples of the different types of programs that are used across the world. Programs for multilingual learners of English (MLEs) are usually determined at the district or school leadership level.

Dual Language Immersion Programs

- **Overview**: These programs balance instruction in English and a partner language (e.g., Spanish, Chinese), fostering bilingualism and biliteracy. Students are taught academic content in both languages.
- **Why it works**: It supports both English language development and preservation of the home language, leading to cognitive benefits and higher academic achievement.
- **Example**: Many districts in California have successfully implemented dual immersion programs to support both MLEs and fluent English speakers.

Newcomer Programs

- **Overview**: These programs are designed for students who are recent immigrants, providing intensive language support and helping them acclimate to U.S. schools and culture. Newcomer programs can range from 1 year to multiple years.
- **Why it works**: By addressing the immediate needs of students who are new to the United States, these programs provide a supportive space to adjust socially, emotionally, and academically.
- **Example**: The International High Schools in New York City are well known for their newcomer model, which integrates language instruction and content learning.

Transitional Bilingual Education (TBE)

- **Overview**: TBE programs use the student's home language to deliver instruction for a certain period, transitioning them gradually to English instruction. The home language is phased out as the student's English proficiency grows.
- **Why it works**: TBE builds a strong foundation in the home language, helping students access content and succeed academically while they develop English skills.
- **Example**: Texas has been a leader in implementing TBE programs, particularly for Spanish-speaking students.

English as a Second Language (ESL) Pull-Out Programs

- **Overview**: These programs pull students out of the general classroom for part of the day to receive focused English instruction.
- **Why it works:** It allows for targeted, small-group instruction that focuses on language development while the students also participate in mainstream classes.
- **Example**: ESL pull-out programs are common in districts with a lower density of MLEs, offering flexibility to meet individual needs.

References

Ajjawi, R., Tai, J., Dollinger, M., Dawson, P., Boud, D., & Bearman, M. (2024). From authentic assessment to authenticity in assessment: Broadening perspectives. *Assessment & Evaluation in Higher Education, 49*(4), 499–510. https://doi.org/10.1080/02602938.2023.2271193

Alim, H. S., Rickford, J. R., & Ball, A. F. (Eds.). (2016). *Raciolinguistics: How language shapes our ideas about race.* Oxford University Press. https://doi.org/10.1093/acprof:oso/9780190625696.001.0001

Allman, B. (2019). *Principles of language acquisition.* Equity Press. https://edtechbooks.org/language_acquisition

Andrews, T. (2024, September 10). *Which language is richest in words?* Interpreters and Translators. https://ititranslates.com/which-language-is-richest-in-words/

Banks, J. A. (2015). *Cultural diversity and education: Foundations, curriculum, and teaching* (6th ed.). Routledge. https://doi.org/10.4324/9781315622255

Banks, J. A. (2019). *An introduction to multicultural education* (6th ed.). Pearson.

Banks, J. A., & Banks, C. A. M. (Eds.). (2019). *Multicultural education: Issues and perspectives* (10th ed.). Wiley.

Barfoot, J. R. (ca. 1840). *People with baskets and sacks pick cotton on a plantation* [Lithograph]. Wellcome Collection. https://wellcomecollection.org/works/mf7r354u/images?id=dctev2ms

Beck, I. L., McKeown, M. G., & Omanson, R. C. (1987). The effects and uses of diverse vocabulary instructional techniques. In M. G. McKeown & M. E. Curtis (Eds.), *The nature of vocabulary acquisition* (pp. 147–163). Lawrence Erlbaum Associates.

Berson, I. R., & Berson, M. J. (2003). Digital literacy for cybersafety, digital awareness, and media literacy. *Social Education, 67*(3), 164–167.

Bialystok, E. (2001). *Bilingualism in development: Language, literacy, and cognition.* Cambridge University Press. https://doi.org/10.1017/CBO9780511605963

Braithwaite, W. (1878). *Cottage at Adel* [Illustration]. Leeds Libraries. https://commons.wikimedia.org/wiki/File:1878_Cottage_at_Adel.jpg

Brockedon, W. (ca. 1787–1854). *A study from nature (Horse-drawn cart with two men)* [Illustration]. Yale Center for British Art, Paul Mellon Collection, B1977.14.1490(47). https://collections.britishart.yale.edu/catalog/tms:13255

Brophy, J., & Alleman, J. (2007). *Powerful social studies for elementary students* (2nd ed.). Wadsworth Publishing.

Browne, C., Culligan, B., & Phillips, J. (2013). *The new academic wordlist.* The New General Service List Project. www.newgeneralservicelist.com/new-general-service-list-1

Callahan, R. M., & Gándara, P. C. (Eds.). (2014). *The bilingual advantage: Language, literacy, and the U.S. labor market.* Multilingual Matters.

Callison, C. (2020). The twelve-year warning. *Isis, 111*(1), 129–137. https://doi.org/10.1086/707823

Canva (13 January 2025). Dream Lab [AI image generator]. www.canva.com/dream-lab

Chapelle, C. A. (2024). Open generative AI changes a lot, but not everything. *The Modern Language Journal, 108*(2), 534–540. https://doi.org/10.1111/modl.12927

Cipper, G. (1725). *Häusliche Szene mit Musikanten und Spinnerin* [Painting]. Städel Museum https://sammlung.staedelmuseum.de/en/work/domestic-scene-with-musicians-and-woman-spinning

Colorín Colorado. (2018, February 1). *What it feels like to be an ELL: Event archive* [Video]. YouTube. www.youtube.com/watch?v=pzTbdw3bV7M

Coxhead, A. (2000). A new academic word list. *TESOL Quarterly, 34*(2), 213–238. https://doi.org/10.2307/3587951

Cristall, J. (1825). *A cottage on the side of Symond's Rock near Goodrich, Herefordshire* [Painting]. Wikimedia https://commons.wikimedia.org/wiki/File:Joshua_Cristall_A_Cottage_on_the_side_of_Symond%27s_Rock.jpg

Cummins, J. (2000). *Language, power, and pedagogy: Bilingual children in the crossfire*. Multilingual Matters.

DeCapua, A., & Marshall, H. W. (2011). *Breaking new ground: Teaching students with limited or interrupted formal education in U.S. secondary schools*. University of Michigan Press.

Delano, J. (1941, October). *White Plains, Greene County, Georgia. The three-teacher Negro school* [Photograph]. Library of Congress. www.loc.gov/item/2017796644/

Delano, J. (1941, October). *White Plains, Greene County, Georgia. Studying insects in a classroom at the school* [Photograph]. Library of Congress. www.loc.gov/item/2017796546/

Detroit Publishing Co. (1890, October). *Plantation Residence, Louisiana* [Photograph]. Library of Congress. www.loc.gov/item/2016818856

Dovidio, J. F., Glick, P., & Rudman, L. A. (Eds.). (2005). *On the nature of prejudice: Fifty years after Allport*. Blackwell Publishing. https://doi.org/10.1002/9780470773963

Echevarria, J., Vogt, M., & Short, D. J. (2017). *Making content comprehensible for English learners: The SIOP model* (5th ed.). Pearson.

Engels, F. (1845). *The Condition of the Working-Class in England in 1844* (F. Kelley, Trans.). Project Gutenberg. https://www.gutenberg.org/ebooks/17306

Engels, F. (1845). *The condition of the working-class of England* (F. Kelley, Trans.). Project Gutenberg. https://www.gutenberg.org/ebooks/17306

English imperialism octopus [Illustration]. (1888). Wikimedia Commons. https://commons.wikimedia.org/wiki/File:English_imperialism_octopus.jpg

Fadel, C. (2008). *Multimodal learning through media: What the research says* [White paper]. Cisco Systems. https://curriculumredesign.org/wp-content/uploads/Multimodal_learning_through_media.pdf

Flores, N., & García, E. S. (2020). Power, language, and bilingual learners. In N. S. Nasir, C. D. Lee, R.

Pea, & M. M. de Royston (Eds.), *Handbook of the cultural foundations of learning* (pp. 178–191). Routledge.

Flores, N., & Rosa, J. (2015). Undoing appropriateness: Raciolinguistic ideologies and language diversity in education. *Harvard Educational Review, 85*(2), 149–171. https://doi.org/10.17763/0017-8055.85.2.149

FOX Soccer. (2022, November 20). *Morgan Freeman kicks off the 2022 FIFA World Cup opening ceremony in Qatar* [Video]. YouTube. www.youtube.com/watch?v=fy3jjN0D5iQ

Gao, X. (2024). Language education in a brave new world: A dialectical imagination. *The Modern Language Journal, 108*(2), 556–562. https://doi.org/10.1111/modl.12930

García, O., & Kleyn, T. (2016). *Translanguaging with multilingual students: Learning from classroom moments.* Routledge. https://doi.org/10.4324/9781315695242

García, O., Johnson, S. I., & Seltzer, K. (2016). *The translanguaging classroom: Leveraging student bilingualism for learning.* Brookes Publishing.

Gardner, R. C. (2001). Language learning motivation: The student, the teacher, and the researcher. *Texas Papers in Foreign Language Education, 6*(1), 1–18.

Gastineau, H. G., & Lacey, S. (ca. 1830). *Nant y Glo, Monmouthshire* [Engraving]. Llyfrgell Genedlaethol Cymru—National Library of Wales. http://hdl.handle.net/10107/1131349

Gay, G. (2000). *Culturally responsive teaching: Theory, research, and practice* (1st ed.). Teachers College Press.

Gay, G. (2002). Preparing for culturally responsive teaching. *Journal of Teacher Education, 53*(2), 106–116. https://doi.org/10.1177/0022487102053002003

Gay, G. (2010). *Culturally responsive teaching: Theory, research, and practice* (2nd ed.). Teachers College Press.

Gay, G. (2018). *Culturally responsive teaching: Theory, research, and practice* (3rd ed.). Teachers College Press.

Gillborn, D. (2005). Education policy as an act of white supremacy: Whiteness, critical race theory and education reform. *Journal of Education Policy, 20*(4), 485–505. https://doi.org/10.1080/02680930500132346

Glackens, L. M. (1909, September 22). *No limit* [Illustration]. *Puck, 66*(1699). Library of Congress. www.loc.gov/resource/ppmsca.26411

Godwin-Jones, R. (2024). Distributed agency in second language learning and teaching through generative AI. *Language Learning & Technology, 28*(2), 5–31. https://hdl.handle.net/10125/73570

Gonzalez-Lloret, M. (2024). The future of language learning teaching in a technology-mediated 21st century. *The Modern Language Journal, 108*(2), 541–547. https://doi.org/10.1111/modl.12928

Gunn, A. A., Bennett, S. V., Alley, K. M., Barrera, E. S., IV, Cantrell, S. C., Moore, L., & Welsh, J. L. (2021). Revisiting culturally responsive teaching practices for early childhood preservice teachers. *Journal of Early Childhood Teacher Education, 42*(3), 265–280. https://doi.org/10.1080/10901027.2020.1735586

Hall, E. T. (1976). *Beyond culture.* Anchor Books/Doubleday.

Hammond, Z. (2015). *Culturally responsive teaching and the brain: Promoting authentic engagement and rigor among culturally and linguistically diverse students.* Corwin.

Harris & Ewing. (1917). *Mary Winsor (Penn.) '17* [Photograph]. Library of Congress. https://www.loc.gov/item/mnwp000225/

Harris, K. (2015). *Integrating digital literacy into English language instruction: Issue brief.* Literacy Information and Communication System. https://lincs.ed.gov/sites/default/files/ELL_Digital_Literacy_508.pdf

Heath, D. B. (Ed.). (1963). *A journal of the pilgrims at Plymouth: Mourt's relation.* Corinth Books. https://www.gutenberg.org/files/66359/66359-h/66359-h.htm

Heineke, A. J., & Davin, K. J. (2020). *The seal of biliteracy: Case studies and considerations for policy implementation.* Information Age Publishing.

Hine, L. (1908). *Child labour Vivian Cotton Mills.* Leiden University Libraries. https://digitalcollections.universiteitleiden.nl/view/item/1659529

Hine, L. (1911, September). *Crowded tenement used by cranberry pickers* [Photograph]. Library of Congress. www.loc.gov/item/2018676025

Hsu, W. (2014). The effects of audiovisual support on EFL learners' productive vocabulary. *ReCALL, 26*(1), 62–79. https://doi.org/10.1017/S0958344013000220

Human Rights Watch. (2021, April 27). *A threshold crossed: Israeli authorities and the crimes of apartheid and persecution.* www.hrw.org/report/2021/04/27/threshold-crossed/israeli-authorities-and-crimes-apartheid-and-persecution

Huynh, T., & Skelton, B. (2023). *Long-term success for experienced multilinguals.* Corwin.

[Illustration of machine works of Richard Hartmann in Chemnitz, Germany]. (1868). Wikimedia Commons. https://commons.wikimedia.org/wiki/File:Hartmann_Maschinenhalle_1868_(01).jpg

Jensen, E. (2009). *Teaching with poverty in mind: What being poor does to kids' brains and what schools can do about it.* ASCD.

Jim Crow [Illustration]. (ca. 1835–1845). Library of Congress. www.loc.gov/item/2004669584

Keppler, U. J. (1898, February 16). *A new legend in an old dress* [Illustration]. *Puck, 43*(1093). Library of Congress. www.loc.gov/item/2012647516

Keppler, U. J. (1904). Next! [Illustration]. *Puck, 56*(1436). www.loc.gov/item/2001695241.

Kitson, C. (2025). *TESOL zip guide: AI in English language teaching.* TESOL Press.

Krashen, S. D. (1982). *Principles and practice in second language acquisition.* Pergamon Press.

Kress, G., & van Leeuwen, T. (2006). *Reading images: The grammar of visual design* (2nd ed.). Routledge.

Kristina, M., & Nagara, E. S. (2023). The use of visual media as one alternative to improve students' learning motivation. *Journal of Ethics and Character Education, 1*(2), 49–58. https://www.journal.yhmm.or.id/index.php/JECE/article/view/33

Kumashiro, K. K. (2015). *Against common sense: Teaching and learning toward social justice* (3rd ed.). Routledge. https://doi.org/10.4324/9781315765525

Kurz & Allison. (1891). *Battle of Kenesaw Mountain* [Lithograph]. Library of Congress www.loc.gov/item/91482215

Ladson-Billings, G. (1995). Toward a theory of culturally relevant pedagogy. *American Educational Research Journal, 32*(3), 465–491. https://doi.org/10.3102/00028312032003465

Ladson-Billings, G. (2021). Three decades of culturally relevant, responsive, & sustaining pedagogy: What lies ahead? *The Educational Forum, 85*(4), 351–354. https://doi.org/10.1080/00131725.2021.1957632

Langan, E., & Lawrence, S. A. (2021). Which came first: Literacy or social studies? How primary sources can bridge the divide. *Excelsior: Leadership in Teaching and Learning, 13*(3), 182–197. https://doi.org/10.14305/jn.19440413.2021.13.3.01

Le, V. (2023, October 3). *Race-aware algorithms: Paving the way for a more equitable future.* The Greenlining Institute. https://greenlining.org/2023/race-aware-algorithms-paving-the-way-for-a-more-equitable-future/

Lee, R. (1939). *Negro drinking at "colored" water cooler in streetcar terminal, Oklahoma City, Oklahoma* [Photograph]. Library of Congress. www.loc.gov/item/2017740552

Lewin, K. M. (2007). *Improving access, equity, and transitions in education: Creating a research agenda.* Centre for International Education, University of Sussex. http://www.create-rpc.org/pdf_documents/PTA1.pdf

Lucas, T., & Villegas, A. M. (2013). Preparing linguistically responsive teachers: Laying the foundation in preservice teacher education. *Theory Into Practice, 52*(2), 98–109. https://doi.org/10.1080/00405841.2013.770327

marissaorton. (2008). *Sweatshop Project* [Photograph]. Flickr. www.flickr.com/photos/28876688@N03/2697297072.

Marzano, R. J., Pickering, D. J., & Pollock, J. E. (2001). *Classroom instruction that works: Research-based strategies for increasing student achievement.* Association for Supervision & Curriculum Development.

Mayer & Stetfield. (ca. 1861). *Union generals* [Lithograph]. Library of Congress. www.loc.gov/item/90714113

Mayer, R. E. (2009). *Multimedia learning* (2nd ed.). Cambridge University Press. https://doi.org/10.1017/CBO9780511811678

Mayflower 400. (n.d.). *The story of Thanksgiving and the National Day of Mourning.* www.mayflower400uk.org/education/who-were-the-pilgrims/2019/july/the-story-of-thanksgiving-and-the-national-day-of-mourning

McLaren, P. (1998). *Life in schools: An introduction to critical pedagogy in the foundations of education* (3rd ed.). Longman.

McQuillan, J. (2019). Where do we get our academic vocabulary? Comparing the efficiency of direct instruction and free voluntary reading. *The Reading Matrix: An International Online Journal, 19*(1), 129–138. www.readingmatrix.com/files/20-d7ceydef.pdf

McVay, L. (2017, November 22). *Everyone's history matters: The Wampanoag Indian Thanksgiving story deserves to be known*. Smithsonian Magazine. www.smithsonianmag.com/blogs/national-museum-american-indian/2017/11/23/everyones-history-matters-and-wampanoag-indian-thanksgiving-story-deserves-be-known/

Menken, K., & García, O. (Eds.). (2010). *Negotiating language policies in schools: Educators as policymakers*. Routledge. https://doi.org/10.4324/9780203855874

Menken, K., & Solorza, C. (2014). No child left bilingual: Accountability and the elimination of bilingual education programs in New York City schools. *Educational Policy, 28*(1), 96–125.

Merriam-Webster. (n.d.-a). Democracy. In *Merriam-Webster.com dictionary*. Retrieved June 16, 2025, from www.merriam-webster.com/dictionary/democracy

Merriam-Webster. (n.d.-a). *How many words are there in English?* www.merriam-webster.com/help/faq-how-many-english-words

Merriam-Webster. (n.d-c). Say. In *Merriam-Webster.com dictionary*. Retrieved June 16, 2025, from www.merriam-webster.com/thesaurus/say

Mohamed, N. (2024, March 14). *Every teacher is a language teacher: Strategies for supporting multilingual learners of English in the mainstream classroom*. The TESOL Blog. www.tesol.org/blog/posts/every-teacher-is-a-language-teacher-strategies-for-supporting-multilingual-learners-of-english-in-the-mainstream-classroom/

Monte-Sano, C. (2010). Disciplinary literacy in history: An exploration of the historical nature of adolescents' writing. *Journal of the Learning Sciences, 19*(4), 539–568. https://doi.org/10.1080/10508406.2010.481014

Moya, G., & Le, V. (2021). *Algorithmic bias explained: How automated decision-making becomes automated discrimination*. The Greenlining Institute. https://greenlining.org/wp-content/uploads/2021/04/Greenlining-Institute-Algorithmic-Bias-Explained-Report-Feb-2021.pdf

Mueller, J. (2010). *Authentic assessment toolbox*. https://jonfmueller.com/toolbox/

Mulligan, C. J., Quinn, E. B., Hamadmad, D., Dutton, C. L., Nevell, L., Binder, A. M., Panter-Brick, C., & Dajani, R. (2025). Epigenetic signatures of intergenerational exposure to violence in three generations of Syrian refugees. *Scientific Reports, 15*, Article 5945. https://doi.org/10.1038/s41598-025-89818-z

Murad, N. L. (2024, October 8). Educators beware: The Anti-Defamation League is not the social justice partner it claims to be. *Rethinking Schools, 39*(1).

Museum and Library Services Act of 2018. Pub. L. No. 115-410, 132 Stat. 5412 (2018). www.govinfo.gov/app/details/PLAW-115publ410

National Archives and Records Administration. (ca. 1800). [Photograph of farm workers in the 1800s]. Flickr. www.flickr.com/photos/usdagov/6510688255

National Archives. (2021, November 22). Thanksgiving: Historical perspectives. https://visit. archives.gov/whats-on/explore-exhibits/thanksgiving-historical-perspectives

National Center for Education Statistics. (2024). *English learners in public schools.* U.S. Department of Education, Institute of Education Sciences. https://nces.ed.gov/programs/coe/indicator/cgf

National Council for the Social Studies. (2013). *The college, career, and civic life (C3) framework for social studies state standards: Guidance for enhancing the rigor of K–12 civics, economic, geography, and history.*

National Museum of the American Indian. (n.d.). *Harvest ceremony: Beyond the Thanksgiving myth.* https://americanindian.si.edu/nk360/resources/Harvest-Ceremony

Negro expulsion from railway car, Philadelphia [Illustration]. (1856). The Illustrated London News. Library of Congress. www.loc.gov/item/2007678048

Newmann, F. M. (1996). Authentic assessment in social studies: Standards and examples. In G. D. Phye (Ed.), *Handbook of classroom assessment: Learning, achievement, and adjustment* (pp. 359–380). https://doi.org/10.1016/B978–012554155–8/50014–4

Nieto, S. (2010). *The light in their eyes: Creating multicultural learning communities* (10th ed.). Teachers College Press.

Oklahoma City Public Schools Native American Student Services. (n.d.). *A Story of survival: The Wampanoag and the English.* www.okcps.org/cms/lib/OK01913268/Centricity/Domain/130/NASS%20Thanksgiving%20Lesson%20Plan%20Booklet.pdf

Paine, T. (1776). *Common sense.* Project Gutenberg. https://www.gutenberg.org/ebooks/3755

Paivio, A. (1990). *Mental representations: A dual coding approach.* Oxford University Press. https://doi.org/10.1093/acprof:oso/9780195066661.001.0001

Paris, D., & Alim, H. S. (Eds.). (2017). *Culturally sustaining pedagogies: Teaching and learning for justice in a changing world.* Teachers College Press.

Powelson, B. F. (ca. 1868–1869). *Harriet Tubman* [Photograph]. Library of Congress. www.loc.gov/item/2018645050

Qin, K., & Llosa, L. (2023). Translingual caring and translingual aggression: (Re)centering criticality in the research and practice of translanguaging pedagogy. *The Modern Language Journal, 107*(3), 713–733. https://doi.org/10.1111/modl.12868

Recht, D. R., & Leslie, L. (1988). Effect of prior knowledge on good and poor readers' memory of text. *Journal of Educational Psychology, 80*(1), 16–20. https://doi.org/10.1037/0022–0663.80.1.16

Richards, H. V., Brown, A. F., & Forde, T. B. (2007). Addressing diversity in schools: Culturally responsive pedagogy. *Teaching Exceptional Children, 39*(3), 64–68. https://doi.org/10.1177/004005990703900310

Rizzuto, K. C. (2017). Teachers' perceptions of ELL students: Do their attitudes shape their instruction? *The Teacher Education, 52*(3), 182–202. https://doi.org/10.1080/08878730.2017.1296912

Robespierre, M. (1794, February 5). *Rapport sur les principes de morale politique qui doivent guider la Convention nationale dans l'administration intérieure de la République* [On political morality]. Digital Public Library of America. https://dp.la/item/2a8c010fe2b3666c8073af3dceed64f5

Romanowski, M. H. (2009). What you don't know *can* hurt you: Textbook omissions and 9/11. *The Clearing House, 82*(6), 290–296. https://doi.org/10.3200/TCHS.82.6.290–296

Sadker, D. M., & Zittleman, K. R. (2009). *Teachers, schools and society* (9th ed.). McGraw-Hill.

Santa Monica College. (2025). *Bias.* https://admin.smc.edu/administration/human-resources/diversity-equity-inclusivity/bias.php

Schwartz, R., Vassilev, A., Greene, K., Perine, L., Burt, A., & Hall, P. (2022). *Towards a standard for identifying and managing bias in artificial intelligence* (NIST Special Publication 1270). National Institute of Standards and Technology. https://doi.org/10.6028/NIST.SP.1270

Shanahan, T., & Shanahan, C. (2012). What is disciplinary literacy and why does it matter. *Top Lang Disorders, 32*(1), 7–18. https://ceedar.education.ufl.edu/wp-content/uploads/2014/10/Shanahan-Shanahan-2012-What-is-Disciplinary-Literacy.pdf

Sherman, S. (2019, November 11). The Thanksgiving tale we tell is a harmful lie. As a Native American, I've found a better way to celebrate the holiday. *TIME.* https://time.com/5457183/thanksgiving-native-american-holiday

Shoman, S. (2024). *Teaching Palestine/Israel: A multiple narratives approach.* Middle East Children's Alliance. https://teachpalestine.org/teaching-palestine-israel/

Simpson, J. (ca. 1917–1919). *Your motherland will never forget* [Illustration]. *Canada in khaki.* British Library. Wikimedia. https://commons.wikimedia.org/wiki/File:Your_motherland_will_never_forget.jpg

Sleeter, C. (2018). Multicultural education past, present, and future: Struggles for dialog and power-sharing. *International Journal of Multicultural Education, 20*(1), 5–20. https://files.eric.ed.gov/fulltext/EJ1173724.pdf

Sleeter, C. E. (2017). Critical race theory and the whiteness of teacher education. *Urban Education, 52*(2), 155–169. https://doi.org/10.1177/0042085916668957

Strobridge & Co. (ca. 1888). *Abraham Lincoln and his Emancipation Proclamation* [Illustration]. Library of Congress. www.loc.gov/item/97507511

Taylor, J. A., & Duran, M. (2006). Teaching social studies with technology: New research on collaborative approaches. *The History Teacher, 40*(1), 9–25. https://doi.org/10.2307/30036936

TESOL International Association. (2024). *The 6 principles for exemplary teaching of English learners: Grades K–12* (2nd ed.). TESOL Press.

Thomas, W. P., & Collier, V. P. (2002). *A national study of school effectiveness for language minority students' long-term academic achievement.* Center for Research on Education, Diversity and Excellence. https://escholarship.org/uc/item/65j213pt

Turner, B. (2019, November 19). *Thanksgiving: Practicing gratitude and honoring the real story*. PBS Kids for Parents. www.pbs.org/parents/thrive/thanksgiving-practicing-gratitude-and-honoring-the-real-story

U.S. Department of Education. (2023, November 16). *Biden-Harris Administration launches "Being bilingual is a superpower" to promote multilingual education for a diverse workforce*. Retrieved November 17, 2024 from https://web.archive.org/web/20241117190912/www.ed.gov/about/news/press-release/biden-harris-administration-launches-being-bilingual-superpower-promote

Unidentified Soldier in Confederate Uniform [Photograph]. (ca. 1861–1865). Library of Congress. www.loc.gov/item/2022633084

Unidentified soldier in Union uniform [Photograph]. (ca. 1861–1865). Library of Congress. www.loc.gov/item/2022642437

Ure, A., & Simmonds, P. L. (1861). *The cotton manufacture of Great Britain: Investigated and illustrated* (Vol. 1). Internet Archive. https://archive.org/details/dli.ministry.01503

UsingEnglish.com (n.d.). *37 English phrasal verbs with "COME."* www.usingenglish.com/reference/phrasal-verbs/come.html

Valenzuela, A. (1999). *Subtractive schooling: U.S.–Mexican youth and the politics of caring*. SUNY Press.

Vera, E. M., Israel, M. S., Coyle, L., Cross, J., Knight-Lynn, L., Moallem, I., Bartucci, G., & Goldberger, N. (2012). Exploring the educational involvement of parents of English learners. *School Community Journal*, *22*(2), 183–202. https://files.eric.ed.gov/fulltext/EJ1001618.pdf

Virginia & Truckee Railroad 11, Reno, with the Lightning Express at Virginia City [Photograph]. (ca. 1880). Wikimedia. https://commons.wikimedia.org/wiki/File:Virginia_%26_Truckee_Railroad_11,_Reno,_with_the_Lightning_Express_at_Virginia_City_(early_1880s%3F).jpg

Vizetelly, F. (1862, October 4). *The Civil War in America* [Engraving]. The New York Public Library. https://digitalcollections.nypl.org/items/510d47e0-f9ca-a3d9-e040-e00a18064a99

Walsh, R. (2013, May 14). *Does background knowledge matter to reading comprehension*. Russ on Reading. https://russonreading.blogspot.com/2013/05/does-background-knowledge-matter-to.html

Winchester, S. (2011, May 28). A verb for our frantic Times. *The New York Times*. www.nytimes.com/2011/05/29/opinion/29winchester.html

Wineburg, S. (2001). *Historical thinking and other unnatural acts: Charting the future of teaching the past*. Temple University Press.

Wineburg, S. S. (1991). On the reading of historical texts: Notes on the breach between school and academy. *American Educational Research Journal*, *28*(3), 495–519.

Woman Suffrage Button [Photograph]. (n.d.). National Museum of American History. https://www.si.edu/object/nmah_1437164

Women miners in the English coal pits. (1842). In *Parliamentary Papers: Vol. XVI*. Internet Modern History Sourcebook, Fordham University. https://origin.web.fordham.edu/Halsall/mod/1842womenminers.asp

Wootton, A. J. (2021). Authentic assessment: A foundation year case study. *Journal of the Foundation Year Network*, *4*, 75–85. https://jfyn.co.uk/index.php/ukfyn/article/view/67/57

Xia, N. (2024). The impact of bilingual education on young children's cognitive development. *Transactions on Social Science, Education, and Humanities Research*, *11*, 919–928. https://doi.org/10.62051/p2j7f435

Zhu, M., & Wang, C. (2025). A systematic review of research on AI in language education: Current status and future implications. *Language Learning & Technology*, *29*(1), 1–29. https://hdl.handle.net/10125/73606

About the Authors

Dr. Fatima Aldajani is an experienced education professional with 15+ years of expertise in supporting multilingual learners and fostering inclusive, culturally responsive classrooms. Holding a PhD in curriculum and instruction, she has worked globally, integrating her international insights into curriculum development, teacher training, and social-emotional learning. Her research focuses on equity, anti-racism, and the impacts of professional development on student success. A passionate advocate for educational justice, she addresses anti-Arab racism, Islamophobia, and antisemitism while promoting intersectional pedagogy. Additionally, she explores the ethical applications of AI in education, leveraging technology to enhance personalized learning and promote digital equity.

Mary Brennan is an accomplished educator with more than 20 years of classroom experience and 6 years as a district administrator. She is dedicated to making learning engaging and meaningful for both educators and students, and she views learners as the greatest assets in every classroom. Mary's goal is to inspire a lifelong love of learning in all students. Outside of her professional role, she enjoys spending time with her three grandchildren, hiking, and crafting.

Peggie Cypher is a veteran instructor of multilingual learners of English, from kindergarteners in Toledo, Ohio, to college-level students in Tokyo, Japan. Her specialty is working with content area teachers to make instruction comprehensible. Peggie is also a widely published author whose work has appeared in diverse publications, from *Ladies Home Journal* to the narrative series *Legacy* for the Bill and Melinda Gates Foundation's project on small schools. She is a cowinner of two Wilmer Shields Rich Awards for Excellence in Communications, and recipient of a Parenting Publications of America award for drinking water safety and a *Guinness Toast* award at Mickey Finn's pub.

Kaedmon Fulton speaks four languages and holds certifications in three content areas: Teaching English to Speakers of Other Languages, Social Studies, and English Language Arts. Their 10+ years of teaching experience include rural, suburban, and urban public schools in New York state, where they specialize in making challenging content in Social Studies and English literature accessible to students with beginning English proficiency and interrupted formal education. Their research interests include disciplinary literacy, curriculum development, and bridging cultural gaps between families and school. In 2023, they were named the Middle School ESOL Teacher of the Year by New York State TESOL.

Andy Jiahao Liu was an award-winning global professor of English at the University of Arizona at the time of writing. He is now a PhD student in language, literacy, and social studies education at the University of Iowa. His research centers on second language writing, English for research publication purposes, and language testing and assessment. He is coeditor of the *Journal of Second*

Language Writing special issue on Emotions in Teaching Second Language Writing. An active member of professional communities, he has served as chair of the Second Language Writing Interest Section at TESOL International Association and chair of the Council of Writing Program Administrators' Graduate Research Award Committee.

www.ingramcontent.com/pod-product-compliance
Lightning Source LLC
Chambersburg PA
CBHW080126150626
46550CB00017B/2691